<u>TABLE OF CONTENTS</u>

PREFACE

THE CASTING COUCH, SEXUAL ABUSE AND THE QUEST FOR POWER

ASSAULT AND PEPPERED

NEVER HIT A WOMAN?

HOW WOMEN GET LAID AND PAID

Signs that a Man is Bad-in-Bed: An Analysis
The Foundation: Disguised "Misandry"

- The Woman Hater's Club" – The 3 Stooges
- On-Going Misandry Gets "Flipped"

The Black Woman and the Rise of the 'Sister Dyke'

- Popular Culture

The 'Pussy Principle': Concepts and Characteristics

- The Economic Reality of "Getting Laid and Paid"

  - **Professional Athletes and 'Mistresses'**
  - **Politicians and "Mistresses"**

    - *George Washington & Venus*
    - *Abraham Lincoln & Joshua Speed*
    - *JFK & Mimi Alford*
    - *JFK & Marilyn Monroe*
    - *JFK & Judith Campbell Exier*
    - *JFK & Ellen Rometsch*
    - *Grover Cleveland & Maria Crofts Halpin*
    - *Bill Clinton & Monica Lewinsky*
    - *James Buchanan a& William Rufus King*
    - *Warren G. Hardin & Nan Britton*
    - *Warren G. Harding & Carrie Fulton Phillips*
    - *Dwight D. Eisenhower & Kay Summersby*
    - *Thomas Jefferson & Sally Hemings*
    - *FDR & Lucy Mercer*
    - *James Garfield & Lucia Calhoun*
    - *John Tyler & The Majority of His Slaves*
    - *George H.W. Bush & Jennifer Fitzgerald*
    - *LBJ & Alice Glass*
    - *JFK & Angie Dickinson*
    - *Marion Barry, D.C. Mayor*
    - *Cory Booker, Newark Mayor*
    - *Rev. Ben Chavis, NAACP*
    - *Henry Cisneros, HUD Director*
    - *Eliot Spitzer, N.Y. Governor*
    - *Anthony Weiner, N.Y. State Rep*

  - **The Richest Women in the World**

- **The Grown Man as "Child"**

Rise of the "Chicken Heads": Even Ugly Women Get Laid and Paid
The Reality of Alimony: Ka-Ching!
The Reality of Child Support Payments: Ka-Ching!

- *Little Bow-Wow*
- *Jermaine DuPree*
- *Chief Keef*
- *Allen Iverson*
- *Terrell Owens*
- *Evander Holyfield*
- *Bobby Brown*
- *Dennis Rodman*
- *Flavor Flav*
- *Shawte Lo*

Don't Hate the Playa OR the Game: Hate the System That Produced and Endorses Both!

- The Side Chick

Conclusion
References

CLOSING REMARKS

PREFACE

The American Casting Couch is more than just a title of this book, but an accurate description of "relations" in America. In this case the emphasis is on male-female relations and how men use the power they have to seduce and otherwise sexually malign females. But the attitude behind the act has other applications which is one reason I know what this society is going to do to Harvey

Weinstein, the Hollywood mogul exposed in October 2017 of harassing scores of women and even raping a few of them. He did all this after luring them to his office or apartment, having co-workers help him set up the "meetings" and then convincing the women that sex with him would land them lucrative contracts and roles in major movies.

Weinstein is a typical male in a society that is driven by various forms of privilege. But he is going to be used as a scapegoat in much the same way that these white people point to the Nazis and the Ku Klux Klan and shout "white supremacists!" The fact of the matter is, all white people are white supremacists on some level because they have accepted it and passed it on to their children, whether consciously or not. By blaming these "right wing groups," the majority of whites – who also believe in white supremacy – can be absolved of being "the kind of racist" that is represented by the hood, the robe and the swastika.

This is the same type of trick that is now being used after Harvey Weinstein has been "exposed." Exposed after everyone in Hollywood knew what was taking place. Just like with the white supremacists: white folks knew black people were being enslaved, lynched and raped and their silence gave their consent. Not only that, but the system that was constructed as a result of black degradation, enslavement and exploitation is one that most whites benefit from to this very day. So on some level, all of them are beneficiaries of white supremacy. And to accept the benefit is the give your endorsement.

Sexual misconduct, harassment and rape work in a similar way. Men have been taking advantage of women for centuries. It's a cultural universal and even the so-called Bible is filled with sexist bullshit. Be that as it may, Weinstein is being used as the scapegoat to pay for all the "sins" of a system of female denial and degradation that is based on "tradition, reason, and acceptance" (Karenga, 1967).

All men are in on it on some level. Women have been accepting it claiming that there was nothing they could do. In the case of white women, their situation is different in my view: this was their man committing these atrocities. Many of the men committing these acts were married to white women who had to know what their man was capable of. Just like Hillary knew about the kind of man her husband (President) Bill Clinton was, just the wives of Roger Ailes (CEO of Fox News, who was married three times) and Bill O'Reilly, who was married 14 years before divorcing. These white women knew and kept quiet just like the wife and children of Bernie Madoff clammed up and acted as if they didn't know that Madoff had stolen over 50 billion dollars!

These white people are experts at "diversion." And black people and other people in this country are so entranced by the media's manipulated manifestations of reality that they refuse to see what is taking place. To personalize an issue ("he did it!") that is centuries old, universal and obvious to the naked eye does the victims of that issue a disservice.

INTRODUCTION

As a thinker and a scholar, I find myself wondering about the origins of things. I know that to know how something started gives you an idea of why it functions the way it does today. Malcolm X said long ago that, "Of all our studies, history is best qualified to reward our research."

Both politics and popular culture reign supreme in American society because these two institutions are paramount in the maintenance of white supremacy domination. My job is to share information and insights with black people who simply do not understand that gravity of the race war we are in. Continuing to claim to be "Americans" (although in need of civil rights), they continue to believe that all is well and that ignorance is bliss. Meanwhile the white man is killing us on both an overt and covert level. This paper is aimed at raising an issue that continues to exist, one that has to do with how the powerful take advantage of the powerless and how fame and fortune and the quest for both have blown the minds of millions of people in this country and all over the world. And most don't understand what they've gotten themselves into until it's too late.

From time to time you hear pundits talking about "the casting couch" and how long it has been in existence. One has to wonder how such a situation can have such a long and twisted history and in order to exist for so long there had to be a process in place that guaranteed its longevity. As Pickert (2014) cogently explained the situation:

> The casting couch is as old as Hollywood itself. Ever since there have been aspiring actors eager for a chance to break into the business, there have been powerful producers and directors offering opportunity and access in exchange for sexual favors. But in the wake of accusations that *X-Men* director Bryan Singer sexually abused underage boys, there's a re-examination now going on in Hollywood of exploitation in all its forms. Some of it concerns the alleged abuse of minors, but the scandal has also thrown a spotlight on the places where the line between Hollywood networking and the casting couch is sometimes blurry, if not obscured altogether. (Pickert, 2014)

As metaphor, the concept of a "casting couch" has existed in almost any situation where men are in a position where women must come to them seeking employment on some level. Black women who were enslaved and those who later worked as housekeepers have horror stories about their "interviews" and how many had to "audition," not only in terms of performing chores and showing their cooking skills, but also would be left alone with the "master of the house" while the white wife drifted off into another room as the man conducted his "interview."

The fact is, and a point that this paper hopes to point out, is that the key to the success of any casting couch situation is the degree of desperation of the people who are "applying" for a given position. I recall a quote from Henry Wadsworth Longfellow who once said, "The strength of criticism lies in the weakness of the thing criticized." In like manner, one's desperation will show what one is willing to do to acquire what one wants. Karenga (1980) wrote that, "He who has the ability to satisfy human needs controls the humans that have those needs." Put these two ideas together and what do we have: people with power using the resources at their disposal to get whatever it is they happen to want, sex included.

The four essays that follow address sexual abuse, harassment, stereotypes, values and beliefs in divergent ways. The first essay, "The Casting Couch, sexual Abuse and the Quest for Power" provides some background and some case studies of how Hollywood has functioned long before Harvey Weinstein got busted in October of 2017. The section also offers that along with sexual harassment, these Hollywood hucksters were also pedophiles in many instances.

The second essay, "Assault and Peppered," provides views on "sexual assault" and the social psychology of same. "Never Hit a Woman" is the third essay, and it is an argument against the gender biased belief that men should never hit women. No human being should ever hit another human being without expecting to get hit back, Fourth and finally, "How Women Get Laid and Paid." Of what good would a book about sexual misconduct and abuse be if somebody didn't tell the truth about the kind of Pimp-Prostitute relationships that Americans have been duped into referring to as "courting," "dating" or "hooking up"?

This will be established throughout this book.

THE CASTING COUCH, SEXUAL ABUSE AND THE QUEST FOR POWER

<u>INTRODUCTION</u>

The term "casting couch" may have originated in the motion picture industry (run by Jews, or course), but the concept has been alive and well for a long time.

White men have been in positions of authority and power and were therefore in positions to determine who would get interviewed, who would get the jobs, who would get the best positions at the job and so on.

And the casting couch, as we now know, didn't only apply to getting some head or some ass from a woman. These white boys were on the downlow and were gay from day one. They allowed men to become stars in exchange for sexual favors and then these decision makers in Hollywood covered it up. That is why we are just now finding out about Rock Hudson, Randolph Scott and so many others who were being presented on screen as male studs when, in real life, they were using their huge mansions to take it up the ass behind closed doors.

In simpler terms what began taking place in the public case of Hollywood's Harvey Weinstein is neither new or nerve-shattering. But before you can understand the hypocrisy of the same media that assisted in covering up the sexual harassment and rapes of women by this Hollywood mogul and the complicity of all the people who knew about his activities and yet said nothing about it, you need some background on his predecessors and the contextual conditions that shape the type of conduct and consciousness that made Weinstein's actions possible in the first place.

<u>THE CASTING COUCH "SYNDROME"</u>

One reliable source provides us with an excellent operational definition of the casting couch mentality or "casting couch syndrome" as it has come to be known.

> The casting couch, casting-couch syndrome, or casting-couch mentality is the trading of sexual favors by an aspirant, apprentice employee, or subordinate to a superior in return for entry into an occupation, or for other career advancement within an organization. The term *casting couch* originated in the motion picture industry, with specific reference to couches in offices that could be used for sexual activity between casting directors or film producers and aspiring actors (Wikipedia, 2016).

According to one source, "It [the casting couch] … is not to be confused with the adult entertainment industry where such actions may be a prerequisite, although many pornographic films and pornographic websites play on the casting couch theme and allude to similarities one may find in casting couch scenarios in the film industry." (Wikipedia, 2016). However,

> The term is now often used to refer to other industries besides entertainment, though careers which are highly desirable and

traditionally difficult to break into, such as the movie, television
and music industries, have been the subject of casting couch stories
in popular culture. Such trading of favors can be an abuse of
power—possibly even statutory rape—and can become a wider sex
scandal if deemed newsworthy. (Wikipedia, 2016).

It doesn't matter what industry you're talking about: white men in general and those in power, in particular, use their power to get whatever they want or feel as if they need. This has been going on for centuries and many women kept quiet because if they were to tell their husbands, those white men would get their asses kicked and possibly killed. If the man meting out the beating was black, the woman would fear retaliation from other whites and a lynching of the black man, based on her testimony, would be the result.

Now you can see all of the Hollywood hypocrites and other powerful men who have long been guilty of sexually harassing and abusing women who were seeking jobs or some other position, coming out and claiming to be surprised. This talk, when combined with the myth that a man "should never hit a woman," is what perpetuates the existing state of affairs. To personalize an issue that is ideological, attitudinal and social is to demean or distort any chance there might be toward a resolution. But as long as men are in power there ain't gonna be any resolutions because "sexist is as sexist does."

But let me be clear: one thing about the "casting couch syndrome" that should not be overlooked: it's a two way street. Henry Wadsworth Longfellow once wrote that, "The strength of criticism lies in the weakness of the person criticized." Using this paradigm as it relates to the casting couch, let's put it like this: "The power of being able to get a person to give up that ass or some head lies in the desperation of the person who is being ordered to do so." Feel me?

THE CASTING COUCH: CASE STUDIES AND ANALYSIS

The following case studies of people who have experience with "the casting couch" would be moot to black people if they weren't tied in to the politics of Hollywood and how "race" and "ethnicity" play a part in the application, interview and selection process. The casting couch does not only pertain to those who want a part in a movie, a play or some other public spectacle; it is a philosophy where those in power have willfully and by design used such an undertaking as a key component of "screening." White men have been doing it for centuries both in the United States and other countries, but it can be said that any institutional arrangement or system where men are in charge will have a "casting couch" approach to not only "interviews" with women, but also with young boys and men, since large numbers of these decision m**akers have both overt and cover**t homosexual leanings.

From Wikipedia I looked up "casting couch" figuring that there would be some case studies that I could rely upon to show the long-time existence and application of the "casting couch" concept. And sure enough, I found plenty, some of which I'll share below with my commentary filtering in and out. But let me just say before we get into the following testimonies: almost every single example of having been approached via the "casting couch" approach was a piece of shit him/herself. In other words, they may have been exploited but once we look at their character before, during or after their "experience" we find that their claims are akin to a street walker calling a corporate call girl a "ho."

Now, let us look at the Hollywood-related examples of "the casting couch":

> In her book *You'll Never Eat Lunch in This Town Again* (1991),
> Oscar-winning producer Julia Phillips attempted to expose many of
> the underground Hollywood institutions and confirmed that a
> "casting couch" mentality was alive and well in Hollywood.
> (Wikipedia, 2016).

Here's my question: what did she do about the "casting couch mentality" before writing her book? As a producer she must have seen numerous examples of it. What did she do once she heard about these incidents? Did she file any kind of grievance? Did she pull the alleged victims to the side and work with them to sue the responsible parties? No. She did nothing. She decided to WRITE about "the underground Hollywood institutions" so that she could do what? Make money.

Let us continue:

> In a 1995 article, journalist Peter Keough described Hollywood as
> "a town where everyone is selling body and soul for fame and
> fortune and all – especially women – are considered
> commodities".(Wikipedia, 2016).

What Keough is describing is not just Hollywood – he's describing American society's methods as a whole! In a capitalist society, every human being becomes a commodity: either a tangible asset or a crippling liability. How is this new insight as it relates specifically to Hollywood? Again, the accuser commits his "whistle blowing" to the publication of an article. Where is the direct, physical action that would expose and bring down the "casting couch"?

Let's keep going:

> In a 1996 interview, actor Woody Harrelson declared "every
> [acting] business I ever entered into in New York seemed to have a

casting couch ... I've seen so many people sleep with people they
loathe in order to further their ambition." (Wikipedia, 2016).

How would Woody know about the casting couch? Did he actually see it? Did he participate? When you look back on how his career seemed to skyrocket, it seems as if he was screwing somebody! It was one hit after another following the NBC TV comedy "Cheers" (1987-1991) where he was nominated for Emmys, winning twice. But after that there was "White Men Can't Jump," Indecent Proposal," "Natural Born Killers," ""Kingpin", "People vs. Larry Flynt," "and they list continues all the way to "Hunger Games" (2014) and "LBJ" (2016). That's a lot of movies and a lot of very different roles. Was he on the "couch" as well?

Continuing:

> In 2003, Italian actress Asia Argento stated that Hollywood
> producers expect oral sex from young starlets in exchange for roles
> … Her semi-autobiographical film *Scarlet Diva* (2000) features a
> scene along these lines with painter Joe Coleman playing a
> lecherous producer. (Wikipedia, 2016).

White women suck dick the way most women shake hands. Black men know that and this is the "mystique" that society talks about when discussing the so-called "attraction" that black men have for white women. It's as simple as that: white women suck dick and most black women don't unless they know the male for a long period of time. Ask the bruthas – they know what I'm talking about. Even men from other countries come to America with the expectation of screwing a white woman because, thanks to the Jewish media, the white women is being propped up as an international whore, ripe for the pluckin'. Just look at Melania Trump: she even LOOKS like a whore, but that's the way the white man likes them.

What does this have to do with the "casting couch" you may ask? Who do you think controls the casting process? When there is a "part" in a movie and women apply, who do you think does the interviewing. Even when the person in the room is another female, she could well be just a referral point, a "pre-interview" before she "directs you to the boss." This is how it works in my opinion. Look at some of these white women getting these roles in major movies. You be the judge.

The evidence is in abundance:

> At a 2005 class reunion, producer Chris Hanley told his former
> classmates that "almost every leading actress in all of [his] 24 films
> has slept with a director or producer or a leading actor to get the
> part that launched her career". (Wikipedia, 2016).

Don't get it twisted: when white people say "slept with" or "sleeping with" they mean "fucking." It's just like the use of the term "dating." You hear it all the time: "I used to DATE her," or "he and I used to DATE back in the day." Date? You mean fuck, don't you? Why else would a mere date have any relevance? What do you expect them to say: "I went to dinner with him? He did a good job"? Or "I went to the movies and had some coffee with her. She did good work"?

Continuing:

> In her autobiography *Ich habe ja gewusst, dass ich fliegen kann* (2006), Austrian actress Senta Berger (b. 1941) claimed that in a New York hotel suite in 1965 producer Darryl F. Zanuck (b. 1902) exposed himself to her beneath his silk dressing gown and offered to forgive her for the atrocities of the Nazis if she slept with him. (Wikipedia, 2016).

It just doesn't get any lower than that. These white boys – mostly Jewish men – know they, like the cartoon He-Man, "have the power!" They control the auditions, they control the entire interview and selection process and their fellow Jewish pals control the banks that decide whether or not to "greenlight" a particular project. Hence, the casting couch is a sign of total control, preying on the desperation of people who want to become "movie stars." The casting couch is a sexual version of the "American Greed," show that addresses some of the white collar financial scams that are being run all over the world.

Moving on:

> In 2009, Megan Fox stated that leading film directors made sexual propositions while casting for film roles. (Wikipedia, 2016).

Now don't get me wrong: Megan Fox carries herself like a slut. She is one of those white girls who knows she's fine and plays the part. That's just my opinion. Every movie she's in she plays a wherefrom kiddie flicks like "Transformers" (2004) and "Teenage Mutant Ninja Turtles" (2004) to moves with names like "Whore" (2008), "Jennifer's Body"(2007), "Confessions of a Teenage Drama Queen" (2004) and even "Jonah Hex" (2007), where she played a whore named "Lilah" (short for "Delilah"?)

I think that the casting couch was waiting for Jennifer's "audition." The world has seen her butt naked and she plays roles where she has sex with men. She went to an audition and what were they supposed to do: cast her as a nun?

Then there's Cherlize Theron,born in South Africa and had the gall to say during a standup on "Saturday Night Live" that she was an American but was born in Africa so that makes her an "African-American." But unlike Megan Fox, she has talent. I saw her undergo a near total metamorphosis in a movie called, "Monster," where she played a female serial killer and dyke. Convincingly.

At any rate, her story is:

> In a 2009 interview with *OK! Magazine*, actress Charlize Theron claimed that when she was 18 she was propositioned at an audition by a pajama-clad Hollywood director … "I thought it was a little odd that the audition was on a Saturday night at his house in Los Angeles, but I thought maybe that was normal." (Wikipedia, 2016)

That bitch knew better. She has a nice face but is short on breasts with the typical white girl flat ass. Maybe he had some other actresses in mind and wanted to see what the goods looked like. These white bitches (read: Megan Fox, Cherlize Theron) always want to play victim when, up on that huge screen, they are showing their asses to millions of people and if they have a defect of any kind (like Cherlize) they shoot the scenes to avoid that flaw so that the white supremacy system can continue to promote the myth of white female universal beauty.

Continuing with the Hollywood sob story:

> In a 2009 interview, actor Mickey Rourke declared: "There's definitely something called a casting couch... if you take a girl from the Midwest with a pretty face and instead of inviting them in for an audition in the morning, the directors invite them for dinner at night? ... I can recall with certain women, we'd go out, I'd park the car on Sunset and by the time I'd got to the curb there'd be three or four producers handing them cards. ... There's ways you get a job and ways you get a job." (Wikipedia, 2016).

When someone like Mickey Rourke makes these kinds of statements, you have to take it with a grain of salt. This muthafucka was a racist from day one, and Hollywood has his back. When he started taking injections and steroids to bulk up and you end up looking like a monster, Hollywood will still find parts and roles for you if you "play ball." And it is clear to me that Rourke may have been on that casting couch himself. After all, many of the Hollywood decision makers are gay.

But back to the previous statements by Rourke and those guys handing the girls cards to get a job. There is a show called "American Greed" and it documents various white collar crimes that have been committed where con artists bilk people out of millions of dollars. But the "American greed" does not refer to the con artists; it refers to the people who thought they could get something for nothing and as a result, were ripe for getting scammed by the con men.

In like manner, these girls who take the cards from those producers – they are the ones at fault. The producers know that for the most part, they are whores and are desperate. So they appeal to the GREED of these women who want to become "movie stars." These are women who have been told for most or all of their lives that they are beautiful, that they are "movie star" material and so on. It goes to their heads. They start looking at television and saying, "I look better than she does." And then they make the move to Hollywood with no connections, no contacts, no network. And they get swooped on like a vulture on the dying prey. It's still a casting couch but its more informal than the traditional one that takes place within the studio or the director's office.

Here's another example:

> In a 2010 interview with *Elle magazine*, Gwyneth Paltrow revealed that early in her career a film executive suggested that a business meeting should finish "in the bedroom". (Wikipedia, 2016)

So? She presents herself like a slut. Look at the photos she takes for People magazine and other rags. She doesn't even have a decent body but she's usually got on a skirt up the crack of her ass or some bikini top. Why? Because she's blonde, that's why. In fact, People magazine gave this boney slag the title of "The Sexiest Woman in the World" in 2013. To deflect this title which she knows she didn't deserve (at least not physically) she says that "my family makes me beautiful." Say what? Unless your family has some padded bras, push up panties, mascara, sun tan lotion and collagen for lip buildup, she is going to be very disappointed.

Furthermore, a film executive suggests that they should finish the meeting in the bedroom. This bitch wasn't married. She knows the score and she knows what it takes. Why would she act surprised or shocked?

Moving on:

> In April 2010, actor Ryan Phillippe admitted on the *Howard Stern Show* that he had had to flee a "creepy" casting-couch session when he was 18 or 19. (Wikipedia, 2016)

This is one of those white boys that you can just look at and tell he's taken it up the ass more than a few times. But to white bitches, this is sexy – they refer to guys like this as being "sensitive." Phillippe didn't "flee" – it's not like he can get quality work whenever he wants to. They try to macho him up in a few movies like "Catch Hell," "Way of the Gun" and "Crash," but for the most part he's what the white folks call a "pretty boy" and in my book that's a synonym for "metro male" which is another synonym for "rump roaster."

The next piece of "evidence" is especially interesting:

> In a 2010 interview with *Access Hollywood*, actress Lisa Rinna
> said a producer had asked her for "a quickie" when she was a 24-
> year-old candidate for a role on a prominent television series … At
> the same interview, Rinna's husband Harry Hamlin claimed that a
> female casting director attempted to seduce him in the late 1970s
> when he was 27. (Wikipedia, 2016).

Lisa Rinna is married to Harry Hamlin. If that's not a "closeted relationship," then I don't know what is. Hamlin is one of those white boys who appears to be a metrosexual. Rinna has her own issues – like the ones she has with her lips (the ones on her face). Check it out:

> While sitting in for Kathie Lee Gifford on "Today" on Monday,
> Lisa was taken by surprise when co-host Hoda Kotb interrupted the
> "Celebrity Apprentice" star and said, "Wait, can I ask about your
> lips?" Of course, this is a topic the 49-year-old has gotten used to
> talking about over and over again, but she kindly rehashed the
> issue for Hoda: "Here's the story: 25 years ago, I had my lips
> injected with silicone. Stupid thing to do at 24. I saw 'Beaches.'
> Remember that movie 'Beaches'? I did it with my best girlfriend,
> so she and I go and we get our lips done. Fine. I have it like that
> for my whole career, right? So then cut to a couple of years ago, I
> have a doctor remove as much as they possibly can because it got
> to the point where they were yucky. You know, they get hard. It's
> gross. They are now whatever that was after they took out as much
> of the silicone as they could." (Adams, 2013).

She said that her injected lips got "to the point where they get yucky." Well bitch, that's whatcha get when you see black people's lips and you want to imitate them. No, she didn't say it, but we all know what these white bitches crave for. Even the otherwise tommish and conservative Ebony magazine did a special story for the April 1991 issue with the following heading: "They Took Our Music – Now They're 'Taking' Our Lips." The sub heading of the story inside the magazine read, "As beauty standards change, some White women are seeking large voluptuous lips with injections and cosmetics." Pictured to the right of the sub-heading were Cher, Michelle Pfeiffer, Kim Basinger and Barbara Hershey.

What does this have to do with the casting couch, you may ask? Anybody who would go this far to "improve" their looks so that they could appear sexier and land various TV and movie roles is not above using those lips (the ones on their face and between their legs) to land those roles. You've seen her movies: they are mediocre at best. How do you think she beat out natural beauties with lips that made her look like a white version of Jimmy Walker?

Another "celebrity" had this to say about the casting couch:

> In the November 2012 issue of *Elle*, Susan Sarandon spoke of a
> "really disgusting" casting-couch experience in New York in the
> late 1960s or early 1970s. "I just went into a room and a guy
> practically threw me on the desk. It was my early days in New
> York and it was really disgusting. It wasn't like I gave it a second
> thought. It was so badly done." (Wikipedia, 2016).

What did she mean that the act of throwing her on a desk was "so badly done"? Is there a scripted technique that she was used to? Notice that she didn't complain about it – she just described it. By her own admission she "didn't give it a second thought" meaning that she knew it was par for the course. After all, you can't rape the willing.

Sarandon's story sounds like the following one:

> Theresa Russell has alleged in multiple interviews that she was
> propositioned by legendary producer Sam Spiegel during her first
> casting session for *The Last Tycoon*. (Wikipedia, 2016).

Teresa Russell was a clone of Katherine Turner except that the former had bigger breasts. Whatever that producer did must have worked because according to my research, Russell had a major part in the movie. So when he propositioned her, she must have said "yeah, I'll suck it."

Lovely Latina Rita Moreno, one of only a handful of people who have won an Emmy, Grammy, Oscar and Tony awarded, made the following claim:

> In 2015, in an interview on *Access Hollywood*, iconic actress Rita
> Moreno declared that Buddy Adler, former production head for
> 20th Century Fox studios, made constant calls to her which she
> refused to accept, as she "knew what he was after." (Wikipedia,
> 2016)

Yeah. She refused? Did she refuse when she was nominated for those four major awards as well? Did she "refuse" to get her first appearance on the Ed Sullivan Show in 1948 or Perry Como in the same year? Did she "refuse" in order to land that appearance on "The Jack Benny Show" in 1950? Let's skip ahead to the movies.

Playing stereotyped roles for the most part, Rita auditioned for, and won parts in "The Toast of New Orleans" (1950), and "The Fabulous Senorita" (1952, the latter where she played "Manuela Rodriguez." So a Latina gets Latina parts. Was she harassed during audition? Did they want a "hot Latina" for the part? Did she have to take off her clothes or flash her breasts?

In 1952 she was in the classic "Singing in the Rain" playing a Latina named Zelda Zonders. In 1953 came two more movies: "Fort Vengeance" and "Latin Lovers" the latter where she played "Christina." She knew what these roles were, but she was looking for work, right? She made many more movies but check these out: in 1961 there was "Summer and Smoke" playing Rosa Zacharias, and in 1981 she made two: Evita Peron (which was a TV movie) and "The Four Seasons" where she played Claudia Zimmer." Did she have to audition? What did she go through to get these parts?

Now she turned down a part where she felt she was being harassed, but look at the garbage roles she ACCEPTED. We have to ask "why"?

And it's not just going on in America, either:

> On an episode of *The Word* in 1994, English actress Kate O'Mara claimed American producer Judd Bernard pulled down her panties during a hotel-room audition for the Elvis Presley vehicle *Double Trouble* (1967) … In her autobiography *Vamp Until Ready: A Life Laid Bare* (2003), O'Mara described this alleged casting couch incident (p. 61) and "many other close encounters with... this very unpleasant and humiliating procedure" …. including a well-known television casting director …. the boss of Associated Television at Elstree Studios …. and the director of *Great Catherine* ….

So this woman is auditioning for a part to star with one of the biggest cockhounds in history, Elvis Presley. Behind closed doors some Jew pulls down her panties. How did he arrange that? Did she audition in a dress? Since it was the sixties, perhaps it was a mini-skirt. Then she talks about future casting couch incidents and of course, since she's white she HAS to be a victim.

And these white boys aren't just in it for vaginal action, either. Check out the following:

> In 1998, writer-director Bruce Robinson described how as a 20-year-old young actor he was given a role in *Romeo and Juliet* (1968) after Franco Zeffirelli went down on him in Rome …

So who was the real ho: Robinson or Zeffirelli? It's a two way street in many of these cases, and that gives the concept of the "casting couch" an entirely different "texture" (no pun intended). Continuing:

> In 2002, actress Lesley-Anne Down (b. 1954) spoke of finding fame in the late 1960s: "The casting couch was in full swing, people expected it... My teen-age years were pretty intense, a lot of pressure and a lot of horrible old men out there" … In a 1977 interview, she had also said: "I was promised lots of lovely big

> film parts by American producers if I went to bed with them...
> Believe me, the casting couch is no myth … "

Lesley Ann Down was a ho from way back. Now here she is playing the role of casting couch victim. And guess what? Down had a ten year relationship with the same guy who, in an earlier passage, claimed that Franco Zefferelli gave him some head! She had this relationship with this guy, Bruce Robinson, then got out of it and married Enrique Gabriel, but their marriage ended in a year and a half. So she HAS no morals, and it gets worse:

> In 2015, Down discussed her experiences of sexual harassment in the 1970s by an unnamed legendary Hollywood actor and also by producer Sam Spiegel, saying that she had never really enjoyed her acting career: "Partly that was because of all the lecherous men, studio executives, producers and directors. There was so much running away and hiding under tables. Anyway, I started when I was ten and I've been doing it for 50 years"

Here's what I think: I think Lesley Ann Down has sucked a lot of dick in order to get her roles. I think she was more particular than some of the women who auditioned and when she was approached by a man that she didn't find attractive, she considered it harassment. But when you audition for the kinds of parts she's had – seductress, prostitute, wife, average white woman on the prowl – what do you expect people to assume? These white women give head the way most people shake hands! And it starts in high school, way before black girls learn the trade!

But the sistahs (Black women) get harassed as well. For instance,

> In 2013, Thandie Newton told CNN of how, aged 18, she was auditioned by a male director and a female casting director. "The director asked me to sit with my legs apart – the camera was positioned where it could see up my skirt – to put my leg over the arm of the chair and before I started my dialogue, [I was told] to think about the character I was supposed to be having the dialogue with and how it felt to be made love to by this person. It turned out the director used to show that video late at night to interested parties at his house – a video of me touching myself with a camera up my skirt." She declined to name the director.

This pencil-thin beauty must have done something because she's gotten some pretty juicy (no pun intended) parts with some serious cockhounding co-stars: Tom Cruise, Tim Roth, Christian Bale, Tupac Shakur, Jason Patric, and Cillian Murphy – to name but a few. But keep the previous quote in mind because it shows you how these white boys act and what goes on behind closed doors. It is akin to what they used to do to our mothers when they would go out to clean their homes and the wives of the white man was not available. Our mothers were assaulted and raped and could say nothing because our fathers would have killed that peckerwood and then gotten lynched. But this casting couch, taking advantage of a lone sistah, is an extension of that "man with the gold makes the rules" edict that the white man has historically lived by.

Case Study: Henry Wilson – Hollywood Predator

As part of my case study let me quote from and analyze some key points from the website article, "The Casting Couch: True Story of a Hollywood Predator" (2010). The author claims that it is the true story of Henry Wilson, a casting agent who used his "casting couch" for 30 years. Again, one has to wonder how something so terribly tawdry, so maniacally manipulative and immoral, could persist for so long.

The article begins, thusly:

> The true story of Henry Willson, casting agent whose couch was, for thirty years the only way an actor would get a break. There really was a predator in Hollywood who demanded sex before taking on a client or sending an actor on a casting call. (Kaylar, 2010).

So then it was a matter of quid quo pro. The real pimp was the person that would submit to such a "deal" in the first place, right? The degree of desperation is going to determine just what you are willing to do in order to get sent on a casting call. In another context think about the job situation and all those people, especially the sistahs, who have to sit there and undergo scrutiny by some white man. In many instances it may be legit; but that depends on the status of the position being applied for and how competitive the applications for the job are, does it not? More on that later.

Kaylar continues:

> Willson was born into a prominent show business family in the East. His father, Horace, was vice president of the Columbia Phonograph Company and became president of Columbia Gramophone Mfg. Co. in 1922. Henry displayed his orientation very early, and his father sent him to Asheville School in North Carolina, where he thought the rough sports and rugged weekend activities such as rock climbing would 'straighten him out'. It didn't. (Kaylar, 2010).

It sounds to me as though Henry's father thought he was a little "too light in the pants," a might "too soft in the loafers" or "too sweet for his own good." In other words, a fag. So he wanted to toughen him up, which was the way that parents handled that kind of suspicion back in the day. In fact, Bernie Mac's skit on his sister's kids bears this out. He says that the young boy he had to adopt because the boy's mother was on drugs was suspected to be gay. As part of the skit Bernie says, "Don't nobody walk around like this here! Do some damn pushups or somethin'!"

Moving on:

> It was mutually agreed that Henry would go away, and he went to Hollywood. He didn't go overland. He cleverly booked himself onto a cruise ship on which Bing Crosby and his wife Dixie Lee were traveling. He ingratiated himself into a friendship with Dixie, and she undertook to introduce him to Hollywood elite and secured him a job at *Photoplay.* (Kaylar, 2010).

So the kid was a manipulator and it's not specifically stated how he "ingratiated himself." We know that a young boy can act in a way that is so self-deprecating that older women adopt a motherly attitude toward them. Not only that, but I'm sure there was more to it than that. After all, Bing was big time cockhound and Dixie Lee. He had four boys by her before they divorced, and from what one son wrote, he used to beat the shit out of them as punishment.

In his 1983 book, *Going My Own Way*, the eldest Gary shared the following:

> I dropped my pants, pulled down my undershorts and bent over. Then he went at it with the belt dotted with metal studs he kept reserved for the occasion. Quite dispassionately, without the least display of emotion or loss of self-control, he whacked away until he drew the first drop of blood, and then he stopped. It normally took between twelve and fifteen strokes. I counted them off one by one and hoped I would bleed early. To keep my mind off the hurt, I would conjure up different schemes to get back at him, ways to murder him.

As Black people we are raised around white folks and we pick up on a lot. Notice how I knew something was weird about the fact that Dixie just "picked up on" Henry's ingratiating behavior. That prompted me to do some research on the Crosby clan and found out that Dixie and Bing divorced. I figured that because Bing was getting all kinds of pussy in Hollywood, especially after he started making movies after meeting Frank Sinatra. So just add two and two. And it is clear that he was cold-hearted towards his boys and who knows how he treated Dixie.

At any rate Dixie was used to be surrounded by testosterone and Henry played on it long enough to get to Hollywood. Once there,

> He began writing for *The Hollywood Reporter* and *The New Movie Magazine*, then became a junior agent at the Joyce & Polimer Agency. Horace, wanting to insure that Henry didn't come back, purchased a house for him in Beverly Hills. With his job, his house, and his contacts, Henry Willson became the scourge of Sunset Strip gay bars. (Kaylar, 2010).

There are too many gaps in this story. Horace, Henry's father, wanted to get rid of him so what does he do? He buys him a house and I believe that by this time the father knew the son was a straight up fag. He just wanted the kid out of his sight. And Henry took full advantage. By "scourge of the gay bars" I presume it to mean that he was a man-whore who gave up ass and head to scores of other men.

And so his career begins:

> From Junior to Lana
> One of his first clients and lovers was Junior Durkin, who was killed in an automobile accident on May 4, 1935. Willson, behaving in a manner which proved Durkin far more than just a client, drew the wrong attention. To mask his proclivities, Henry searched for a female he could turn into a major star and discovered Lana Turner. This rocketed him to fame, squelched negative hype. No less than David O. Selznick hired Willson to head the talent division of his newly formed **Vanguard** Pictures. This gave Willson more credibility, and much more power. (Kaylar, 2010).

So in order to cover up the fact that he was gay, he decided to make it appear as if he was heterosexual, at least in terms of his business client inclinations and preferences. Enter: Lana Turner. He was able to play down the gay rumors. When he was hired by David O. Selznick he gained power and credibility. In case you don't remember, he was notorious for popping amphetamines and perhaps as a result he suffered several heart attacks. He won a major award for is production of "Gone With The Wind."

Wilson wasn't finished:

> The first film Willson cast was the World War II drama ***Since You Went Away*** with Claudette Colbert, Jennifer Jones, and Shirley

Temple. He placed three of his lovers, Guy Madison, Craig
Stevens, and John Derek (billed as Dare Harris) in small
supporting roles. (Kaylar, 2010).

Take note that Jennifer Jones was cast in this movie. She would later move
on to marry Selznick, the pill popper mentioned earlier. At any rate, Willson never
put away his homosexuality – he simply exploited it. You may remember the three
guys mentioned above. Guy Madison, who I remember was "Wild Bill Hickok"
and a rough and tumble cowboy type; Craig Stevens, who I watched on television
as a boy as Peter Gunn. He was married to a woman, but as you can see, he was
going both ways. John Derek, who would end up marrying Bo, also took it up the
ass or so it would appear. He would also marry Linda Evans, famous for her role as
Crystal Carrington on the long-running night time soap opera, "Dynasty."
Willson's power kept increasing:

> This proved to the Sunset crowd that Willson could deliver.
> Flushed with this power, Henry Willson opened his own talent
> agency, where he nurtured the careers of his young finds, coercing
> them into sexual relationships in exchange for publicity and film
> roles. (Kaylar, 2010).

Coercing them? If I'm a prostitute and you offer me money for sex, have I
been "coerced"? Here we are in Hollywood, a veritable hotbed of hubris, ego and
conspicuous consumption. All of this has to be combined into a package that will
allow those seeking "stardom" to be able to appear on screen. Self-confidence
means nothing unless one can link it to evidence f talent. And that talent is defined
by people like Willson and in return for the marketing of that talent, he wants sex
and money in return. This is the way America operates in general.
Furthermore:

> Richard Barrios, In his book, **Screened Out: Playing Gay in
> Hollywood from Edison to Stonewall (2002)**, wrote, "Talent
> agent Henry Willson... had a singular knack for discovering and
> renaming young actors whose visual appeal transcended any lack
> of ability. Under his tutelage, Robert Mosely became Guy
> Madison, Arthur Gelien was changed to Tab Hunter, and Roy
> Fitzgerald turned into Rock Hudson." (Kaylar, 2010).

They had to be ideals in terms of their looks. And, of course, they had to be
white. In other words, these are the types of men who became known as "sex
symbols." Many times the names were changed for macho-oriented reasons but
there had long been a tradition in America and in Hollywood to change your last
name if you were a Jew, to make yourself sound more "American." In other words,

a race of chameleons, so Hollywood was no exception and with the advent of plastic surgery, the "changes" became even more evident and pervasive. But that is another story for another time.

Let us take the case of Rock Hudson. According to Kaylar (2010),

> Roy Fitzgerald was a clumsy, naive, Chicago-born truck driver. Willson, in over lust, molded him into one of Hollywood's most popular leading men. Creating another of his super macho names, Roy became Rock Hudson. (Kaylar, 2010).

In other words, white hillbilly by way of white privilege is molded into white stardom. Don't forget that when Hudson was a star America was in various stages of racial segregation. Not that black people gave a damn, but the point is that Hudson's homosexuality was hidden from white people as he proceeded, at least according to the rumor, to marry none other than Jim "Gomer Pyle" Nabors! I had heard that a long time ago but thought it as a joke. But here's what's not a joke:

> Marc Christian MacGinnis, who won a multimillion-dollar settlement in 1991 from the estate of his ex-lover, actor Rock Hudson, after convincing a jury Hudson had knowingly exposed him to AIDS, has died. He was 56.Dec 5, 2009 (Wikipedia, 2017).

All this is taking place while black people are marching for civil rights and looking for black role models on television. Be careful what you ask for. But the Rock Hudson story is a long way from over. As Kaylar (2010) claims, When in 1955 Confidential magazine threatened to publish an expose about Hudson's homosexuality, Willson disclosed information about two of his other clients; Rory Calhoun's years in prison and Tab Hunter's arrest at a gay party. Willson would do anything to protect Hudson. (Kaylar, 2010).

Rory Calhoun was one of my mother's favorite stars. How could that old lady know what was going on his warped life? But I'm thinking about Doris Day and all those movies she made with Rock. I'm wondering about how pervasive AIDS was at the time and how many people got infected by Hudson:

> It was Willson who organised the marriage of Hudson to his secretary, Phyllis Gates. This killed the rumors. Although the marriage only lasted three years, (Gates was a lesbian), it was sufficient to end the questions of Rock Hudson's sexuality. Most of Willson's clients married. Some more than once, others fathered children to dispel the question of their orientation. (Kaylar, 2010).

So it was widespread. So when these naïve black people claim, as they do, that "he's not gay – he's married," don't you believe a thing. I had a good friend in college who was openly gay on campus and became a lawyer. He also got married and had a kid. And the point made here is that the strategy is not a new one; if these peckerwoods could set up Rock Hudson with a dyke and make all these other arrangements to keep fag news out of the tabloids, when what else are they capable of ? And how many of our people, fronting like macho stars and beautiful starlets, are switch hitters behind closed doors?

This is just the tip of the iceberg. Kaylar (2010) writes:

> For nearly thirty years, Henry Willson exploited young attractive males. Promising stardom in return for sex, making it clear to Gay and Straight alike that there was only one way to get into pictures. By the late sixties, Willson was a drug addict, had bouts of alcoholism, paranoia, and weight problems. As his own homosexuality was well known, many of his clients abandoned him(Kaylar, 2010).

For nearly thirty years this cracker got away with this shit. And there are hundreds like him doing the same thing, and it's far more pervasive in places other than Hollywood and in situations beyond filmmaking and media. The "casting couch" is a metaphor for how people can be controlled and how their dreams can be pimped and their lives controlled.

In the case of Willson it was promising stardom for sex. But "stardom" can mean different things to different people. For many it can be a job interview, access to a student loan, a new dress or a pair of shoes – depending on one's socioeconomic status. The casting couch means that on one end you sacrifice yourself and compromise what little morality you may have and this is done in return for something you deem more important than these things. In most cases it is material and if not, then it is economic or financial and in a capitalist setting that translates to mean material.

Whatever happened to Willson?

> In 1974, unemployed and destitute he moved into the Motion Picture & Television Country House and Hospital, where he remained until he died of cirrhosis of the liver. With no money to cover the cost of a tombstone, he was interred in an unmarked grave, in Valhalla Memorial Park Cemetery, in North Hollywood, California. (Kaylar, 2010).

He died broke, but that's not the point of this information I am sharing with you. What I am sharing is but a metaphor for what these white people and their negro lackey are up to and in far too many cases it's being done behind closed doors. In far too many cases the concept of "fame and fortune" are goals of our young people who aspire to be what they see on the silver screen and on television. These young people are given promises of movie stardom and then some "B-rated" opportunity comes up and they have to strip down, do what the "director" says (who, by the way, is the real pervert) and then they can boast to their friends about being "in the movies." They never share the part about the degradation ceremony they were exposed to and forced to participate in.

<u>CORPORATE AMERICA AS "POLITICAL CASTING COUCH"</u>

As yet another teaching moment, let me now share an article by Philip Rucker and Karen Tumulty from the Washington Post, dated December 22, 2016. The headline of the article is, "Donald Trump is Holding a Government Casting Call. He's Seeking 'The Look.' It contains a lesson for our young people and other aspiring folk who think that "success" can be obtained based on looks and a willingness to do whatever it takes to get what it is you seek.

The article begins, thusly:

> Donald Trump believes that those who aspire to the most visible
> spots in his administration should not just be able to do the job, but
> also look the part. Given Trump's own background as a master
> brander and showman who ran beauty pageants as a sideline, it was
> probably inevitable that he would be looking beyond their résumés
> for a certain aesthetic in his supporting players. (Rucker &
> Tumulty, 2016).

The people with this kind of power are essentially pimps. The Hollywood version has a "pay for play" approach to the casting couch. With Donald Trump it's more of an opportunity for him to get laid and to flaunt the women he hires to other guys so that he can come off looking like some kind of "playboy." Boasting about this to Billy Bush during an interview is how he got busted on national television degrading women and claiming that he can just walk up to them and kiss them or just grab them by the pussy. This is not only the mentality of a wannabe pimp, but also of a misogynist.

The article continues: "Presentation is very important because you're representing America not only on the national stage but also the international stage, depending on the position," said Trump transition spokesman Jason Miller." . (Rucker & Tumulty, 2016). But in 2017 Trump is now president and his personal life is a matter of public record. He's a pig. What he was just quoted as saying is just a façade: he could care less about how America is "presented." Look at his wife, Melania: she has all the appearance and presentation of a high-class whore. And Trump knows it. He doesn't touch her in public and vice-versa. It's all for show. The fact is, after seeing some photos of him with his daughter Ivanka, I think she's the one he's screwing.

But I have always said that Trump was a closet homosexual and that he has homoerotic thoughts about none other than Barack Obama. He is so envious of Obama that his apparent dislike for the former president is reminiscent of the disdain that a woman has for a man after she's been rejected or dismissed. More on that later.

According to Rucker & Tumulty (2016), it's not just about female physical attractiveness when it comes to the public 'casting couch':

> To lead the Pentagon, Trump chose a rugged combat general, whom he compares to a historic one. At the United Nations, his ambassador will be a poised and elegant Indian American with a compelling immigrant backstory. As secretary of state, Trump tapped a neophyte to international diplomacy, but one whose silvery hair and boardroom bearing project authority. . (Rucker & Tumulty, 2016).

The men he chose were silver-haired old geezers. The sister from India is nice looking and her name is Nikki Haley. Trump doesn't want to hire anyone who is so physically attractive that he takes attention away from him. After all, he has a tan that produced orange skin, bleached blonde hair and so it is apparent that he spends a lot of time in the mirror. He then sits in judgment of others, as the following paragraph makes clear:

> The parade of potential job-seekers passing a bank of media cameras to board the elevators at Trump Tower has the feel of a casting call. It is no coincidence that a disproportionate share of the names most mentioned for jobs at the upper echelon of the Trump administration are familiar faces to obsessive viewers of cable news — of whom the president-elect is one. "He likes people who present themselves very well, and he's very impressed when somebody has a background of being good on television because he thinks it's a very important medium for public policy," said Chris Ruddy, chief executive of Newsmax Media and a longtime friend of Trump. "Don't forget, he's a showbiz guy. He was at the pinnacle of showbiz, and he thinks about showbiz. He sees this as a business that relates to the public." . (Rucker & Tumulty, 2016).

Trump is overrated. In my view, just because you appear on television for a few minutes or because people interview you doesn't make you a "showbiz guy."

Trump chased the spotlight time and time again. According to reports he made up a persona named John Miller and would call newspapers, masquerading as a publicist, and talk about how great Donald Trump was, especially with women. What kind of sick asshole does that? And now does this obvious narcissism impact on his decisions to select and hire other people?

The article claims:

> "The look might not necessarily be somebody who should be on the cover of GQ magazine or Vanity Fair," Ruddy said. "It's more about the look and the demeanor and the swagger." . (Rucker & Tumulty, 2016).

Trump has a fragile ego and doesn't want to be upstaged or outshined, so I don't know where the authors got their information. Trump might just say this kind of thing and tell others to relay the information so that he (Trump) will appear less petty and more professional than he really is. Demeanor and swagger: two characteristics that black men, even low-income street brothers, are in abundance of. And this is one group that Trump despises. The only blacks he can tolerate are the ones who are stiff, out of touch and in love with white folks like Omarosa Manigault, Dr. Ben Carson, Paris Dennard and a few others.

Trump's homoeroticism may have been evident in his decision to choose Mike Pence for Vice-President. Check it out:

> As Trump formally announced his vice presidential pick in July, he said that Mike Pence's economic record as Indiana governor was "the primary reason I wanted Mike, other than he looks very good, other than he's got an incredible family, incredible wife and family." . (Rucker & Tumulty, 2016).

He looks very good? Pence has white hair. Rex Tillerson (Secretary of State), graying, as is James Mattis, Secretary of Defense. John Kelly moved from Homeland Security to being Trump's babysitter is both balding and gray; Jeff Sessions, old man; Sony Perdue (Secretary of Agriculture), balding. Gray and overweight; Will Ross (Secretary of Commerce) is bald and cartoon looking Steve Mnuchin who, somehow married a blonde model/actress with a fucked up attitude. As ugly as Trump is, all of these guys, on some level, look worse.

Homoeroticism reigns with Trump and not a single pundit has said anything about it, even though that "Steele Dossier" alleges that he paid some Russian prostitutes to stand on a bed that Barack and Michelle Obama slept in while they were in Russia (Ritz-Carlton Hotel) and pissed on it while he (Trump) watched! What was that about? Was he fantasizing that he and Barack were having sex?

Moving on:

> And in picking retired Marine Gen. James Mattis as his nominee for defense, Trump lauded him as "the closest thing to General George Patton that we have." Mattis has a passing physical resemblance to the legendary World War II commander, as well as to the late actor George C. Scott, who won an Academy Award for his portrayal of Patton in the 1970 biopic. Trump also seems particularly enamored with a nickname that Mattis is said to privately dislike. "You know he's known as 'Mad Dog' Mattis, right? 'Mad Dog' for a reason," Trump said in a recent interview with the New York Times. . (Rucker & Tumulty, 2016).

"Mad Dog" Mattis. He's not acting like a mad dog when Trump starts pulling his antics. He just sits there like the old fart that he is. It's easy for these white boys to be heroes when they sit back, bark out orders and push buttons. The kids in the field are the ones getting their arms and legs blown off and the old dudes get all the credit. Patton was notorious for craving photo ops whenever he could get them – just like that egomaniac Donald Trump. Trump ran from the draft and dodged it five times, but he's always talking about being a "counter puncher" and a "fighter." My sons could whip his ass with one hand tied behind their backs.

Back to the importance of physical appearance:

> On the other hand, in Trump's book, not having the right kind of appearance is tantamount to a disqualifier. During the presidential campaign, he stirred a controversy when he pronounced that Democratic nominee Hillary Clinton lacked "a presidential look, and you need a presidential look." Battling through the GOP primary, Trump frequently made barbed comments about his opponents' appearances. . (Rucker & Tumulty, 2016).

Trump must not have a mirror in his house. Not only is he morbidly obese (he hides it under his oversized suits), he has a sun tan that makes him look like an alien. His bleached hair is ridiculously unkempt and uncombed, and the fact that he had the nerve to insult Hillary was an attempt to camouflage his own slouchiness. And remember that on the Trump "casting couch," he will not allow anyone who may appear to be better looking than he is. As a petty and shallow curmudgeon, he judges other people but never takes a look at himself, physically or internally.

And because far too many white people are unkempt (though they think they are well dressed), Trump comes off as being "GQ." For instance, note the following paragraph:

> Those kind of skin-deep standards helped make Trump a success
> as a reality-television star and international brand, but his critics
> say they are worrisome in the Oval Office. His personnel choices
> show signs of being "cast for the TV show of his administration,"
> said Bob Killian, founder of a branding agency based in Chicago.
> "They are all perfectly coifed people who look like they belong on
> a set." . (Rucker & Tumulty, 2016).

In Trump's world there is no real difference between "casting" and "hiring," especially when the person being interviewed is a woman. Why should there be? She comes in knowing the kind of person this asshole is. He clears the room and asks a few questions. She probably has on a dress so short you can see her cootchie and breasts exposed. He might hint around to getting some head or meeting later at a hotel. It doesn't matter. He knows that she needs a job and she knows that he has the power to provide her with one. How is this any different than the casting couch?

Now come the lies and attempted cover-ups of Trump's shallowness:

> But Trump spokesman Miller insisted that some qualifications do
> not lend themselves to lines on a résumé: "People who are being
> selected for these key positions need to be able to hold their own,
> need to be doers and not wallflowers, and need to convey a clear
> sense of purpose and commitment." . (Rucker & Tumulty, 2016).

Steve Miller is a right wing flunky, akin to Steve Bannon, who is lying through his teeth in the previous excerpt. To begin with the "qualifications" that Trump has are almost totally subjective and white oriented. As you can see there are no black people in his direct circle and only one (Dr. Ben Carson) on his cabinet. And that one black person is one that during the Republican campaign Trump referred to as a pedophile. Ironically, the subject was "pathology" and Trump – of all people – attacked Carson's claims. On November 1, 2015 it was reported:

> Donald Trump says rival Republican presidential hopeful Ben
> Carson has a 'pathological' temper that can't be cured any more
> than a pedophile can be cured. Speaking at a campaign rally in Fort
> Dodge Iowa, Trump discusses Carson's admission about having a
> 'pathological temper – a disease' in his 1992 memoir Gifted Hands
> and questions his suitability for becoming president (The
> Guardian, 2015).

Some important points should be made here.

First of all, Dr. Ben Carson is an utter idiot. He is so passive and low-key – such a milquetoast – that he wrote about his temper in 1992 so he wouldn't come off like a sissy. His words came back to haunt him.

Secondly, Trump says that pathology can't be cured, and well he should know. If there was ever a pathological liar, it is Donald Trump. And no matter how much people tell him, no matter how many news casts call his sanity into question, he continues lying. As of August of 2017 the New York Times has documented over 1,000 lies that Trump has told.

And third, comparing this black man to a pedophile? That is a serious charge and in fact, the statement constitutes slander. Again, Trump has nerve because in my view he is not only a pedophile as it relates to his daughter Ivanka, but he has also committed incest with her. Their relationship is far too publicly intimate (check out some photos they took together when she was but a young teen) for my tastes.

But this is the one black person in Trump's cabinet. So Miller's claim about Trump looking for people who can "hold their own" and have a sense of purpose is bullshit. Trump was a willing thrall, hence his on-going queries to people testing and asking them about their "loyalty" to him. Not to the country – to HIM.

One lie begats another. If you buy into Miller's bullshit, then the next statement is a follow-up and reinforcement of that same lie:

> All of which has led him to some unconventional picks. If
> confirmed by the Senate, ExxonMobil chief executive Rex
> Tillerson will become the first secretary of state in modern history
> to come to the job with no experience in government. Then again,
> Trump himself has none. . (Rucker & Tumulty, 2016).

These old white men are ultra-rich, and that is what they have in common. He's out of Exxon-Mobil, the largest oil company in the world. And he's also got serious ties with Trump's homoerotic boyfriend, Vladimir Putin. These two facts in and of themselves made him a prime candidate since Trump's administration is about stockpiling money and wealth and little else. Tillerson's experience is about building up oil reserves all over the world and he's looking to the ice cold Antarctic, an area that Putin wants as well. But Obama's sanctions stopped it which is why it is imperative that Tillerson do his job and work with Trump to get those sanctions lifted.

Continuing:

> South Carolina Gov. Nikki Haley (R) has little obvious foreign
> policy experience to qualify her for United Nations ambassador,
> but she is a rising political star who brings diversity to Trump's

largely white and male picks for top jobs. Given how she and the
president-elect had clashed during the 2016 campaign, Haley's
selection also suggests that Trump is willing to bring adversaries
into the fold when they suit his needs. . (Rucker & Tumulty, 2016).

Nikki Haley is brilliant and bold and doesn't really jibe with Trump's concept of beauty. She's brown and dark but she has just enough color to make Trump's cabinet appear to be diverse. But make no mistake about it: Trump has gay tendencies and his on-going "man-watching" manifests itself in his descriptions of men, his jealousy of Barack Obama and in other ways. For instance, the following instance:

> In hiring, Trump has long trusted his own impressions, at times
> more than a candidate's expertise or experience. In 1981, he saw a
> security guard at the U.S. Open tennis championships masterfully
> eject some hecklers. Trump asked Barbara Res, one of his top
> construction executives, to hire the man. "But you've never even
> met him!" she protested. Trump said he liked how the man looked
> when he handled the situation. . (Rucker & Tumulty, 2016).

To begin with, Trump trusts his own impressions. Those who make decisions regarding the casting couch usually do. And their impressions are primarily sexual and social, not talent wise. Look at all the worthless people, especially in politics and popular culture, who hold positions of power. And when you see and hear them you ask yourself, "whose dick did he/she suck to get that job"? As black people we can tell because we've been kowtowing to white people for years, so we have a kind of intrinsic expertise.

Furthermore, take a look at the example above. Trump is a man who sees another man and likes what he sees. What kind of homoerotic bullshit is that? He told his executive that "he liked the way the man looked when he handled the situation." Can you see where I'm coming from? It's a less formal version of the casting call; that man wasn't auditioning, or at least he wasn't conscious that he was auditioning. But a homoerotic cockhound had "observed" him and that's all it took. You can hear and see the same homoerotic response from these white boys at sporting events as they watch powerful black men run, jump and engage in other athletic activities.

More on the security guard that Trump hired:

> That security guard, Matthew Calamari, has worked for Trump for
> 35 years and is now chief operating officer of Trump Properties.
> His son, Matthew Calamari Jr., started with Trump five years ago
> as a security guard and is now the Trump Organization's director
> of surveillance. . (Rucker & Tumulty, 2016).

This is that old peckerwood who tossed Univision reporter Jorge Ramos out of a Trump rally.

> In August 2015, a month into Trump's presidential campaign, the then-candidate had a verbal altercation with Univision reporter Jorge Ramos during a press conference. Ramos told Trump he "cannot deport 11 million people, you cannot build a 1,900 mile wall, you cannot deny citizenship in this country." Trump aggressively told Ramos to "Go back to Univision," and then moved on to another reporter. But Ramos wouldn't remain silent. He demanded an answer until he was forcefully removed from the press conference by Trump aides. (Perry, 2017).

The 6'7" bald headed old peckerwood who was bogarting Ramos was none other than Calamari. Trump's decision to hire Calamari was based on both race and homoerotic attraction. And you can tell by what he said about Ramos that racism was also something that Calamari has to agree with in order to have worked for Trump for 35 years. This has to do with Trump's idea of the"type" of people Trump finds acceptable:

> Trump's closest aides have come to accept that he is likely to rule out candidates if they are not attractive or not do not match his image of the type of person who should hold a certain job. "That's the language he speaks. He's very aesthetic," said one person familiar with the transition team's internal deliberations who spoke on the condition of anonymity. "You can come with somebody who is very much qualified for the job, but if they don't look the part, they're not going anywhere." . (Rucker & Tumulty, 2016).

Now pay close attention to this where one employee says of Trump's tastes, perceptions and choices: "You can come with somebody who is very much qualified for the job, but if they don't look the part they're not going anywhere." This is a classic definition of racial discrimination over the years, is it not? Even after the laws were changed, the "aesthetic" became light skinned blacks or mulattoes selected over darker blacks. This means that Omorosa must have sucked a lot of dick to get her position because although she's gorgeous, she's also dark in complexion. And she is surrounded by blondes. You do the math.

Trump has some serious issues when it comes to sexuality. In addition to that golden shower ordeal in Russia, he seems to have an attraction to men and to women that he has power over. Those beauty contests provide him with free reign to ogle, feel on and harass young girls who have entered his contests. His young wives are willing thralls and hail from other countries – no American bitch would have his goony ass. He boasts about women using a fake voice and personality, and the Billy Bush interview makes it clear what he thinks of them.

I believe he has the same fascination when it comes to men. After all, all genders are sooner or later involved in 'central casting,' right? Check it out:

> Trump was drawn to Tillerson and 2012 GOP nominee Mitt Romney for secretary of state because of their presence and the way they command a room when they walk in. The president-elect considered Romney despite the former Massachusetts governor's scathing criticism of him during the presidential campaign. Several Trump associates say he was drawn to Romney, and later to Tillerson, by their "central casting" quality, a phrase the president-elect uses frequently in his private deliberations. . (Rucker & Tumulty, 2016).

Drawn to other men because of "their presence" and "the way they command a room when they walk in." What kind of fag is this guy? He's scoping out other men while all the while trying to present himself as some international playboy? I've never seen him kiss Melania a single time and they hardly even touch or hold hands as they enter or exit a room. You can tell that it's all for show. Just like she showed that ass while modeling for GQ magazine a few years back.

Back to Trump and his version of central casting;

> People close to Trump said he has been eager to appoint a telegenic woman as press secretary or in some other public-facing role in his White House — both because he thinks it would attract viewers and would help inoculate him from the charges of sexism that trailed his presidential campaign. . His first choice was his campaign manager, Kellyanne Conway, who has resisted the offer. On Thursday, Trump announced that she would be counselor to the president (Rucker & Tumulty, 2016).

The homoerotic honky originally went with Sean Spicer which was a horrible decision on a number of fronts. But he settled on a woman who is anything BUT "telegenic." Her name is Sarah Huckabee Sanders and she is average looking at best.

<u>CONCLUSION</u>

America is a den of sin and the world knows it. Foreign students come here and the first thing they want to do is "mingle with the Americans" and do the things that they see on TV. And what do they see on TV? White bitches giving up pussy left and right and white men going after anything in a skirt. And even after humans who are male. It doesn't matter in America, and the "casting couch" concept feeds on this concept as a way to "audition" people who seek success, riches, fame and publicity. It's another form of "if you wanna play, you gotta pay.

The casting couch, on any level, is going to exist as long as there are people who want or need something. As the saying goes, "Those with the power to control human needs control the humans with those needs." And so it goes. People apply for something, seek out something or need something and those who have it or can get it are going to give it to them – for a price.

<u>REFERENCES</u>

Adams, Rebecca (2013, March 19). Lisa Rinna lip trouble is the topic of conversation on 'Today'. *The Huffington Post.* Retrieved from http://www.huffingtonpost.com/2013/03/19/lisa-rinna-lip-trouble-today_n_2906183.html

Akst, Daniel (2005, December 18). Review: Old Hollywood's gay Pygmalion: Tale of agent for Hudson both uneven and engaging. *Boston Globe.* Retrieved from https://www.highbeam.com/doc/1P2-7936191.html

Ebony. They Took Our Music – Now They're "Taking" Our Lips. *Ebony.* Retrieved from https://books.google.com/books?id=0MsDAAAAMBAJ&pg=PA118&lpg=PA118&dq=Kim+basinger+on+cover+of+Ebony&source=bl&ots=ferRsdp2pN&sig=BgIvZo56_Cjo7nCJIuvR6XI02bo&hl=en&sa=X&ved=0ahUKEwi69uv3orvTAhVrzIMKHT4XDHYQ6AEIPTAJ#v=onepage&q=Kim%20basinger%20on%20cover%20of%20Ebony&f=false

Gallagher, Brenden (2013, September 25). 20 classic Hollywood stars who make Lindsay Lohan look like a saint. Retrieved from https://www.google.com/search?site=&tbm=isch&source=hp&biw=1248&bih=875&q=Hollywood+casting+couch&oq=Hollywood+casting+couch&gs_l=img.3...7472.12417.0.13109.23.16.0.7.3.0.156.1750.3j12.15.0....0...1ac.1.64.img..1.17.1696.gIt2PSyPdWU#imgrc=byehT5en2MqABM%3A

Garland, Benjamin (2016, March 21). Hollywood Jews repeatedly tried to rape Shirley Temple. Daily Stormer. Retrieved from http://www.dailystormer.com/hollywood-jews-repeatedly-tried-to-rape-shirley-temple/

Guardian, The. (2015, November 13). Donald Trump compares Ben Carson's 'pathological temper' to 'child molesting.' The Guardian. Retrieved from https://www.theguardian.com/us-news/video/2015/nov/13/trump-compares-ben-carsons-pathological-temper-to-child-molesting-video

Kaylar (2010, September 5). The casting couch: True story of a Hollywood Predator. Retrieved from http://celebrities.wikinut.com/The-Casting-Couch;-True-Story-of-a-Hollywood-Predator/1w2chkea/

McKay, Hollie (2011, December 14). Are Hollywood stars enabling sexual predators by not naming names? Foxnews.com. Retrieved from http://www.foxnews.com/entertainment/2011/12/14/are-hollywood-stars-enabling-sexual-predators-by-not-naming-names/

Perry, Tod. (2017 February 2). Trump Aide Tells Univision Reporter To 'Get Out Of My Country' Good Worldwide. Retrieved from https://www.good.is/articles/trump-aide-get-out-of-my-country

Pickert, Kate (2014, May 5). What the Bryan Singer scandal says about Hollywood. Time.com. Retrieved from http://time.com/88234/bryan-singer-hollywood-scandal/

Rucker, Philip & Tumulty, Karen (2016, December 22). Donald Trump is holding a government casting call. He's seeking 'the look.' *The Washington Post*. Retrieved from https://www.washingtonpost.com/politics/donald-trump-is-holding-a-government-casting-call-hes-seeking-the-look/2016/12/21/703ae8a4-c795-11e6-bf4b-2c064d32a4bf_story.html?utm_term=.e44eade9f7e0&wpisrc=nl_most-draw6&wpmm=1

Wikipedia (2016). Casting couch. Retrieved from https://en.wikipedia.org/wiki/Casting_couch

ASSAULT AND PEPPERED
Sexual Assault, Romance and the American Tradition of Abuse

INTRODUCTION

All of us know about the world's oldest profession, where men give women money in exchange for sex. No, I'm not talking about prostitution: *I'm talking about marriage!* Think about it: a racket where men (especially in America) turn "trick" by wooing, dining and dating these women, proposing to them, giving them diamond rings from the mines of South Africa where African men earn about fifty cents an hour, and have this woman gushing with happiness, bragging to all of her friends and her parents about the "trick" and how she's finally trapped a man for the rest of his life.

That's what it boils down to, although most people don't see it this way until long after they've been seduced by the mystique and materialism and a long life sleeping next to and staring at the same old individual again and again and again and again … You get it: 'til death do us part.'

This essay is a primer that I hope will inform and hopefully save the people who are smart enough to read it from cover to cover. It deals with a small slice of the sexual system in America, one that deals with what has grown to be known as "sexual misconduct." Some refer to it as "sexual abuse," but it's essentially the same thing: men taking advantage of women and threatening them for booty. But there's another side, too: the sexual misconduct of women who are smart enough to know that most men aren't about shit and therefore appeal to our cockhounding natures and offer us something in exchange for something: our souls!

To be "peppered" with something means "to sprinkle liberally, to scatter." And that is just what the issue of assault and the topic of various forms of abuse are doing: they are being scattered about but rarely discussed. The issue of assault is being used to generate grant dollars, to get members of the opposite sex arrested, to stockpile restraining orders, to be used as part of a divorce case and other social issues that don't get to the basic facts as I see them: men, in general, do not like women, in general. And vice-versa. Look at the record and that is what it looks like to me.

Being "peppered" with talk of assaults and other conflicts that impair and impede male-female relationships are the "spice" that flavors American society, no matter where you live or how you live. So in this short essay let me share some "preliminary notes" about sexual misconduct and how it impacts on male-female relationships and the family system.

THE TRADITION OF SEXUAL ASSAULT

The recent case of Tiger Woods and Ben Roethlisberger seem to be different. In the former case, you have a man who had numerous relationships with women outside of his marriage. In the latter case, a single man who apparently forced himself on young girls on at least two occasions. But stripped of its pomp and rather impious ceremony, people who are running their mouths seem to miss the point; that point is, "Something is WRONG."

If you know something is wrong, then you have an obligation to do something about it. That's the way it works for me. And since so many people are a part of what's "wrong" with this picture, I am going to spend the next seven weeks (not counting this introduction) sharing with you my views on what I view as very related issues: romance, sex, love and assaults.

I am going to show you how most of us (I say "us" for the sake of social courtesy) have been bamboozled and mummified by a set of values, ethics and false "norms" that pave the way for "affairs," "infidelity," "rape," "adultery," "pornography" and ultimately, assaults and death. We're all in it, and not just here in America – all over the world.

Being who I am and being able to do what I do affords me the time and talent to share ideas with you that you may have considered, but were too busy or gutless to do anything about. But in the next few months, just follow my logic and I'm going to show you how male-female relationships decayed to their present status and how money is made and power is maintained because of the manipulation of the THINKING of those involved in these relationships.

What makes me an authority? What gives me the right to offer these views are not the numerous degrees, the high IQ or knowledge of the issues involved. It is simply because I give a damn enough to put myself and my views out there for inspection and analysis and, from there, no one will be able to say that "nobody told me" or "somebody should have said something" – the same utterances most of you made when Senator Chambers was in office protecting and warning you. But as they say, "You never miss your water until the well runs dry."

If you care about black people (or I guess any people, for that matter), then your purpose is to reject in detail, defiance and self-determination the BS that is hurled at them from all over. Most people are imbeciles, six levels below the category of fools; they believe anything. W.C. Fields once said, "There's a sucker born every minute." He ain't never lied!

If you see a child in the street and a car is coming and you do nothing to save that child, you are responsible for what happens. Sen. Chambers used to teach that if you elect Jesse James to office, and he harms someone, you are responsible for what Jesse did. In this case, I know my people are busy and, for the most part, ignorant of the REAL issues, too busy concentrating on maintaining false status, trying to look good, looking for a baby daddy, out creating more baby mamas, chasing after a white man to adopt them (i.e., seeking a job instead of creating one), and/or a combination of all of the above.

But even in that, they still deserve to be informed and protected. So, like nasty medicine that you are forced to take, you're gonna read this series and you're going to get well for having read it. I don't believe in "trial and error" for people if there are leaders who can protect those people from making the errors. Why should you have to go through what I went through if I can help you avoid the pitfalls, obstacles and detours? I'm gonna do what the parents, teachers, preachers, counselors, advisors, mentors and scholars ought to be doing: unveiling male-female relationships and how they have been manipulated to represent the biggest scam in the known universe.

It's unfortunate that Tiger and Big Ben had to make asses out of themselves to get people talking. But if you're talking about particular situations, then you can't arrive at collective solutions. Only when you show a pattern of persistence, an ideology of imposition, a philosophy of philandering can you intelligently deal with what I'm going to be dealing with.

Now it's going to hurt some people. But simple analysis and deduction will set you free. As men, we have to look at what other men have done and ask ourselves: why do we follow suit? As fathers, we have to look at what other fathers did in their circumstances and ask, "What have I done to improve those circumstances?" And the reason I'm directing these prefatory remarks at the males is because the origins of all this rancor and rigmarole is male inspired! Maybe it wasn't our ancestors, but we had our own version of keeping women down, a woman's place is in the bedroom and the kitchen, and man is king. If you know the source of a problem, you can deal with it – we need to stop looking at the symptoms (teen pregnancy, infidelity, monogamous marriage, etc.)

These simple philosophies, which your grandparents believed in and promoted, are at the root of the problem. If you know this much, then you really need to know nothing else. Those in power keep it because they are able to manipulate these male-female realities and control the product of the way we relate to one another. This is in operation in every single nation on earth – and yet nobody is doing anything about or saying anything. Why?

Because those in power have linked male-female relationships and the control that has been "ordained" for men with religion and politics. Since most people claim to believe in a higher power, charlatans come along claiming to have a special "religious FedEx" from the Supreme Being. The message inside the Holy Box is simple: man on top, woman on the bottom (figuratively and literally speaking). And people eat it up, accept it, and then impose it through laws, rules and regulations.

This is the ROOT of the problem. An old cultural nationalist, Maulana Karenga, once wrote, *"We say that male supremacy is based on three things: tradition, reason and acceptance."* Karenga claims to have altered those views but the components of what I am writing about are essentially the same.

You know what I'm talking about: "A man is the head of the household." "The man's word is final." "A man always follows his money." "Don't ever ask a man where he's been." You've heard these sayings before and if you haven't, then ask your grandparents. It's the basis of a certain **tradition.** As for the **"reason,"** it was based on physical force, and I'll discuss that in an upcoming segment. Talk back and "pow! Right in the kisser. It is so prominent that it's even in the movies (Cagney, Bogart, etc.). And because of the success of the tradition and the reason, **acceptance** was therefore inevitable. *And a person who can control your relationship with your mate controls YOU.*

USA TODAY identified 164 athletes and former athletes who faced sexual assault allegations in the past dozen years. This is but the tip of the iceberg; assault is more than just physical: it is also ideological, philosophical and attitudinal. What Frederick Douglass said over a century ago still rings true, folks: *"Find out just what the people will submit to, and you have found out the exact amount of injustice and wrong which will be imposed upon them; and these will continue until they are resisted with either words or blows, or with both. The limits of tyrants are prescribed by the endurance of those whom they oppress."*

Next week: Gifts, Goons and Ideological "Game"

GIFTS, GOONS AND IDEOLOGICAL "GAME"

Part 1. Okay, with last week's preface out of the way (appeared in the Omaha Star week before last) let's get something straight right off the bat with part one: in my book, it's ALL about "sexual misconduct" when all is said and done. If we agree with Malcolm X that "of all our studies, history is best qualified to reward our research," then we know how important it is to go to the source of things. But, I ask, what if the source it, itself, poisoned or distorted? What if the history or the ideology of what we have been led to believe in his intentionally maladjusted?

Since nobody knows for sure and can only point to words in books that claim to be divinely inspired in order to validate what is "right" or wrong" or what took place "in the beginning," then let me advance a theory of my own. Let's call it the "Flip the Script" theory.

The first man that saw the first woman giving birth probably didn't know what the hell was going on. All he knew was that from her body was coming something that he could not replicate. He didn't even know that he had a role in producing it; all he knew was that this was a life producing another life. Now, from that realization can come two responses: one can be a renewed and positive vision of this female creature and from there, much respect and love as a result of what she has just done, OR jealousy because she could do something he could not do. And as far as he knew, his not being able to do it must be some kind of curse. If that was the case, then she, not him, must be truly BLESSED.

The adage teaches us that "the man with the gold makes the rules." The script had to be flipped because it was man who was always angry and at war and man that was the strongest in a physical sense. He could beat her up if she got out of line and that was the way that "God" wanted it. And so to justify physical strength, something had to be done to take that advantage and make it universal: to transform it into God-ordained power that existed across the board.

So along comes a book that claims that yes, indeed, at one point, a MAN also produced life. That's right – from the rib of the MAN came – woman, the same one that produces life to this very day. If people can be led to believe that, then superiority across the board, from the supernatural to the more mundane, is made clear. Woman's incredible ability to carry children is offset by the fact that "man" is made in the image of – God himself! It says so right here!

These then, are the ideological underpinnings of what is viewed as sexual misconduct. How? Because if the basis of something is flawed, fabricated or "F****ed up," then anything that is produced from that entity is going to be the same way! How can you have a "beginning" that is rooted in blaming a woman for "causing" man to take a bite out of an apple, and not set in motion an entire universal system aimed at defining, defiling, deflating and deforming her?

Several pseudo-intellectuals oftentimes are in chat rooms or on line debating their specious views of male-female relationships. But they never get to the root of it because they, too, accept the premises of the ideology I've just outlined. They are among the first to point to "man as the head of household" – I ask, based on what? As a sociologist I learned and teach that the division of labor is the way that gender differences were used in the favor of men, and it continues that way.

What, pray tell, does this have to do with sexual misconduct?

Misconduct is operationally defined here as, "intentional wrongdoing, a deliberate violation of a law or standard." In other words, "improper behavior." So if the origins or basis of relationships between the sexes is considered wrong or immoral (with one gender being responsible for duping the other one into "sin"), then where are the standards? Where is the normative conduct? That's right: the relationships were weird from the beginning because there was no UNDERSTANDING. This left the door open for manipulations of definitions that made sure that man was on top and in control and that woman, no matter how many miracles she pulled off, would always be in an inferior position.

So what we have is misconduct as a norm: because even at its best, relationships between men and woman are based on inequality. Just look around the world at the "arranged marriages" and look at "romantic love" in the United States. The two are very different, but they both share a common denominator: the legal system, which the man controls, being viewed as the "standards." So in absence of any moral sensibility or common sense, those in power invoke LAW as the norm. And it is from this kind of zaniness that the concept of "being married" takes form and function.

As I view it, the very concept of "sexual misconduct" describes human activity from the very beginning – even before there were rules and regulations to govern the conduct. So in my view, ALL sexual activity is evidence of "misconduct" because it's intentional, it's improper and it's deliberate. Because of its flawed base and inconsistent application, then, there are holes where "gifts, goons and ideological game" can be interjected to make the myth of male superiority even stronger and more pervasive than it already is. Remember: this is just a theory.

GIFTS

America is a young nation, but gets its values and vigor from jolly old Europe. Needless to say, Europe is one continent where morals are in short supply. But when it comes to male-female relationships, Africa isn't far behind as far as the treatment of women. But one thing about the Mother land: women were at least "allowed" to participate in social development. But that's not to say that every nation where men were in power was a nation where women were treated like objects. No doubt about it.

So we come here in chains. Not the kind that black people were bought over here in; the kind of mental chains that lead to alienated arrangements instead of relationships. Over here came every kind of pervert known to humankind and as a result, entire subcultures and systems were created. It is because of this beginning, one replete with disease, moral decadence and destructive tendencies, that America is in the shape it is in today.

To offset or perhaps veil the utter contempt that men had for women (and the jealousy that also existed), gifts were used to make it appear as if women were truly appreciated. Apparently, they fell for it.

So enter the concept of "romantic love." In sociology we provided students with an outline of what it entailed, but they don't go into the details because it would sound too "communistic." But the fact is, romantic love is nothing but a capitalist venture that forces one person to turn a trick with another. That's what it comes down to: paying for sex. In the early days it was paying for marriage and long-term commitment. Today, the formula goes more like this: pay and prove that you're stable, woo me and dine me, then we have sex until you're just about to get fed up with me, then I'll either "allow" you to marry me or I'll set you up with a kid and thereby squeeze 18 years of child support payments out of you.

I know: crude, cruel and crazy. But quite accurate.

The old folks used to teach us that what's done in the dark will come to the light. Well that's true about sexual misconduct; actions that originate in insanity will produce insanity. And that's what's going on today: 21st century prostitution being disguised as "wedded bliss" and "holy matrimony." A new set of chains replaces the ones that most of those who immigrated here already had on their minds, values and cultural belief systems. This nastiness would later be imposed on blacks as well.

Gifts: From kindergarten "play dates" to high school proms to college dating and then on to marriage, it's all about turning a trick. That's why this society moves on the sexes through capitalist holidays and movies that glorify dating and courting: it's an appeal to hormones, not the heart. When you're young, guaranteed long-term sex with the same person is an ideal that you'll buy into. If you wait until your 30s or 40s to get married, you've got sense enough to realize that sexual intercourse is a finite act! Who wants to give up their life for 30 minutes in the hay? (an hour, max).

The point here is simple: use gifts to disguise the grotesqueness of these alienated arrangements. Link these gifts to being evidence of "love." Valentine's Day, Mother's Day, Father's Day, Christmas, and even Thanksgiving: love in America means spending money and giving people things. And all this is how sexual misconduct is legitimized: it is perfectly normal. It is the way things are done. What I have just described are examples and prototypes for sexual misconduct that is perfectly acceptable. When The Beatles crooned, "Money Can't Buy Me Love" in 1964, and the Spinners later claimed, "Ain't No Price on Happiness," all I can say is: they were both wrong.

GOONS

A goon is a stupid person or someone who is hired to terrorize or eliminate an opponent. When it comes to sexual misconduct as a universal norm and certainly an American way of life, both definitions fit the male of the species like a glove.

Goons come in many forms in America, but the purpose or function of these individuals is the same: to eliminate common sense, to place a shroud around logic, and to mystify stupidity and raise it to the level of sacred observance. The key to the role of the goon is to link "security" and "satisfaction" to the institution of marriage. Although monogamous marriage makes no sense for the most part, the world has nevertheless latched onto it by again, using women as scapegoats: "Well if ya don't get married, ya won't know who the kid's daddy is." Well guess what folks: there are no guarantees even if you ARE married. Remember: Mama's baby, daddy's MAYBE."

Marriage is what young girls are duped into striving for. Their mothers teach them well: "why should he marry the cow if you're giving away the milk for free." In other words, MAKE HIM PAY FOR IT. The goons will provide enforcement and collect the money: blood test, marriage certificate, wedding gowns, wedding costs, reception, and so on. Money generated for the same system that tells you that "Valentine's Day" is the time to show someone you love them. Sex for sale in America is not an act of misconduct – unless it's on the streets and can't be taxed. At that level it's a crime; but when you're a housewife or a married woman, you can sell all the sex you want in the name of "marriage" and all is well.

The goons come in many forms, and that includes their presence in the pulpit, but that is best dealt with in the next area under "ideological game." Let it suffice to say that marriage is enforced from the womb to the tomb, and the only logical reason is that it generates money: the system can get two workers for the price of one, tie the couple to the economy through home purchases, furnishings, cars and other major items. The divorce rate, hovering near 60%, is a wakeup call telling us all that these "alienated arrangements" are not working and that sexual misconduct has been exposed. But nope. America is too arrogant to see the forest for the trees. And it's only going to get worse.

IDEOLOGICAL GAME

The dominant ideology in this system is capitalism, but its twin sister, religion, is not far behind. In fact, the two are oftentimes the same thing: if you don't believe it, ask yourself this: when was the last time you went to church and a collection plate wasn't passed around?

As "ideological game," religion is the root of sexual misconduct on a number of fronts. It is a philosophy that enables some, while disabling others; it is the ultimate confounding of things in many respects: it makes small things look big, weak things look strong, and stupid people appear intelligent. And all of this plays a role in justifying one's existence in a society that is permeated (and dependent on) with case after case of sexual misconduct.

Religion is used to tell you when you can have sex, who you can have sex with and so on. Religion was used to ban interracial sex, and religion is still a major reason for the dearth of interreligious marriages. Religion absolves child abusers and pedophiles for their crimes if they "repent," say a certain number of "hail Mary's" and so on. In the major religion of this country, you can sin all you want, do what you please – then say "I'm sorry" and all is forgiven. That is how sexual misconduct continues on unabated despite this being a supposedly "Christian nation."

So there you have it: the first installment. I know it's a lot to take in, but Rome (a sexual haven if there ever was one) wasn't built in a day. Through gifts, goons and ideological game, we can't even see that sexual misconduct is as normal as crossing the street; it's just hidden so well from plain view.

But on a regular basis, examples appear that clearly show that this misconduct is infecting all of us. And in next week's installment, we'll talk about "The Economics of Sexual Misconduct."

SEXUAL MISCONDUCT: ECONOMIC AND LEGAL LESSONS

Again, my thesis is clear: sexual assault and sexual misconduct are Americans norms, and the values that support this cultural system reinforce this fact. In America, politics are not becoming more moral but indeed, morality has always been political. This is quite clear in the area of America's economic development. Let me explain.

In the preface of this series I provided an operational definition of sexual misconduct (go to the Omaha Star, get a copy and look it up). That definition made more sense than the "legal" definition that follows:

"Sexual misconduct encompasses a range of behavior used to obtain sexual gratification against another's will or at the expense of another. Sexual Misconduct includes sexual harassment, sexual assault, and any conduct of a sexual nature that is without consent, or has the effect of threatening or intimidating the person against whom such conduct is directed." The problem with this definition is that it posits that sexual misconduct is activity that is "without consent." But here is where the power to define bamboozles most of us into investing into a false morality that does not exist.

Let me explain.

We live in a capitalist society and, as I've written elsewhere, money is basically the "ultimate confounding of things" making the weak appear strong, the little appear large and so on. The belief that sexual misconduct can only exist "without consent" is ridiculous. Sexual misconduct, as I allege, is normative behavior in American society and is not only psychologically, but economically motivated. "Without consent"? That implies that if you give consent, then it's not sexual misconduct! How ludicrous. A child that consents to sex with an adult as that adult waves a $10 bill in his face doesn't negate the fact that the adult is engaging in sexual misconduct. A man who gets the consent of a woman who needs money and has ten children to feed in exchange for some money is, in my book, committing sexual misconduct.

Some would refer to these as business transactions. But if one of the individuals involved is under aged or oppressed, then those who are adult and members of the oppressor class commit sexual misconduct every time they take advantage of their superior economic position! Feel me? And that is what American "romance," "erotic exchange," "prostitution" and, yes, "marriage," are all about: those with the gold making the rules and in this case, the rules involve the manipulation of the consent of those who don't have any gold!

The economics of sexual misconduct, as I see it, are inextricably bound to the American way of life. It may start off with dolls for little girls and guns for little boys. But that whole sex role stratification thing plays a key part: an entire culture "consenting" to this way of life, and in comes the color pink for the girls and blue for the boys. Once you have an entire population agreeing to division between the genders, then you pave the way for sexual misconduct; if that was not the case, then there would be no need for the divisions in the first place!

The economics are not just embryonic and traditional – they are also justified and consented to by a public that still, to this day, believes that you should open a door for someone because they are of a particular gender; that you should never hit someone (even if they hit you) because they are of a certain gender; that if you are a certain gender then you should be given a break because "boys will be boys." Songs that speak of what little girls are made of, or the boys being "back in town." All this is consented to and supported with school-based education, church-backed parables, and mass merchandising. All with the consent of a gratuitously goony American public.

Now, look at the rest of the "legal" definition. A second problem inherent in the definition is where it speaks of sexual misconduct having, *"the effect of threatening or intimidating the person against whom such conduct is directed."* As I have clearly shown, a person need not feel threatened or intimidated in order for sexual misconduct to be taking place: if you believe that a person's role is to submit to another person because of your gender, and you do it, you are still a victim of sexual misconduct even if you're told that God ordained it! If you believe that a person is the "head of the household" or "the boss" because of gender, then you're a victim of sexual misconduct even if you buy into this bull!

There are "threats" woven into American society that are subliminal, and perpetuate the way of life that most people feel most comfortable with. Sexual misconduct is directed at, and endorsed by, the vast majority of the public whether they want to admit it or not. Sexual misconduct, like racism, doesn't just affect the victims of the legislation or the actions – it affects those who impose it because they have to continually promote more lies and pseudo-science in order to keep the public confused. And it's working to perfection.

Dupes are in abundance. Did you know, for instance, that April was "sexual assault awareness month?" and that sexual assaults spiked during the winter Olympic Games; during the 17 day period, with 27 taking place. This implies that sexual assaults only take place when they are identified or visible. No one wants to admit that assaults and misconduct (synonymous in my book), are ideological, philosophical – and pervasive.

I've shown where the law "bites its tongue" when dealing with a definition of such misconduct. And I've provided examples of the role that money plays in propping up this parasitic problem. But its all around us, and to single out Ben Roethlisberger, Tiger Woods or any of the female teachers that assault their students other folks (I deal with this type of behavior in a later segment), is like busting a drug dealer selling joints on the corner while the kingpin down the street ships kilos all over the country. Feel me?

America is a nation of followers and flunkies. Salesmen know it and so did W.C Fields when he uttered, many decades ago, "There's a sucker born every minute." But the biggest sales scam ever waged was the one that pitted men against women, gave men all the power (including the legal power of definition) and then force-fed women and the children that they raise into buying into it.

Sexual misconduct? How can there be such a thing when the very norms surrounding sex and the sexes are grotesquely gruesome, sadistically unsisterly and brutally unbrotherly? It's a long-standing dupe: give people a false sense of morality and then take immoral concepts and pawn them off as 'acceptable.' Then, apply a ranking system where some deviance is acceptable but other forms are not. Then give discretion to define which is which to one gender and one race: white men. And there you have it.

Two last titillating examples (that will be addressed in dynamic detail later in this series) will give you something to talk about in the bedroom, bathroom or breakfast table.

FACT: Sexual assaults are on the rise in the military, so much to the point where they now have standing committees to deal with the issue. Why do I mention this? Simply to show that sexual misconduct exists in every single institution (and institutions are designed to perpetuate systems, not condemn them, right?) So if the institution practices it, it's because the system endorses it. And the military is filled with pistol-packing patriots who, evidently, still harbor perversions.

FACT: Child trafficking is a $5=$6 billion dollar a year industry, according to a recent report on MSNBC. And America is in the thick of it. I always believed that the way a nation treats its children is a standard on which that nation can be built – or buried.

Next time around we'll deal with the subject of, "Role Models, Race and Sexual Misconduct. Stay tuned.

RACE, ROLE MODELS AND SEXUAL MISCONDUCT

Kobe Brant. Ben Roethlisberger. Tiger Woods. Ray Rice. Joe Mixon. The talk is that they are not good role models despite claims by each that they want to be. Forget it: unless you're a male willing to admit that how we've treated women – and allowed them to be treated by other men – is wrong, then you ARE a role model. Why? Because by perpetuating the system – and the sexual misconduct that is normative behavior within that system -- *you are just what the doctor ordered.* By doing *nothing,* you are serving as a model for future confused boys to continue to do what you and YOUR role models have ordained, through their words and deeds, to be "perfectly acceptable."

Those who claim to be shocked when they hear about acts of "sexual misconduct" on the part of these so-called celebrity athletes are abysmally ignorant, lying or just plain stupid. Let's look at three areas that I just came up with: (1) control, (2) leadership, and (3) situational ethics.

CONTROL

When it comes to control, even in a democratic society that claims to be rule by the people, the fact is, those at the top have responsibility for what takes place among the rank and file. **Control is herein defined as "exercising** restraining or directing influence." While there's not much restraining taking place (except in times of control when race or gender are concerned), there is a whole lot of "directing" taking place, and its done overtly as well as subliminally.

Sexual misconduct is controlled and directed in different ways, depending on who the audience is. Those in power have defined such misconduct as totally alright, depending on the circumstances. In the case of these athlete role models, such misconduct is patterned after the behaviors of the rich and famous: "you can do whatever you want to anybody you want as long as you don't get caught." And this is the way it has been in this country for centuries.

When the victims were black men and women, sexual misconduct had its heyday, since both groups were in various forms of servitude (black folks as enslaved workers and white women as sperm spittoons). Sexual misconduct, as a form of control, was meted out to both groups whenever and wherever the white man felt like it. Let it suffice to say that the groups that were victimized were not the only ones watching; there were other witnesses, which is why all over America, such behavior is taking place regardless of gender or race. The common variable in these cases, however, is that the people getting caught have money and visibility – they got caught because they violated the basic rule of sexual misconduct: use the money and wealth bestowed upon you to break the rules behind closed doors – not in public.

The people catching the most hell are celebrities on some level: athletes and entertainers. But as has always been the case, others are watching. So now you have white female teachers who look like models going after young boys; you have priests going after the same group; you have television programs that offer up hours of sexual innuendo that is immediately mocked and mimicked by viewers; and of course, you have the legitimacy of celebrity sexual misconduct since most of them – almost all – get off with a light fine, an air sandwich "punishment" or some decision maker looking the other way. The actions, therefore, are legitimized, pervasive and powerful influences to new generations who view sexual misconduct as a cruel joke rather than a perversely parasitic product of a particular (male) mindset. So-called "role models" lead the charge in this on-going onslaught, aided by the gullibility of the American public and the powerlessness of its victims.

LEADERSHIP

As a result, leadership within such a context boils down to those making decisions becoming nothing short of "control freaks," defined by Merriam Webster as, "a person whose behavior indicates a powerful need to control people or circumstances in everyday matters." Those in power do what they know will keep the people confused and keep attention off of what they (the powerful) are up to. So they give legitimacy to sexual misconduct, with even the political casualties (senators, governors, teachers, nannies) becoming famous, receiving pity, and then disappearing even as a new crop of "leaders" is ushered forth to labor under the same set of sexually perverse conditions ("conditions shape both conduct and consciousness").

Leadership in America is nothing more than the ability to convince people of what they already know and believe. If a single leader stood up and said, "America is a sexually perverse nation and we need legislation to stop, once and for all, all forms of sexual misconduct," that person would be assassinated. Why? Because Americans don't believe that for one minute. They TALK a good game and they go to church; the claim to be a moral nation but when all is said and done, every waking minute, on some level, is spent endorsing sexual misconduct. The ones who get caught at the top get the blame and then America relaxes, goes to bed, and then wakes the next morning believing that things are better when, indeed, things remain exactly the same.

Leadership in such a context is more about deflecting blame and criticism than it is about correcting the problem. Sexual misconduct is so pervasive that it is taking place even by those who have a great deal to risk: John Edwards, Marion Barry, Mike Tyson, Anthony Mason, Bill Clinton, Lawrence Taylor, And for you Big Red fans, don't forget the names Christian Peters, Shaven Wiggins, and Lawrence Phillips.

The control is the attitude, the aura and atmosphere that leads to the behavior, which manifests itself in leaders who should know better nevertheless buying into sexual misconduct because they fall prey to it in the same way that young people are socialized into believing that white is good and black is bad. It's just that traditional and extensive – and it's just that acceptable. It may come in different degrees or different levels, but as I wrote earlier, sexual misconduct is as American as apple pie.

SITUATIONAL ETHICS

As sociologists we learned that Joseph Fletcher came up with this concept called "situational ethics." Now, whether you accept it or not, essentially it states that, "decision-making should be based upon the circumstances of a particular situation, and not upon fixed Law." But then it goes one step further by claiming that, "The only absolute is Love. Love should be the motive behind every decision. As long as Love is your intention, the end justifies the means. Justice is not in the letter of the Law, it is in the distribution of Love."

This is a clone philosophy behind the pervasiveness of sexual misconduct: the ends justify the means. Sexual misconduct in a society that equates love and sex on the same level, is bound to take precedence, since sexual misconduct is usually about the here and now and the immediate. Look at the examples above: men with power, money and some with lovely wives at home, still as yet risking it all for what? Love? No. They risk it all so that they can conquer that which they yearn for. It's as simple as that.

And since men are hardly the only ones with such philosophies – risk it all for sexual gratification – then it should be clear, by now, that my theory about sexual misconduct being a social norm hits the nail right on the head. Even our children are inundated with the message which explains everything from teen pregnancy and under-aged sex to drug abuse and belonging to gangs: everybody wants pleasure, but no one wants the pain associated with it.

When you combine control, leadership and situational ethics, you have a dangerous recipe for sexual misconduct, it seems to me.

And as for "role models"? They are merely representatives and prototypes of this society: they do not serve as people who OPPOSE sexual misconduct. Indeed, they are the embodiment of such activity.

SEXUAL MISCONDUCT AS NORMATIVE BEHAVIOR: THE SOCIAL ACCEPTANCE OF LEGALIZED PROSTITUTION

As an American norm, sexual misconduct is usually associated with one gender: the male. The fact is, as I've postulated in the first four parts of this series, we are responsible for establishing the conditions that foster the kind of perverse and parasitic conduct and consciousness that, in turn, maintains the conditions that are rife for this kind of conduct. In short, it's a cycle that is self-perpetuating because the actors are all engaged in it on some level.

And that includes the women folk. But I say this: the woman's role in sexual misconduct, even when she's gold digging, sashaying around or engaging in what society views as "immoral" behavior, is nevertheless the role of the victim.

After all, how could you have sexual misconduct without their existence? They raise the children and are there to approve or disapprove of any behaviors or attitudes that the children have. These kids grow up seeing things and a lot of it has to do with what they CHOOSE to emulate. This is not to imply that they can avoid being involved in the misconduct; it merely states that the acceptance of gender differences sets the stage for the misconduct. For the most part, the men are the vultures and women are the victims. But females are also complicit in the shaping of the culture of sexual misconduct. Let me explain how.

Who, for the most part, is involved in the sexual misconduct, either as victim or provocateur? Women. When men set them up with fashions and material possessions, this is but the beginning. For every gift to be fulfilled, there has to be acceptance. So from the womb to the tomb, she's force-fed a dream that her ultimate goal (and test) is to find a man to "adopt" her. From baby color pink and Barbie to promises of being a bride, she never has a chance to distance herself from a culture that bombards here with accepting that fact that sooner or later, she's going to have to "give it up."

Now how she gives it up is another matter, altogether. It can be legitimate (true love they claim), legal (marriage) or as a product of lounging and lollygagging, but sex is going to take place. And when it comes to sexual misconduct, a male-run society defines what is "acceptable" and what is not. And it differs based on class, race and location. But in most instances, it has to do with the power of money (see part 2) and how it turns every single person in America into the same kind of person: a prostitute.

That's right friends. A prostitute is not only Coretta on the corner, Heidi in the hotel suite or liquored-up Lucy. It's a verb AND a noun. Generically stated, a prostitute is someone who is "devoted to corrupt or unworthy purposes" (transitive verb) or as a noun, it's a woman who engages in promiscuous sexual intercourse especially for money. Now, doesn't that just about include every "housewife" in America? And who are their biggest tricks? US, of course!

Most men know how it goes once you've "tied the knot" (more like a hangman's noose). At any rate in far too many homes she controls the money and pays the bills. Even when the man controls the money, the fact that he got married was part of the "economic arrangement" that leads to "legalized prostitution." The process of getting married, also known as a "date," is nothing more than tricking. I know, it sounds crass, course and corrupt, but it's nevertheless the reality. Why do you think they never pay for the date? Why do you think women in bars order from the top shelf? (to see if you can afford the drink)? Why do you think women rarely, if ever, pick up the tab for anything? The answer is clear: they have been programmed, by this society and of course, their parents, that this is the "natural order of things."

And as johns or tricks, we men have been duped. Because it is so clear that we occupy these roles, a façade is created to make it look otherwise. We have been programmed to believe that we "talked out way up on that" or "seduced" some woman. Other than rape, anytime a woman has sex with a man it has been HER decision. The issue is that some have a more subtle way of making it appear as if it was OUR work, not theirs. But trust me: like a prostitute who moves from one pimp to another, it is a matter of choice. And if you're with a woman, the odds are that she chose YOU, not vice-versa.

But if there is a glamorous part of prostitution, it's only on the movies. Those white women who are actresses will publicly state that the roles that they cherish are the roles of bad girls or hookers. Why? So that they can be 'free' to address 'the range of their abilities." The same mentality exists out here on the streets in far too many cases. With the economy being what it is, too many of these young girls think that the best and fastest way to get out of the house is a welfare check and the fastest way to get one is to find some sucker to impregnate you. In this age of hi-tech and ready-made birth control, any "accidental pregnancy" is not always an "accident."

When you approach a woman, what is one of the first things she wants to know? Where you work. And in this day and age, men want to know the same thing about her. Where you date, where you go on vacation prior to marriage – these are all about paving the way for long-term exchange of money for "life" in America. But to paraphrase Shakespeare, "A trick, by any other name, would pay just as much."

If you get pregnant, you've got 18 years of child support from some source. You've sold your body to someone who you believe has the wherewithal to "take care of you for life." So the thing to do, according to society, is for the trick and the hooker to get married – and that way, you can get the sex for free. But can you? No. Society will see that you both pay: utilities, rent, mortgage, car note, baby clothes and food, and so on. Every payment is a part of the "trick" being turned. Today, however, the "two income family" is just another way of saying that this society gets "two hookers for the price of one."

The woman is still the victim for the most part. Even when the trick is tricked, he still gets free reign. Since 60% of all marriages end in divorce, and since most divorces claim to be about "irreconcilable differences," those differences are usually issues of sex and/or money. And what did we say a prostitute was earlier: someone who trades sex for money! Now are you beginning to get it?

In this day and age no one "gives away" sex. Even the most promiscuous among us is either selling it or paving the way for future benefits (e.g., dates, loans that never get paid back, a nice gift, etc.). I'm telling you what people from other countries think of us, and they think that way courtesy of the American media in general, and the American movie industry, in particular. Men from other countries arrive here with one major perception of American women: that they are whores. Ask them.

If what I just described has any value or validity, then maybe you understand where this series on "sexual misconduct as an American norm" is coming from: we can all see it, but we've been bamboozled into thinking that we're a Christian nation. And in case you haven't been to church lately, those sermons aren't free; there's a little thing called a "collection plate" and last time I looked, it's still being passed around!

As I wrote in an earlier installment, money is the "ultimate confounding" of things. It makes the little look big, the weak look strong and, check this out: it makes the immoral appear moral. Sexual misconduct is so rampant that it can only be trumped with dreams of religion and piety. The only problem is that the biggest pimps and prostitutes in this society are also some of the most consistent church members. You know it's true.

Meet, date, get married, have kids that you teach to accept this process as "the way things are." Rather than critically looking at it, we just keep on trickin.' As the saying teaches us, "Whom the gods would destroy, they first make mad."

SEXUAL MISCONDUCT: THE CHILDREN

Every thought which genius and piety throw into the world alters the world.

--Ralph Waldo Emerson

Sexual misconduct is a social norm that no one wants to accept. In fact, to deviate from this norm one is assumed to be some kind of moralist or religious fanatic. But to see the obvious and then understand its nature is the role of any thinking human being. We see what is taking place and yet refuse to act upon that which we see. *Yet we condemn it when we see it in other people. And our children are condemning us because of our hypocrisy.* This, in my view, is a key beyond youth homicide and general rebellion.

I looked into a concept called "bystander apathy," which I picked up from an episode of "The Practice," which used to be one of my favorite shows. It's not that I have an abiding respect for the legal profession or lawyers, but I view law as an area that has fallen down in the face of what I've written about in the previous five installments. Even our leaders, religious people and teachers have fallen prey to believing that social misconduct is "deviant" behavior. As I argue, it is not sexual misconduct that is deviant: *it is doing the right thing in the face of it,* that is.

Bystander apathy is how I view the inability of this society to see that sexual misconduct is everywhere, even in the denials of its existence. Bystander apathy and the bystander effect are explained by experts who say that "witnesses are often reluctant to help someone in obvious distress because they either fear for their own safety or figure someone else will help if others are around."

In the case of sexual misconduct, I contend that people who say what I am saying are going to viewed with disdain-and-how-dare-you, and that they fear alienation from others. Not me. I know what I see.

The children know. They watch, and they imitate what they see. We all know this and we understand the power of various forms of socialization; but the institutions responsible for this socialization are the keys to justifying that sexual misconduct is alright. Sure, there are varying levels and degrees of it, but the children are "broken in" with the subtle forms, forms that gradually become more overt as the child becomes older.

We know how boys and girls are divided up from infancy. From the "blue for boys and pink for girls" divisions to all that takes place from that point on: boys are rough and girls are 'gentle;' girls play with dolls and the boys get guns and sporting equipment. The girls have to get "pretty" while boys can wear whatever they choose including jeans with holes and dirty t-shirts. But one theme weaves its way through it all: boys have "roles" and girls have a "place."

As they mature, sexual misconduct creeps in because added to the divisions cited earlier are various types of ways to make girls "dependent" on a male-dominated system. Ask yourself this: with over 60% of black households being headed by a single parent, what kind of image do you think that single parents paints of the opposite sex? What do mothers tell their daughters and sons about "daddy"? What do single fathers tell their kids about "dey mama"? Sexual misconduct is not just an activity but, as I've pointed out elsewhere, it is an ATTITUDE.

If a girl is a virgin, the boy's goal is to make sure that she doesn't remain one for long. If the boy is a virgin, his job is to lie and claim that he's not. In any case, sex, even before the ripe old age of ten years old, is a part of young people's lives like never before. They see it on television, in the movies, on their video games and in their reading material. And, because mama and daddy are single, far too many are getting a live version of sexuality long before they are old to understand what is really taking place.

All they know is this: it's okay for mama and daddy to "date," which means having a friend of the opposite sex. Unfortunately, it's also okay for either parent to have "lots of friends." They see different people hugging and kissing on one another and they see it reinforced on television. They see a babysitter coming over while that parent "goes out" and who may or may not come home that evening. Kids see all this and we think we're fooling them. They will remember. And they will internalize it and imitate it.

The rape and sexual assault of black boys and girls is rampant, yet understated, in our community. In the name of not wanting to "air dirty laundry," there are far too many family secrets, and many of those secrets are linked to sexual misconduct of various types. Because the parents are so busy working to make ends meet, a lot of what these kids get away with is not even noticed. Many of those "adventures" or activities enjoy dangerous, deadly or near death experiences that the kids may get away with, but will always remember. These experiences shape the way they view one another, authority figures, and it impacts on how they respond to rules and regulations.

What does all this have to do with sexual misconduct being a social norm?

Churches and schools become a part of their lives. In the case of the former, the Bible and other documents are rife with stories about sexual taboos, liaisons and misconduct. Unfortunately, one religion provides loophole after loophole for such behaviors or abuse. This same religion claims men have an ordained right to rule the household (as the "head"), and that women are responsible for the sin that exists in the world. This same religion offers that even if you commit a sexual crime of some kind, you can pray your way out of it and then start all over again. That is why so many people in the church are some of the biggest perverts in the community: from the Catholic Church to what takes place in secrecy in the black church. You know it's there, and I say it's there because it's a norm – one that is hidden or justified because, after all, "we're only human," "nobody's perfect" or "I'm a work in progress."

Just as the church provides avenues, arenas and the atmosphere for on-going sexual misconduct, so do the schools. As it is with religious institutions, the educational institutions are TRUSTED by the parents of these children, often becoming surrogate parents and babysitters (based on the declining grades and scores of American students, what else could schools be doing?) These schools are also "safe havens" for young people and offer a feeling of security; that is why what is being taught is memorized and pawned off as "the truth." And that is how sexual misconduct, both at school and in the textbook, continues on, unabated.

The third institutional arrangement that paves the way for and perpetuates sexual misconduct is the media. Black kids watch more hours of television per week than any other racial grouping. And they have little recourse and few alternatives on the set: when they try to "watch black folks," what do they find? Black Entertainment Television (BET), TVOne and other insultingly insidious media machinations. Their choices: scantily clad women, pimp like dudes, guns and gut-spilling, or illiterate rappers who couldn't pour piss out of a boot if the instructions were written on the heel.

"Old men can make war, but it is children who make history," the saying teaches us. The more this country continues to engage in raw hedonistic behavior and then mask it with myths about "dating," "marriage" and "holy matrimony," the longer the problem will be distorted and the relationships between men and women, couples in general, will become nothing more than "alienated arrangements."
 If all we can hand to our young people are our sperm-saturated porno magazines, condoms and supposedly religious scriptures and talk about women taking bites out of apples and causing the world's troubles, then maybe, just maybe, the men and women of America deserve the fate that befalls us.

CONCLUSION

Sexual misconduct appears to be a norm in American society and as such, sexual abuse and domestic conflicts are inevitable.

REFERENCES

Karenga, Maulana (1967). *The quotable Karenga*. Los Angeles, California: Kawaida Publications.

Never Hit a Woman?
A Different Take On The Mind-numbing Idiocy Behind the "Domestic Abuse" Rhetoric: Critique and Commentary

FOREWORD: SOME PRELIMINARY NOTES

In an act of supreme grandiosity and idiocy, Dallas Mayor Mike Rawlings decided to organize a domestic violence rally, one that declares that "there is never a time when a man should hit a woman." The name of the rally? "Dallas Men Against Abuse."

Now here you have a city whose culture is steeped in violence against women on all levels. Women earn less, perform most of the menial labor, and are victimized by domestic violence. So bad was the domestic abuse that in 1995 Dallas was the first county in the Texas to establish a specialized Family Violence court. This is one of the most misogynistic states in the country and there is more to violence against women than just kicking their ass: there is social coercion, economic coercion and educational coercion.

On Monday, March 18th, in an "appeal to the men of Dallas," Rawlings said, "We men must say, 'No more. No mas.' According to one reporter, Rawlings said, "Hitting a woman is not acceptable. Strangling a woman is not acceptable, Stabbing a woman is not acceptable," he thundered. "Shooting a woman is not acceptable." (Floyd, 2013). As a sign of the hypocrisy, none other than Dez Bryant of the Dallas Cowboys showed up as a "surprise speaker." You know why it was a surprise? Because if people had known beforehand there may have been a protest of people who are aware of the fact that Bryant hit his own mother in July and was arrested for it. At the rally the pompous and immature wide receiver said simply, "Here's all you need to know: I'm done with domestic abuse." (USA Today, 2013).

The 1931 movie "Public Enemy," aired on the AMC (American Movie Classics) station in November of 2012, carried the following promotional blurb on the menu: "A feisty punk [James Cagney] hits women, shoots men and runs beer during Prohibition." Say what?

The way American society promotes the hitting of women is tantamount to shooting someone. This male-dominated culture actually wants the world to believe that women are never to be hit. Where did that stuff come from? If someone hits you, hit them back. I don't believe in just firing up women because of a belief in physical superiority. I'm talking about the concept of "hitting," period.

The movie "Deadfall" (2012) was aired on a high definition channel on the Dish Network. In one scene, the sheriff's daughter, who is also an officer, has just informed her father that she shot a man in the forest. The father, pissed, walks up to her and says, "If you was one of my boys, I'd hit you." She stares him down (knowing that she won't get hit) and says, "If I was one of your boys, you'd be proud of me." The man's reaction may sound gallant, but it is actually sexist: he says if she was a boy he'd hit her, why not hit her anyway since she's his daughter? A child beater is a child beater so how can it be gender-neutral? This is an extension of that pink blankets for girls and blue blankets for boys bullshit that paves the way for the gender conflicts that follow us through life.

On March 21, 2013 it was reported that Jennifer Capriati, former tennis star and an Olympic gold winner, showed what can happen when you adopt this "hit me when you feel like it" demeanor on the part of men. This 36 year old woman stalked and battered Ivan D. Brannan, Jr. in a gym, hitting him in the chest, punching him and shouting. But first, she stalked him. According to documents, the description for the stalking charge says that the athlete did "willfully, maliciously, and repeatedly follow, harass, or cyberstalk" Brannan between February 16th and February 18th" (People.com, March 21, 2013).

Both of these examples, playing on society's concept of "etiquette," that hitting a woman is on the same level beer running and shooting people. Where did this shit come from? This book believes that it's gone too far and that today, in the year 2012, we have to stop being hypocritical: either we're equal as genders or we're not. If I'm not supposed to hit you just because you're a woman, but I can hit another man, that implies, on some level, that you're "different" on some level. So then, it's up to a male dominated society to define whether or not that "difference" is a deficit, or if it is a matter of the woman being superior.

I don't buy into either one.

Check this out: During the month of November, 2012, a 9-year old girl, Samantha Gordon, was shown all over national television and the internet playing pee wee football with "the boys." She was running touchdowns, taking off for long runs, zigzagging through defenses and even played defense, making some incredible tackles. This, in turn, triggered debate and that included former football players who aired their views on ESPN's "First Take." This girl has raised the issue of whether or not boys should go "all out" and treat her like she was a boy or should they be leery and "not hit her because she's a girl."

This is the kind of issue that lies at the root of what I am writing about in this book. Stephen A. Smith of "First Take," claimed that "we should have a heightened level of sensitivity when it comes to women." I agree: but the basis of that heightened sensitivity should not be patronizing, degrading or sexist. The day of "women are inferior" are over, and anything short of treating them the way that they want to be treated would be an insult.

Instead, you have people like Judge Joe Brown using as a promo for his 30-minute court show (now cancelled), "Protecting womanhood, promoting manhood." What makes him think that men don't need to be protected from some of these crazy bitches who are running around here trying to get paid: set men up with pregnancies, filing false restraining orders and generally doing whatever they can to find a "sugar daddy" to adopt them? Where's the protection for *that,* asshole?

On the same segment of "First Take" that I alluded earlier, Stephen A. Smith added that, "girls are supposed to be treated different from boys" and that, "Girls should be treated with the level of delicacy that they deserve." His fear was that treating women the same on a football field would lead to treating them as equals in everyday life, which would include and "you can take things that apply in sports and think it can apply to everyday life."

What an asshole. This is a society that has created the defensiveness that women exhibit, and it is the one that has fostered this notion of "equality of the sexes," a notion that I happen to believe in. We are not physically equal, but in some cases, as an old saying goes, "equal opportunity means the opportunity to display unequal talents." If women want to play football with boys, let them – and let them reap what they sow. If women want to compete against men in any athletic event, let them, because this is a free country. But in the face of Title IX where women have their own leagues, divisions, competitions, etc., for a woman to want to compete against men is a conscious choice, and it is a choice that is based on, among other things, reality denial.

So let them compete. If they can do so, succeed and be happy, then more power to them. But if they get their asses kicked, they will be getting what any competitor has earned and therefore *deserves.* As this book proves, that applies to any physicality that comes along with male-female relationships. *Any.*
But let's call it what it is. One scholar

> Female athletes in basketball, and presumably other team sports,
> have to negotiate a "contradictory set of cultural images" …. As
> scholars have long noted, women's participation in sport, and in
> particular team sport, is frequently accompanied by a questioning
> of the (hetero)sexuality of athletes … This is in part due to the fact
> that, unlike individual sports such as tennis and gymnastics,
> participation in a team contact sport like basketball is viewed in U.
> S. culture as a "masculine" endeavor … Thus, female athletes are
> often confronted with cultural assumptions regarding their lack of
> femininity, and thus their lack of heterosexuality … (Cooky,
> 2010).

If it runs like a dyke, throws like a dyke, dunks like a dyke and passes like a dyke, it's a dyke! Just like most of the men who engage in skating and swimming are faggots, so it is with women. Why not call it like it is? Look at the WNBA: you're going to tell me that a vast number of these women aren't lesbians? They grow up playing against their older brothers and other guys in the hood and they become good at what they do. They go to school and when they compete against other women, they use the tricks they learned from us and dominate. Being around women becomes their life: playing, practicing, showering and so on. I believe that homosexuality is rampant in the NBA and the NFL as well, but that's another story. But since the playing field is become more equal, so are the secrets. Call it what it is.

In the bed women want to experience orgasms just like we do. They know we, as men, are weak and inferior to them sexually. They know that we have to be in a certain frame of mind to even engage in sex with them, and they know how to use what they've got to get us in that frame of mind. Women, for the most part, lay the framework for when, how and why we will have sex with them; the smart ones are good at making it look like we initiated the relationship when, in reality, they CHOSE us.

They share information about us to one another. It doesn't matter how close you are or in love you are. Let me tell you something: if one woman knows something, then that means at least TWO women know it. And that goes double when it comes to men. I mention this because this kind of interaction is, in my view, psycho-genetic and as such, I have a section in this book where I take a look at "intent." All of this mental and cerebral stuff plays into this "I'm the weaker sex" scam and the "officer he hit me" approach to getting payback. This is what society has devolved into because we – men – were so damn stupid that we created this "sex role socialization" and programmed the entire culture into thinking that women were helpless and in need of men to "take care" of them.

All this is going on and then, out of nowhere, she's got the right to put her hands on me in a violent way and I'm supposed to stand there like a retarded idiot and do nothing? I've heard this everywhere I've gone and, for the most part, I've tolerated the people who spew forth such beliefs. I've even gone so far as to open the door for young women entering a place of business and so on. Now, I do the same for elderly people, men or women. But just opening the door for someone because she's a female, to me, is bullshit. Allowing a woman ahead of you to get on the bus, because she's a woman, is bullshit.

As I express later in this book, fair is fair; a woman, based on gender, holds a political, legal and social "advantage" if she charges that a man "hit her." This is regardless of the situation, what she did beforehand, what she said about him or the harm inflicted upon his person or property. In sum, because of her gender, she gets a free pass.

Let us move on.

INTRODUCTION

According to Gramsci (1971), social order is maintained through a dynamic process of coercion and consent whereby dominant groups produce dominant cultural beliefs, called hegemonic ideologies, and subordinated groups to consent to structural conditions that may be oppressive given the power of hegemonic ideologies. For Gramsci, consent is secured through the "cultural leadership of the dominant grouping" (Curran, 2006 p. 132).

Staged or not, love it or hate it, merely look at an episode of "Jerry Springer" or any of those related programs (e.g., Bill Cunningham, Maury Povich, "Cheaters"). The man on the program exposes that he's seeing someone else, that he's really a woman or that he's homosexual. What is the first thing that the woman, who has been harmed in front of a major audience, do? *She slaps the living shit out of him, that's what.* And why does she do it? A man admits that he's had an affair and that his woman is boring in the bed and his fiancée comes walking out of the back (after being called) and hits the man so hard that I felt it! Why do these women do this? Because they know she's protected by Springer's security team and secondly, she knows that no matter what happens, this man – who may do something different behind closed doors – is not going to strike her in front of the American public. Why? Because the American public says that it's, "wrong." Wrong based on what?

On another episode a man is complaining that his woman, Cassandra, (overweight) doesn't dress up when they go out and walks around the house in moo-moos and sweat pants. This is not so bad I suppose. But then he said that when he comes in the house in the evening, "She hits me and I have to walk away."

Here's my point: *you don't have to walk away!* First of all, if he had done what I recommend in this book, he would have told this fat cow not to put her hands on him in anger or any way that is negative. Had he told her that, she would have been on notice. To be forewarned is to be forearmed. He thinks he has to walk away for the same reason that so many men think they have to do so: because she'll call the cops. And that is why I say if the house is in both of your names, you have to stand up for your part of the house and more importantly, stand up for ALL of your sense of self!

The "castle law" should be modified to not only include burglars, intruders, trespassers or robbers. The "castle law" is so named because a man's (or woman's) home is supposed to be their "castle" and as such, you have the right to defend it from those who would violate it. This should be expanded to include men or women who become physical with their spouse within that "castle." If a woman is throwing things or a man is putting his fist through walls, then you need to have the right to stop that person from devaluing the value of your "castle." If that means busting a cap in his (or her) ass, then so be it.

This society has come a long way from when women were afraid of men, would never talk back and would shrink at even the thought of a man getting angry, let alone striking them. Gone are the days when women were afraid that if they spoke out of turn, said something against the existing system, or did something "unbecoming," they'd get publicly humiliated, lynched, sent to the guillotine, burned at the stake, locked up or banished.

So my question is this: *how can such unsubstantiated bullshit last for so long and among so many different people in a nation as large as this one?*

Now I've always had a philosophy that nobody hits me without getting hit back. A toddler can come up to me and hit me and I will take his or her little hand and tap it, to let that child know, first of all, it ain't good to hit people and secondly, that if you DO hit people, you stand the chance of getting hit back. I do this with everybody on different levels. Now a grown ass muthafucka should know better. And this includes women as well. This shit about "a man should never put his hands on a woman" is nothing more than a license to get your ass kicked by some female. Fuck that shit. If a woman hits you, then you should hit her back. If she thinks you won't hit her back, do you think that's gonna make her more nonviolent or more violent? More violent, of course!

Now remember: *with women the violence can come in many forms.* Many of them will shout and try to over talk you, hoping to get you angry and lose control. Whatever you do, don't lose control. If you put your hands on her, she is then justified to do whatever she wants to do: poison your food, cut you, shoot you or call the cops and charge you with domestic violence. But the shouting and conniption fits are all a part of the subtle violence that they wage when they feel they are losing control.

When you are involved with such a person, you must establish the ground rules early in the relationship – cover all the bases when it comes to all forms of interaction, from intimate to conversational. In that way, "to be forewarned is to be forearmed," and she won't ever be able to claim that she "didn't know he was like that," or "he said that he was nonviolent." You can be nonviolent and still refuse to take shit from somebody.

Next, in a chapter titled, "Justifiable Pent Up Defensiveness," I offer some reasons why black women are understandably "on guard" and as a result, more prone to assume the worst from men. The areas I've created and selected for analysis are: The Pedestal of Endangerment, The "I-Don't-Need-No-Man" Syndrome, Male Neglect Creating Stoicism, Abandonment Issues, Body Image Issues, Deep-Seated Hatred of Interracial Relationships, and the Chilling Effect (Handcuffed by His Holiness).

The pedestal of endangerment is self-explanatory: when you place anything or anyone on a pedestal, it is easy for them to "fall" off of it. Who, therefore, wouldn't be defensive if they were placed up high, out of reach and left to be watched and admired, but never related to?

The next section addresses what I call the "I-don't-need-no-man" syndrome and most black men have seen this at work. As I explain in this book, most black women have been hurt or harmed by at least one man before you meet her. She is not going to give you the benefit of the doubt of being "different" because by the time you've met her, she's slowly but surely turned herself off toward men, period. She may not have reached the "I-don't-need-no-man" level yet, but she's working toward it. She's defensive, for good reason, and in her view, if you're the same gender as "the others," then you're all the same – until proven otherwise by way of plenty of "tests" and other trials.

A related category is the Anglo male and how he may be getting to be an option in the absence of black men and because of the shortage of us. She won't see him as being much different, but what most of them have is one thing many black men don't have: money and/or resources. So these white boys can spend money on things and they can assist her in paying bills. She may encounter a little alienation from the community ("why should you be happy?"), but on the other hand, black people are so locked into the slave mentality they might consider her as a "lucky sister" because she's dating a cracker.

Another reason for pent-up defensiveness is the black male's new recreational activity: the down-low. This is not something that is taking place among "the few;" there are niggas galore doing this shit, and a lot of it has to do with the fact that many were in prison. For the ones who weren't it's just black men doing something that they've always wanted to do, but didn't have the guts. So they do it behind closed doors. Then they lie and claim that they're not gay. I address this contradiction in the book.

Male stoicism is epidemic. Stoicism, succinctly defined, is "an indifference to pleasure or pain." Like zombies men and women are beginning to act as if they are above pain, as if they've never been hurt or that they don't believe in love. If you haven't encountered it yet, you will. What's worse is that our kids play video games and worse, watch on television as our young women parade around butt naked, breasts pumping to the music, while young boys lust after them and treat them like, well, you know – hos. Male stoicism leads to and magnifies the pent-up defensiveness that many black women may feel.

Another basis for black female frustration is that they have body image issues. I'm not talking about teen girls who may be overweight and try to binge like white girls. I'm talking about black women who get depressed, gain weight, and then turn around and justify their obesity by claiming that "men like curves" and related slogans. By having body image issues, as I show, they also engage in putting all that fake shit on their bodies that white women do, from false eyelashes and push up bras to underalls, invisible girdles and fake fingernails.

Back to interracial issues, we find that many black women may be frustrated and angry because of interracial relationships that black men seem to be increasingly becoming a part of. Even black men who talk black are living with and marrying white women. This is pissing the sisters off, especially the ones who are looking for a black man who will love and stick with them. Read on and you'll learn more about how this relates to pent-up defensiveness.

I don't give a shit about who gets mad about my views of religion and Christianity in particular, and how it has negatively impacted on the thinking, attitudes and behaviors of black women and their treatment of black men. At the same time, these black ministers are feeding women a crock of shit and playing a major role in the division of black families. If the husband or boyfriend is at home on Sunday watching the game, she's going to church and is therefore "vulnerable" to the preacher's message. Since most preachers are cockhounds and pimps, this is not going to bode well for the brother who places his sports above what is taking place at church.

JUSTIFIABLE PENT-UP DEFENSIVENESS

Black women are, arguably, very defensive. The ones who are not are becoming so because of what they are seeing, hearing and being exposed to. Many of them live in fear. From young ones to the oldsters, single or married, well-off or ghetto superstars -- black women, in particular, have every reason to be defensive. Look where many of them live, how they live, what they have to do in order to eke out an existence, the powerless of their menfolk and so on.

For those who are novices, what does it mean to be defensive? Defensive is defined as, "made or carried on for the purpose of resisting attack," or more importantly to this examination, *"excessively concerned with guarding against the real or imagined threat of criticism, injury to one's ego."* The black woman, against her will or not, has been placed in a position where she fits both definitions like a glove.

We (meaning men) did this to her. She can deny that she's not defensive but even in her denial there is defensiveness. Were she not defensive, she might have been wiped out by now, because in my educated view, it appears that eliminating black women surely seems to be somebody's goal, ranging from the overt attacks by white men and the seductive "be my pal" approach of white women to the inability (or refusal) to protect her by black men. If she doesn't defend herself (and, as she will say, her children), then who will?

The Pedestal of Endangerment

Black women are angry and everybody wants to know if this is truly the case. I say that it is and that they have reason to be. One of those reasons revolves around what I call "the pedestal of endangerment."
Now look at us: the pedestal of endangerment has most of us locked up, our families divided, kids rebelling and turning on us and communities looking like scenes out of "Night of the Living Dead." I don't know who Wilma Scott Heide is, but she is credited with a quote most germane to this section of the book. She once posited that, *"The pedestal is immobilizing and subtly insulting whether or not some women yet realize it. We must move up from the pedestal."* While some see the pedestal as uplifting, when applied to the Black woman, it is just another example of her plight and predicament here in America.

The pedestal is therefore a term most fitting, and the "pedestal of endangerment" is a term I coined which I believe most accurately defines what is taking place in America as it relates to African-American women. Some will say that black women are not on a pedestal, that indeed, it has been the white woman who has historically enjoyed that position. I used to believe the same thing and in fact, was taught this position after taking a course in Black History at Saint Mary's College in 1974. The course, Sex and Racism in America, used Calvin C. Hernton's book of the same title as the main text. We were taught that the white woman was on a pedestal, but while the Anglo male placed her there, it was only a rationale for not having sex with her while he ventured out back and raped the enslaved black woman.

Now, as a Black Studies scholar myself, I clearly understand that the black woman is in a similar metaphorical position vis-à-vis the myths concocted about her. Even though she is endangered and, in my view, slated for extermination, she is placed "on high" by Anglo women who praise her and Anglo men who claim that she is the sole reason for what little good exists in the black community. And while much of this may be true, the fact of the matter lies in the other aspect of pedestal life: being unapproachable and untouchable by effeminate and cowardly males – black ones – who view black women as "not feminine enough" or "too bossy" or "too confrontational."

You see, these Anglo women were placed on this pedestal as a reason to *ignore* them. They're "up to high" to be able to relate to, or so the mythology goes. Just as the Anglo male during slavery used the pedestal as an excuse to create an angelic and chaste image of the Anglo woman (too good to have sex with, except to produce children), I believe that the males of today are using a similar rationale to avoid dealing with black woman as human beings; hence, what I call "the pedestal of endangerment."

Another aspect of being on a pedestal is that you become objectified or what Kovel (1974) referred to as "thingification." Although he was making reference to what Anglos did to black people during slavery, I liken the same concept to the manner that women have been treated throughout history. In the case of the African-American women, the pedestal was a front that worked any way you wanted it to. It can be what I outlined above – a place for cowardly men to place the woman so that they can play around and ignore her – and it also serves as a convenient way to remind the female that when all is said and done, she exists in name only, nothing more than the sum total of the plethora of platitudes, the multitude of compliments and the many descriptive poems that have been written about her over the years.

If men felt the way about women in real life the way we write about them in songs, things might be a lot better. For the most part, most of the songs about her are about getting into her panties. There are some beautiful love songs that have been written about making it last forever but, as we know, these are unrealistic because they're mostly expressing one side of the story – his. If not that, then the songs are about loss or "if I had one more chance" after having made some kind of mistake.

It's easy to write love songs, poems and sing about women if you view them as beings whose feelings are nothing more than a sum reaction to what YOU, as a man, want! It's easy to be in love and see butterflies and the moon and feel like a thousand bucks after you've gotten a nut! Let me tell you something: *If the woman had not been placed on that pedestal, and, instead, had been in a position to be viewed as the productive and life-bearing being that she was, man would have to accept his position as the simplistic creature that he has worked so hard to portray HER as being!* Think about it: for the most part, we produce nothing more than problems, babies and technology. The rest of the time is spent fighting with each other, fighting with her, trying to get into her panties, engaging in some kind of athletic activity or trying to prove that God doesn't exist!

A Brief Sampling of Some Case Studies

Back in the old days you'd see a white woman slap her man and he'd take it like a punk. She would slap anyone knowing that she was getting her point across because such action was presumed to be her "acting out of character" and as a result, you knew she was angry. Not only has this drastically changed where now she will slap the shit out of anyone, but she is now hitting men with her closed fist and kicking him in the balls. It's becoming so common that it's being deemed as "funny." I don't see anything funny about such action in the face of the society myth that "a man should never hit a woman." If a woman hits me, she's gonna get the shit knocked out of her, plain and simple.

Today it appears to be acceptable (and in some cases promoted) for a woman to slap the shit out of a man. She will walk up on him and put her hand in his face, she will grab him by the ear as if he is a child, she will kick him and, of course, the vintage slap across the face. Women are human beings, so when they engage in this kind of violent behavior, they are doing it to hurt the person they are lashing out against. And since that is the case, they should expect to get the shit knocked out of them in return, not hide behind their gender and some kind of false social chivalry. As the old saying teaches, "do the crime you do the time."

On the September 9, 2014 segment of "The View" something intelligent finally came out of the mouth of Whoopi Goldberg. They were discussing the Ray Rice case after Rice had been banned from pro football. Rice had knocked his wife out during a "domestic dispute" and although the tapes from the elevator showed that she was charging him and violating his space, he was the one who was charged. Goldberg told the audience that she believes that if a woman hits a man, he has every right to hit her back. Truer words (other than mine) were never spoken.

Now, speaking of the Ray Rice case.
In the movie "Thor: __," the so-called demi-god is once again united with the woman he loves (an earth woman, no doubt) played by little Naomi Watts. Upon his return and having expressed the fact that she missed him, she turns around and slaps the living shit out of him, not once but twice. He does nothing about it. He

even goes so far as to take her back to Asgard with him and she proceeds to be the basis for its near destruction and the death of his (Thor's) mother (she was defending the earth woman when she got killed). Does Thor hold his earth ho responsible? No.

During a September 9, 2014 episode of "The Young and the Restless," this ex-GI green beret type guy named "Stitch" is sitting at the table with Victoria Newman discussing the baby she's carrying – which might be his. As he's talking Victoria's younger sister, Abbie, walks up behind him and cuffs him upside the head – hard. Not one of those staged soap opera slaps, but an actual cuff, the kind that snaps when you do it right. She had just hired him for a job and was "angry" because he was talking to her sister – who represents a competing fragrance company. What did he do? He didn't do shit but stand up and star arguing with her.

A key reason why this society claims that a man should never strike a woman is because of the "morality plays" that are pawned off as television shows and movies, and the message that they convey. After watching these movies and programs, I've heard black women make statements like, "you're less than a man if you hit a woman."

My question, once again, is: how can such unsubstantiated bullshit last for so long and among so many different people in a nation as large as this one?

Chad Johnson allegedly head butted his wife of 5 weeks Evelyn __, and went to jail for it. He also lost his job as wide receiver for the Miami Dolphins and got humiliated throughout the media. In fact, this bitch is on every television show still talking shit. On December 5, 2012, Johnson appeared on ESPN's "First Take" and was continuing to beg and then shared with the audience that he was court-ordered "to enroll in and complete 26 weeks of anger management courses."

What kind of bullshit is this? Do you know who this woman Evelyn Lovado is? She was at one time a regular on the program, "Basketball Wives" which stars a bunch of bitches who you wouldn't know from Adam's house cat were it not for the fact that they were married to current and former NBA players, including some players that really weren't that great. At any rate, I saw Evelyn Lovado throw sand at her ex-husband (who threw a glass of water in her face), pull out a bottle to attack another black woman with, call other black women bitches on a regular basis on camera, and basically show that she is just another fine, out-of-control bitch.

Chad Johnson (who changed his name to Chad "Ochocinco" because he was number 85 as a ballplayer) comes along and talks her out of her panties, and on one program one of her colleagues said she was a "ho" and that Johnson wouldn't be faithful. Evelyn went off again. So she marries Johnson and she finds out he's messing around with another woman because she found a condom in the trunk of his car.

This is what started the argument in the car which led to the head butt which he continues to face public ridicule about. Co-host Stephen A. Smith declared, "You don't put your hands on a woman, period!" Why? Because he says so? This bitch didn't have any business trying to confront somebody and getting all up in that man's face, acting as if she was going to whip HIS ass! Chad Johnson was a professional football player. This bitch knew he had other women. Why is she acting as if she's so surprised?

What about this Rihanna? Chris Brown's phone rings while they're in the car and he's behind the wheel. She snatches it to see who it is and they start arguing. She won't give him back his phone so he fires on her ass and it's on. She's fighting him and giving as good as she gets. Check out the lyrics to some of her songs, and you can see what kind of woman this is – those Caribbean bitches, like the Puerto Rican Evelyn Lozado, don't take that shit.

During a May 4, 2013 segment of "Cops," the police were called to a convenience store because a young man and woman were fighting. When the cops got there is was found that she had thrown his phone out of her car window as she was driving down the street. He was the passenger and she claimed he hit her in the mouth. When he asked to get out of the car to get the phone, she stopped and let him out, but then tried to run him over as he backtracked to get his phone.
The cop arrested him for disorderly and the old (black) officer asked her "are you sure you two are just friends or friends with benefits?" She admitted to the latter and added that she was not supposed to be around him anyway because he had hit her before.

At this point the old cop says, "A man ain't never supposed to hit a woman. That's not a man – that's a coward!" And I say, bullshit! Maybe this young buck as wrong for hitting her in this specific instance, but every man who hits a woman is not a coward – not if he's hitting her to defend himself! How is that cowardice? If a woman knows you won't hit her she will fuck you up – or throw your cell phone, with all of your personal information, out of a car window. They will throw caution to the wind because they know that assholes like this cop are going adopt that old ass "men never hit women" attitude.

Steve Wilkos, former protégé of Springer, uses a direct and confrontative approach but even with security guards on stage, there have been a number of programs where the woman, standing directly in front of the man and with Wilkos watching, has been allowed to slither past the guards and knock the shit out of a man.

On the October 5, 2012 segment of "The Steve Wilkos Show," he's trying to offer advice to these two lesbians who are in a relationship. One of them "puts her hands" on the other on a regular basis. Wilkos shares that in his marriage, "If I go home and slap my wife, she's gone. She's not going to give me a second chance."

He said even before they got into the marriage it was agreed that, "If you put your hands on me, it's over." I doubt if Wilkos, who is a big guy and a former cop, said that to her: *that is what she said to him and he did what all men do*: listened and then nodded his head in sheepish agreement. These same women, of course, offer no guarantees that they will, in turn, keep their hands to themselves.

"Jerry Springer" is a show that should be banned, not because of what takes place on the stage when people fight about everything from infidelity and adultery to stealing money, but what could potentially happen when these people leave the studio and return home. On these programs the men stand as the culprits and the women complain. If a woman messes over a man, all he can do is stand there crying and whining and, even if vindicated, he moves on without incident. Women on this show are allowed, not only to fight one another (pull hair, rip off wigs, tear of blouses, wrestle to the floor and expose their panties), but more importantly to this particular essay, they get to slap the living shit out of the man.

 One show featured a young dude who went to California to do porn, got talked into gay porn and had to tell his girl on stage. It was all about the money he claims. When he told her on the stage of "Springer," she looked at him and said, "If we weren't on TV right now, I'd smack you." This means she's smacked him before when they weren't on television, and he didn't hit her back. This is a guy who is athletically built, and she's some little short white woman. So the question is, where is the motivation, where is the inspiration to make these women KNOW that they can strike a man, apparently whenever they want to, and not have to worry about being retaliated against?

Maury Povich, following Springer's lead, adds a different twist: he uses lie detector tests to find out if either party is being truthful or is telling a lie when it comes to the paternity of children. This program has, on a number of occasions, allowed a woman to slap the living shit out of a man or to threaten to do so.

The movie, "Haywire" featured a skilled woman beating the living shit out of man after man and, even when they attacked her or instigated the confrontation, it is clear that she was not only going to defeat them but humiliate her adversary as well. The CW Channel has a show, "Arrow," which is about some wannabe super hero who carries a bow and arrow and fights evil. Lately he's come across a female counterpart (wouldn't you know it) who unmercifully beats the shit out of men. If you get a chance to view it, juxtapose the two "heroes" and their fighting styles: the man head hunts and breaks jaws combined with a few kicks, but this female goes straight for the testicles and lower body shots. What's that about?

There's an old saying in the black community: "Fair exchange ain't no robbery." That basically means when its tit for tat, things are even. Where is the fair exchange when it comes to men and women and physical abuse? Guys do it, or even hit a woman, it's straight to jail, do not pass go, do not collect $200. When a woman does it, she can get away with it if she cries hard enough, lies good enough, and if she calls the cops fast enough. I, for one, don't see anything "fair" about this kind of 'exchange.'

The I –Don't Need-No-Man-Syndrome

The cultural nationalist Maulana Karenga once wrote that, "unless we admit, we cannot alter." This is about pent-up frustration which I believe is really about anger. In sociology we learned about the "frustration-aggression hypothesis," and that simply means that as frustration increases, aggression is more likely to take place.
This seemingly simplistic statement is at the basis of what I believe we can do to put the victory of the vagina and the power of the penis in proper perspective because, when all is said and done, the present-day perspective is distorted and warped – *by design.* The conclusion amidst all the confusion is that black women have adopted an "I-don't-need-no-man" attitude and it shows in almost everything they do and say.

I think about things. And I read a lot. If you do this consistently, you will be able to find the truth about a lot of things that most people do not or cannot accept. I find this to be the case when it comes to something as basic and essential as black male-female relationships. But first, let me share something with you that I recently read.

Stafford (2001), in this Christian magazine, laid out an analogy that I think will help me get my point across. He begins:

> Imagine a house under construction. While the walls are still
> skeletal, with the breeze blowing through freshly cut wood,
> electricians come to install an elaborate network of wires. Later,
> when the walls are solid with Sheetrock, plaster and paint, these
> wires lie hidden. One day, when the house is ready to live in, the
> electric company hooks the wires into a source of power. You can't
> see any change. The wires stay hidden. But suddenly, you can do
> things you couldn't before. You can plug in and blast your stereo,
> do homework after dark, watch your favorite TV show. You can
> also electrocute yourself.

Moving on:

> Your sexuality is something like that. Biologically, your potential
> was wired in at birth. You have the proper organs. You have a
> male or female mix of hormones. That's good … At puberty, your
> wiring gets hooked into power. Suddenly sexuality becomes an

> active potential. Males and females are charged particles, ready to
> bond. That's good too. Because God made you, and that's the way
> you are. When the power turns on, you begin to feel that the
> wonder of the opposite sex is more than something to wonder
> about. If you're a boy, you want a girl for your own. If you're a girl,
> you want a boy. It's a strong and thrilling (sometimes frightening)
> urge. Biologically you want to touch: to hold hands, to kiss,
> ultimately to make love. Psychologically you want to touch, too: to
> explore a personality so distinct from your own, to love and be
> loved, to expose your thoughts and your fears, to be naked and
> unashamed, to never be alone again.

There's much more because it's a story for young people. But it can also be used for the naïve, the fantasizers and the reality deniers. And in our relationships, at least based upon what the statistics clearly show, Americans in general and black folks in particular, are in need of some schooling. So we begin here.

We begin by accepting the fact that although men and women are both human beings, we are not only different, but it is the woman who is sexually superior. Men are not going to willingly accept this, but the facts are right there. *In Beyond Connections: Liberation in Love and Struggle*, Karenga (1980) wrote, "It is a moral and spiritual fact of no meager importance that where we differ the most is where we fit together most profoundly." And that applies to sexuality as well.

The belief in male superiority – sexual or otherwise - is rooted in myth, power and, in my view, misogyny. Let me give you some background as to why I believe this to be the case, and why it has come to be that women, especially black women, have conditioned themselves to accept the fact that men are an expendable commodity.

I advance the theory that the reason why those who wrote the Bible and claim that Eve came from Adam's rib is because *some man realized the power and greatness of women and their incredible ability to carry life around, nurture it and then bring that life into the world.* Someone saw a woman having a child and was awed by the power that such a reality represented. So in order to keep the woman "in her place" (lest she understand that "the hand that rocks the cradle rules the throne"), a myth was concocted where, the very first time a creation took place (other than God's) it was a MAN giving birth to a WOMAN.

This is what happens when a man writes the book: the woman gets short shrift. The young child sits on his father's lap and says, "Father, you read to me all the time about the lion being king of the jungle and yet in all the stories, by the time they end, the hunter is victorious. Why is that?" The father turns to his son and says, "My son, that is the way it will always be: *until the lion learns how to write.*"

This applies to those who have the power of intellectual creativity and imagination, linked to a great deal of evil, and then backed up by one hell of an ink pin. What is written is going to be a reflection of the person writing it. Men, for the most part, don't write books where they concede that women are physically superior – even though they are. Whites don't write books where they concede that blacks are physically superior – although we are. Get my drift? The woman is always going to be short-changed if she sits around relying on her "opponent" (that's how it seems) to write her into history. That's why it's called "**His-Story**"!!!

Take the case of dancing and how the Bible talks against it, unless it is with someone you're married to or women dancing with women during a celebration. But for the most part, the Bible forbids it. I wondered why. But I figure like this: dancing is a part of every culture, and it is a celebratory thing. Sure, Americans take it way too far and have turned it into an occupation, a way of life, a past time, and so on. But if the Bible and the religious men are denouncing it, then can we not conclude that these are the writings of men who simply cannot dance? Who cannot, for the life of themselves, cut rug? Who stumble and fall at the sound of a bass beat?

Why would this not be the case? When I was a cool adolescent and went to school dances, I didn't dance at all. What was my explanation to the many women who wanted to dance with me? "I'm too cool for that stuff." And to back it up, I'd go outside and get high with some fellow "non-dancers" and we'd go back inside and pick up on chicks who thought we were "cool," nevertheless.

Fast forward to other cultures where women can dance with men and men can dance with men and it's totally acceptable. But we live in America, a nation with a great deal of sexual hang-ups. However, because of the shortage of men, it is no surprise to see women dancing with each other in night clubs. And in America, when black women start doing that, it is a sign. And that sign is that they are adapting to the black male shortage and, in fact, have learned how to have a good time with one another *extramarital.* It may be sexual, it may not but one thing is clear: the I-don't-need-no-man syndrome is in full effect, alive and well, and living in the black communities of America.

It's easy to put something down when you, yourself, do not engage in it (or are not good at it or are afraid to engage in it). And if you have a lot of power, you can write your fears, hang-ups and feelings of inadequacy into law. Those who couldn't dunk a basketball outlawed it at the college level when a group came along (black men) who could dunk one. When you enslave a powerful race of warriors, you pass laws and concoct myths that reduce that race to a category of inferiority and top it all off with, "God told me to do it." Remember the Curse of

Ham myth where blackened skin was supposed to be a punishment for all of Ham's descendants because Noah's children saw him naked and laughed at him? If the kids were laughing because Noah had a little penis, then that's one thing, and that would also explain why a few centuries later, pseudo-scientific racists would concoct, among a host of other theories, that there was a "reverse relationship" between penis size and intelligence. (Get it? If your penis was big, you were a moron; if it was small, you were a genius).

The victory of the vagina is genetic and biological. Women don't have to be in a certain frame of mind in order to have sex. Men do. When we are young there's no problem because hormones are raging. But as we get older, issues like the job, studying for an exam, taking care of a family and so on begin to weigh on our minds. And for men, the mind and the penis work hand in hand. *The power of the penis is really a reflection of the power of the mind.*

With such an advantage, women can do as they please when they please. They don't really "need" us. Back in the day we were good at providing them with children but with today's technology, all they have to do is visit a sperm bank and, voila! Conception!

It is for reasons such as these that men use laws to put so many restrictions on them. If there weren't so many social codes, folkways, mores and rules placed on little girls who then grow up to be women, women would be having sex around the clock! Some of them do; but look at how they are reviled and put down, even by their fellow women! In a male-dominated society (as far as laws and institutions), when a man has a lot of women and a lot of sex, he's a stud and a hero; when a woman has a lot of men and a lot of sex, she's viewed as a "slut" or a "ho." This double standard is an extension of what the religious books (Bible, Korean, Talmud) say about women and it is an attempt to take attention away from man's flaws and promote a myth of male superiority. It is an attempt, using religion and truth-claims about morality," to neutralize the victory of the vagina while promoting and defending the power of the penis.

Understanding all this, the claim of not needing the black man carries some truth. We black men say we need black women, and we know it. There are those of us who marry women who are not black, but once we visit home and visit our mothers or think back on the sisters we have gone out with, we realize that what we are doing says much more about our own psycho-social needs than it does with "doing what's right."

The power of the penis can be demonstrated by the sheer fact that so many women spend their lives trying to control it (the penis). And, in fact, most women can do so, in time. The power of the penis is finite, even with the use of drugs. The victory of the vagina is on-going and permanent because no matter what happens, the vagina will always win. This is a fact that I believe men, throughout time, recognized but simply disregarded. As long as we got ours, we could care less about whether or not she experienced an orgasm or not. *But then the word began to spread and women talked and it became understood that there was a way for a woman to explode sexually and feel the way that we do when we, as men, ejaculate.*

Here's another note: masturbation is an option, and don't be afraid of it. I've been an advocate of pre-date masturbation even before Ben Stiller stole the idea and talked about it in "Something About Mary." If you're hot to trot, all of a sudden any woman starts to look good. Relax yourself first and restore some semblance of objectivity. It's also a scientific fact that masturbation, for men and women, yields the strongest orgasm. It's not the same for everybody, but I figure it's because nobody knows your body better than you do. The best thing to do is to talk with who you're in bed with and once they know what you like, there will be no need for masturbation, right?

Wrong. Masturbation keeps you aware that everything is still working and, at least as far as I can figure, it keeps your sex organs strong. I'm not talking about whacking off every hour on the hour; but it helps you relieve any stress you might have and again, it keeps you from climbing walls or falling in love with your pets.

And it also releases you from the games women play when it comes to starving your body. I was with one who knew she was lousy in the bed, so she continually denied me and made me wait. Oh she would tolerate my expertise in foreplay and the like, but was denying me sex. What she was doing was starving my body (or so she thought) and then, when the time is right, by the time she does give it up, it becomes something "extra special."

When it comes to size, I say that my personal belief is that it matters. Too many women have complimented me and you can tell when a woman is serious. But according to studies, the average size is only about six inches long. The key here though is that a woman's truly sensual and erotic areas are all towards the front of her vagina. So anything more than that is just icing on the cake. Size is good for our ego, and perception still wins the game. There's an old joke that the reason why women's depth perception and measuring skills are slightly off is because men keep telling them that six inches is a foot. Get it?

If a woman tells you that size doesn't matter, she's lying. And don't let them compliment you too frequently because as soon as an argument breaks out, or they don't get their way, the first thing they "attack" is your dick. Richard Pryor once joked about an argument that he had with one of his women. He told her, "Fuck it. I'm going to go find me some new pussy." She shouted back, "If you had two more inches of dick you'd find some new pussy HERE!"

The sexual superiority exists throughout life for the sisters, but it really kicks in and becomes most evident when we become older. As men, we are going to experience erectile dysfunction in our lives. But the fact is, aging itself is not a cause of erectile dysfunction. However, one study says that, "diminishing hormone levels do precipitate some changes. A man may need more physical stimulation to become aroused, and his erection may not be quite as firm as when he was younger -- but sex is no less pleasurable." Lazy women ought to remember this fact: the "lay back and take it' mentality is a definite turn off. And this contributes to the rationalization of not needing a man.

So now I've covered some issues that you may have thought about but were too gutless to state out loud or share with anyone. If you don't agree, just blame it on me and tell whomever that I don't know what I'm talking about. If women think that they don't need a man, then they will do whatever it takes to compensate for the absence of one (like they do now after we screw them and then dump them).

Women don't need men and when you look at how the black man has been slowly transferred into a "bitch," then you can somewhat understand why this is the case.

I attended the State of the Race Conference in 1977, and went to a workshop to listen to one of my favorite scholars, Dr. Frances Cress Welsing. She didn't make it, but her sister, Lorraine, delivered her presentation. And during that presentation she discussed some points that I would read later in some of Dr. Welsing's essays in The Isis Papers.

Dr. Welsing talked about black men. She said that there were five levels of humanity: Man, woman, boy and girl and baby. She said that the black man was denied being a man and that he has adapted to other types of humanity. She said the black woman calls him "baby" and he calls her "mama." He said the black man refers to his own home as a "crib." He said that since he cannot be a man, woman or girl, all that leaves is for him to become a baby.

I don't know about that, but maybe it has some validity. Or maybe it's just the fact that so many black men grow up in single parent households, and that black women spoil them, that they grow up like punks and try to find a woman that will "take care of them the way mama did." I don't know. What I do know is that the same people that are dunking from the free throw line, running 99 yard punts back for touchdowns, and setting world's records in the 100-yard dash are not the same warriors when it comes to confronting our oppressor or defending black women. And for that reason alone, I call manhood into question using logic, common sense and what I've observed.

And it ain't pretty.

I look at the way we act and talk. When we get angry, the first thing we want to tell another person is, "Well you can suck my dick!" You've heard it before. And yet this is the one thing that every black man wants his woman to do. So how can the act be one of sensuality and intimacy when it comes to the woman you love and yet be something negative when you're cursing out another man. Either you subconsciously think that the act is negative or maybe you're gay and you really DO want that man to suck your stuff.

Another thing I've noticed is how we refer to women as "bitches," and have done so for decades. Now, all of a sudden, I notice that women, especially younger sisters, are referring to black males as bitches. What's up with that? In other words, "who's the ho, now?"

The article I am about to use as a foundation for my critique and commentary appeared in *The Observer* on August 3, 2008. It was written by a woman, probably a white woman, but as Chancellor Williams wrote in *The Destruction of Black Civilization*, "it is doubtful if even a devil can write a book that is totally without truth." The article is entitled, "Depressed, Repressed, Objectified: Are Men the New Women?"

The article begins by asserting that, "If recent research is anything to go by, 21st century man is in a desperate muddle. In June [2008], men discovered that their libidos are in freefall, prompting a 40 per cent increase in males seeking counseling for impotence problems" (Day, 2003). Don't think women didn't already know this; they've been faking orgasms for centuries and it has been so successful that male arrogance has probably grown exponentially despite us really having no evidence that our abilities have produced these climaxes.

The fact is, the male is on the decline, and I believe that this "freefall" is more than likely the result of one of two things: serious psychological problems in coming to grips with all the "dirt" that we've done (black men and white men) to women over the years or secondly, a result of all that genetically engineered food that we've been consuming. In either case, we must remember that for every action there is an opposite and equal reaction. So if what is written about libido reduction is true, then I anticipate a response in the guise of overblown egotism, out of control machismo or, maybe even epidemic down-low behavior. This much we know: Something's gotta give!

The article continues: "Their existential angst worsened in July, when British men discovered that they have the most unequal paternity rights in Europe. According to Nicola Brewer, chief executive of the Equality and Human Rights Commission, fathers in the UK are seen as 'not essential for parenting'." (Day, 2003).

That is the same way it is becoming in America, and the way that it has been for some time in the black community. But there is one point that is not mentioned: the perception of fathers not being seen as essential for parenting is based on fact, not fantasy. What do fathers really do when it comes to parenting? Discipline has been taken away by social workers and school psychologists. If you touch your little girl the wrong way there's going to be sex therapists all over the place and in some cases, even she and the mother might turn on you. Being a breadwinner is important but not a priority; women would rather just probably have the alimony or the child support checks. Whatever the rationale or reason, we played a role in it. When she says she doesn't need us, she is not just engaging in a cacophony of emotive labeling: she's speaking her true feelings and the reality of the situation!

As for black men, I figure that it's a case of too much of a good thing; we've had more than our fair share of sex in our lifetimes, so any losses that are taking place *are the direct result of our abuse of our bodies in the process of coveting and caressing someone else's body.* Sperm decline would not be the worst thing in the world – unless you have no children and no accomplishments. Then there could be some serious psychological (and suicidal) ramifications.

Black men are becoming increasingly effeminate. Moreover,

> It's not only their internal biology; men are also succumbing to the traditionally female preoccupation of looking good on the outside, too. Sales of male beauty products have leapt 30 per cent over the past decade. Almost 20 per cent more men are having plastic surgery than ever before while, last year, researchers from Harvard discovered that a quarter of anorexia and bulimia sufferers is male.(Day, 2003).

Dr. Frances Welsing reported back in 1974 when she was writing "The Cress Theory of Color Confrontation and Racism" that there was, in development, make up for the white male. But the fact is, I've seen black men on television wearing makeup as well. And when it comes to black men, if there is any doubt our gradual "feminization," then check out my observations.

Explain platform shoes: high heels, right? Explain the jheri curl: straightened and laid to the side like a woman's, right. Please explain this thing with the earrings, and even now they are wearing them in both ears – just like women do. And not to venture far, but here is another important point. Even now there is a fashion trend (so far, only white boys and east coast faggots) to don these "skinny jeans" that are so fight that they look like leotards.

We have slowly moved from hard working family men to men who dress and act more feminine than any other male in the nation (except for the white male). We earn money and it seems that the wealthier we become, the more the "bitch" in us comes out. Look at how we become blind to our own communities as soon as we sign a large contract of some kind. And when we isolate ourselves from those areas, that leaves us prone to perform all kinds of freakishness in the confines of secluded, gated communities. Just like the Anglo.

So when the preceding passage makes the point that looking good on the outside is a "traditionally female preoccupation," that observation is old news. Look at the standards of old Hollywood: Anglos, or so they would have us believe, walked around their homes in suits or in white shirts and ties, just as the white women wore dresses and were not "allowed" to wear slacks. Plastic surgery has been taking place among men for a long time, but those who can afford the face lifts, pectoral transplants, false penises, hair plugs and the like are also people who can afford to keep it out of the newspapers.

The question is why would a woman who needs a man need a man who dresses and thinks like a woman? A man who is "cuter" than she is? Homosexual males want to look like women for the most part. But guess what? Today's heterosexual men are looking that way as well. Some are even wearing false eyelashes; many are getting colored lens contacts, even the "macho men" are being "outed." Nothing surprises me anymore. But I know what I see and the question still remains: "Who's the ho, now?"

Instead of admitting to being overcome by what I call "the process of sissification," the best thing to do is to take the role of the victim and whine – and in doing so, these same males are acting like the very thing (women and children) that they claim do all the whining!

According to the article,

> Every week, it seems as if there are new surveys and studies tripping over themselves to paint the grimmest possible picture of modern masculinity. They tell us that men are more neurotic and less fulfilled than ever before; that they are objectified rather than revered; that they are expected to be more in touch with their emotions and yet are criticized for it. Men appear to be confused about what they are and unsure about who they are meant to be. So with more of them feeling disenfranchised, disillusioned and disempowered, is it feasible to think of men as the new oppressed minority? *Might men, in fact, be the new women?* And, if so, who is to blame for making them feel marginalized? (Day, 2003 -- emphasis added).

You see? New surveys and studies "painting the grimmest picture of modern masculinity" instead of calling it what it is: these surveyors and the people conducting the studies are finally beginning to tell the truth about masculinity: it's a sham! Even the preceding passage is filled with symbolic errors that need to be pointed out before we continue on further with this section of the book.

To begin with, the writer says that the studies and surveys, "tell us that men are more neurotic and less fulfilled than ever before." The question then becomes, are the surveys right or not? If they are correct, then men should take that information as "constructive criticism" and then be about the business of addressing that neuroticism. Are men less fulfilled? If so, how? And whose fault is it.

By leaving the statement as "less fulfilled," this insinuates that it is the woman's fault, and that it is sex related. The fact is, you can be less fulfilled because the demands you are making are unrealistic or unattainable. If a man wants a woman to sprout wings and fly, and she does not do it, he may feel "unfulfilled" because his wish wasn't granted. But was that wish realistic in the first place? Of course not. So the author had an obligation to define what being "fulfilled" was, and furthermore, who that man was seeking fulfillment from.

The statements claims that, "Men appear to be confused about what they are and unsure about who they are meant to be." Based on what? Maybe they are realizing that they are the "ho's" and were all the time! Maybe they see that "woman came from the rib of Adam" stuff as the myth that it is and they concluded, rightfully, that the people that wrote the Holy Book were also men who were either insane or outright liars. Look at the reactions of Christians when they are challenged to use logic on certain passages of the Bible. That is why they are force-fed this thing about "faith," and much of the time its "blind faith." If you don't use your mind and you fall prey to mythology, the logical conclusion will be that you are going to be confused and unsure!

Before asking if men might be the new women and following up with the query, "who is to blame for making them feel marginalized? The article claims that men are feeling disenfranchised, disillusioned and disempowered. All of these are bare-faced lies, linked with a scintilla of truth. Let me explain.

How can the white man feel marginalized or disenfranchised when he is the majority in Congress, the Senate, the Pentagon, and the Cabinet? In European nations he's the majority in Parliament. He runs all the armies and militaries in the so-called modern world. So why couldn't it just be that he has these feelings because maybe he's coming to the realization that he's undeserving; maybe he tires of seeing his fellow Anglo brothers and sisters on the news showing how they can't do very much on their own. Maybe he's just tired of working so hard to maintain a racist and gender biased system. Maybe, after all, it's just his "feelings" that have him feeling so badly because the world dynamic is changing and people of color are taking over. Maybe he's finally realized that on a global level he is, indeed, a racial minority.

What we do know is that something internal is wrong. How else to explain the fact that,

> In the UK, men account for 75 per cent of all suicides. They are
> twice as likely to die from the 10 most common cancers that affect
> both sexes and, typically, develop heart disease 10 years earlier
> than women. Although there is a national screening programme in
> place for cervical and breast cancer, there is no equivalent for men,
> in spite of prostate cancer claiming 6.7 per cent more deaths for
> men than cervical cancer in women (Day, 2003).

In the United States, according to my research, which came out of Johns Hopkins University in 2008, The increase in the overall suicide rate between 1999 and 2005 was due primarily to *an increase in suicides among whites aged 40-64, with white middle-aged women experiencing the largest annual increase.* Whereas the overall suicide rate rose 0.7 percent during this time period, *the rate among middle-aged white men rose 2.7 percent annually and 3.9 percent among middle-aged women.* By contrast, suicide in blacks decreased significantly over the study's time period, and remained stable among Asian and Native Americans.

There you have it: they're killing themselves all over the world. It could be due to the economic conditions, or it could be to some of the new "awareness" that the feminist movement, Black studies and other progressive-thinking groups are bringing to the fore. At any rate, it's not just the United King – it's also in the United States.

Continuing with the attempt at "male victimology," those who are being interviewed and who serve as the basis for the article in question seem not to be able to catch a break. Check out how the information on employment is "interpreted:"

> While women still earn on average 12 per cent less than men and
> are severely under-represented in top-level corporate roles, men in
> full-time employment work an average of 41.9 hours a week,
> compared to women's 37.6 hours. According to the American
> men's-rights author Warren Farrell, there might be a glass ceiling
> for women, but there is also what he calls 'a glass cellar' for men.
> 'What I mean by that is men are both at the top of the economy
> scale and at the bottom. Of the 25 professions ranked the lowest [in
> the US], 24 of them are 85-100 per cent male. That's things like
> roofer, welder, garbage collector, sewer maintenance – jobs with
> very little security, little pay and few people want them.' (Day,
> 2003).

What an asinine series of juxtapositions.

In the first place, the men at the top, even if they were in the minority, are still the same race as the men at the bottom. As a result, the men at the bottom have role models, pals, buddies and others who will "cut them some slack," which explains why they are favored in terms of pay. And then this thing about 25 professions being "ranked lowest" and that 85-100 percent of them are male. Then, behind that, comes a lie. The lie is that a roofer, welder, garbage collector and sewer maintenance have "little security, little pay and few people want them."

To begin with roofers make top dollar and most of them are independent. The roofing business is controlled by white men and the people on the streets are usually Latino males. Furthermore, garbage collectors earn good money – in San Francisco. It is not an across-the-board low paying job. It would depend on what city you work in, what shift and so on. And as for welders, most of them belong to exclusive and racist unions and they earn top dollar – most people know that. As for sewer maintenance, that is usually a civil service job and once again, it not only pays well but has incredible benefits. So the writer of the article is not only mis-informed, but she is also *a liar.*

And more fabrications are on the way. For instance:

> Farrell says that women generally prefer a more flexible work-life balance and that implies 40-hour weeks 'at most'. Often, mothers are able to work fewer hours only because they are financially supported by their male partners. This, he claims, is the real definition of power. 'I define power as "control over one's life". A balanced life is far superior to the male definition of power: earning money someone else spends while he dies sooner.' (Day, 2003).

Did Farrell, the person quoted in the article, bother to ask women what they preferred? And of what relevance is a "preference" when you "know what has to" be done? Hell, I'd prefer a paid work week of ZERO hours, but it ain't gonna happen!

Farrell writes that mothers are often able to work fewer hours because their partners are supporting them. How does that mean fewer hours when, while that partner is out at the workplace (doing who knows what), she's at the house with those bad-ass kids? That's work!!! And then there's the cleaning, the cooking, the shopping, the outside lawn work that many women do, keeping the car cleaned and so on. Just because a woman works fewer hours outside of the home doesn't mean that she automatically gets a pass.

Having "control over one's life" doesn't equate to having power – except over that particular life! You can't make people do what you want them to do even against their will – the way someone with real power could do! You can't get legislation passed, change the mind of a judge or close down something that's public. That's what people with power can do. Control over one's life is nothing more than that – control over one's life!

Can't women deal with their issues without some man coming along claiming that he's a victim because of it? Continuing:

> But much of this remains a resolutely middle-class problem. At the lowest end of the economic scale, women are still attempting to shrug off the yoke of oppression and inequality. Meanwhile for many men, their loss of status in the home and the workplace is twinned with a loss of confidence in themselves. (Day, 2003).

The "yoke of oppression and inequality" affect women at all ends of the economic scale; the only problem is that the ones at the top end are too blind to see that they are a part of their own oppression. Be that as it may, the issue is not who is poor and who is not poor; the issue is why women, no matter how wealthy, have to be accountable to men simply because we are men. It seems that no one wants to reverse that part of reality; at most, women – as well as people of color and other protected classes – simply want the Anglo to scoot over so that we can all share the throne of oppression as opposed to getting rid of the throne!

The statement that men are suffering a "loss in status at home and the workplace' and that this is somehow related to a supposed "loss in confidence in themselves" is a statement that is, at best, specious. Perhaps the ego has taken a blow because men never thought that women would ever stand up and be counted; in fact, if the average man had his way, how many of them would even listen to anything a woman had to say. Now that women are beginning to say what they feel, all of a sudden the Anglo male is having a nervous breakdown and feels like his rights are being violated. What noivz!

The whining continues:

> Neil Oliver, the television historian who has just published *Amazing Tales for Making Men out of Boys*, says that there is a conspicuous dearth of positive male role models. 'I grew up hearing tales of Ernest Shackleton and watching films like Zulu,' he says. 'The world in which I was a little boy was one of clearly defined roles for men and women and we don't have that anymore, so men are struggling to readjust. Manly men have been hunted to near extinction in Britain and the concept of manliness has been outmoded. Yet the urge to be a man is a primal thing and still exists in boys today.' (Day, 2003).

"Manly men"? What is that? Some asshole who can't let go of the past? This woman I know used to make this statement, "he's a man's man." After I got to know a little bit about her history I realized that she was too parochial in her thinking and far too limited in her experiences to even know what a man was, let alone try to define what a "man's man" is. What it is a nice slogan that defines somebody who doesn't give a damn about anything and doesn't play by the rules – a "bad boy," as it were. But breaking rules and acting tough doesn't make you a man; taking care of a family does. And this translates to mean that in order to be a "man's man," you first of all have to be a good enough man to not let a woman define you. Define yourself, do the right thing and you'll have a good life. It has nothing to do with sexual conquests, how many rules you break or how many people you beat up.

When it comes to the claim that there is a dearth of male role models, I ask, "how could there be"? And I ask that directing the question at Anglos. They are everywhere and despite being a worldwide minority, they control the media so you see them on television, hear them on radio, and read about them in newspapers and magazines. They pawn themselves off as the authorities on all matters, experts on all subjects and the most virile, best-looking and smartest beings to ever walk the face of this planet. Knowing this, how could a white boy be lacking in role models?

The article continues:

> In the classroom, too, boys are at risk of losing out on male role models. According to government figures for 2006, the ratio of newly qualified female to male teachers under the age of 25 was approaching seven to one. The introduction of coursework and modular exams is believed to play to traditionally female strengths – girls tend to be more methodical while boys tend to follow high-risk strategies such as cramming the night before an exam (Day, 2003).

Losing out on male role models? How is that the case when the source of the curriculum, the subject of the areas of social studies, government, science and the like – are men? Does it matter of a female is imparting this one-sided information or not? Maybe women will do in the classroom what they would be able to do in other areas of society if given an equal opportunity: provide some balance!

Furthermore, when women dominated the elementary levels of education back during the formative years, that didn't destroy men, did it? More than 95% of all teachers were women, hence the name "school ma'arms." And as for the "introduction of coursework and modular exams" playing into female strengths: if men are so much stronger and so much smarter, then what difference would it make? Why are men whining now? When women have to deal with a male-dominated and patriarchal educational system in the arts and sciences, humanities, education, business administration, engineering, fine arts, and so on, did they whine?

> Some critics argue that this creeping 'feminisation' has led to girls outperforming boys on almost every level: they use more words, speak more fluently in longer sentences and with fewer mistakes. By the age of 11, some 76 per cent of boys have attained government-set literacy standards, compared to 85 per cent of girls. At GCSE level, 66.8 per cent of girls achieved A-C grades in 2007, compared to 59.7 per cent of boys (in real terms, this means they trail behind their female counterparts by nine years). (Day, 2003).

Again, the preceding quote reeks with tricknology, innuendo and half-truths. Let me explain how.

To begin with, the statement that there is "creeping feminization" leading to girls out performing boys on every level. Why don't they just call it what it is: *superior intelligence?* A truly intelligent person cannot be kept down forever! What they consider to be "creeping" is nothing more than a changing of the guard! The statistics cited only bear out what I've been saying all along: *men have been mistaking women who have suppressed their gifts and talents with believing that men are actually more gifted and talented.* But now, the proverbial cat is out of the bag, and excuses and claims of "unfair advantage" are now being leveled by the same people who used an unfair system *for centuries* in an attempt to keep women arbitrarily and unilaterally at the bottom of the socioeconomic ladder!

The whimpering continues:

> Do these statistics have any bearing on the everyday experiences of ordinary men? 'I don't know if I feel oppressed, but there's a sense in which women can talk about us with impunity,' says a 32-year-old male lawyer from London, who does not wish to give his name in case his female colleagues start pelting him with rotten tomatoes. 'I've been in the office on several occasions where sweeping generalisations have been made about the general crapiness of men: "Oh, all men are useless, no wonder he couldn't get the job done in time" – that sort of thing. I don't take it all that seriously – at least, not yet – but I know that I wouldn't get away with saying the same things about women.' (Day, 2003).

The previous passage contains a reflection of an attitude that is based on an oppressor's perspective. Because women had been oppressed, suppressed and repressed by the system for so long, many men believed that it was protocol for them to have no voice at all. A woman who expressed her views was dubbed some kind of militant or radical and was isolated from them mainstream. Having piggy-backed on the civil rights movement and advanced their own feminist causes, women now say what they want to say when they want to say it. All of a sudden here comes the Anglo male, angry and peeved because a human being that happens to be female has an opinion that may run counter to his. His over-inflated sense of worth and ego are therefore infringed upon. Now, all of a sudden, *he* is the victim.

Such hogwash! What does that man mean that women can talk about us with impunity? He means that they can say what they want to say without being punished! Without being stifled! Without being censored! The very fact that he would utter such a comment smacks of arrogance and gender bias.

Now, all of a sudden, these experts and scholars and angry guys want society to believe that men are the weaker sex. But the key is that men were the weaker sex all along, and women knew it. The only difference between now and days gone by is that women are no longer afraid to voice that fact! This, more than anything else, is what is pissing men off!

Moving on:

> For a long time, it wasn't particularly fashionable to stand up for men. Warren Farrell, the daddy of the so-called 'masculinist' movement, has been making his arguments since the late 1970s and frequently attracts outrage. His books –*Why Men Earn More* and his latest, *Does Feminism Discriminate Against Men?* – seek to redress what he sees as an endemic sociocultural bias against his gender. In almost all respects, he believes that men are now the weaker sex: 'The problem with feminism is that it saw man as the enemy. When only one sex wins, both sexes lose.' (Day, 2003).

The preceding passage represents thinking that is spurious.

To begin with, the statement that, "for a long time, it wasn't particularly fashionable to stand up for men." When was that? What constitutes a long time? When did that period begin? Admittedly, it has never been fashionable to stand up for men of color, especially in reference to the historical manner in which they have been dogged and degraded by the Anglo male, but the preceding excerpt isn't about "all men." It is about white men. And we must remember that when those people talk about "men," the only include men of color when there's something negative on the horizon: a war, an alien invasion, some kind of dreaded disease – something of that nature. In this case, the concern is the white male, because it is the white woman that is raining down all this hell on him by telling him the truth about himself.

Secondly, this so-called "masculinist movement," a clear rip off of the concept of a "feminist movement." Why? What is the purpose? Men control

Congress and the Senate. They control the armed forces, the International Monetary Fund, Fort Knox and the Treasury. These Anglo men have control over entire international organizations. Why then, for reasons other than spite, would this group see the need for a "masculinist movement"?

Third, as a result of the second point, where is this "endemic sociocultural bias against" men? Something that is endemic is something that is natural or built-in – how can a nation dominated by men be inherently biased? How can a nation that is socioculturally oriented toward men, especially white men, have a bias against them? So what is there to seek redress against, and how will it be done?

A fourth point is important for noting, where Farrell is quoted as saying that in almost all respects, men are now the weaker sex. This is an important note because, in case you haven't noticed, this book has proven that this was always the case. Men were always the weaker sex and they knew it all along. Even today, they know it. All we have to do is have sex with a woman and then notice who "finishes" first. Isn't that evidence enough? Those days of going all night long were great for our egos, but even after she had multiple orgasms, she was still ready to get going again. We weren't.

He is also wrong when he says feminism saw man as the enemy. No, feminism saw a patriarchal system that was operated by men as the enemy. Men were just the soldiers in the war. Men were not the enemy as far as black women were concerned – it was the white woman who was going around imitating her war-like man and selling wolf tickets, sounding more and more like him even as she screamed.

Sixth, he claims that, "when only one sex wins, both sexes lose. Again, a flawed conclusion. In such a battle, *there can be no winners*. Even when one claims victory – as men have done throughout history – everybody lost in the process. Women were oppressed and as such, that oppression was reflected in a system that was global and in children who adopted the same kinds of notions. Everyone ends up being wrong and as such, no one can or should be able to claim a victory of any kind.

Even in this "awakening period" where women are claiming their rightful roles in the human family, there will not be any winners because the white man would rather destroy *everything* than to lose his position of power. That is why, as I allege, he is out to get rid of the black woman. Once he does that, the white woman will feel better because she's *always* been jealous of the sister and many of them have always wanted a man of color. Since the Anglo male appears to crave power more than sex, he will gladly let us go at each other while he rules the "sex roost," as it were.

And it is only going to get worse for men. According to the next passage, "Apparently, men are stymied by biology as well – human genetics experts estimate that man will be extinct within 125,000 years owing to their declining sperm count and the mutation of the Y chromosome." If men die out, it will not be due to low sperm counts, but to massive and collective greed and lust for power. Furthermore, the Anglo male is not going to go quietly into the night; once he's exterminated the sister, that leaves the black man doing the menial work and the white woman lusting after men of color, he still has his test tubes, laboratories and cloning devices. As Earth, Wind and Fire would have sang, "That's the way of the world."

In the meantime, more rejection of the obvious continues, and more specious arguments dominate most of the arguments regarding the "gender wars." For instance, take note of the following idiotic passage:

> So – although women hold only 17 per cent of parliamentary positions across the globe, despite there being only 10 female CEOs of Fortune 500 companies and ignoring the fact that it is still illegal for a woman to drive a car in Saudi Arabia – it seems that, sometimes, it is harder to be a man. (Day, 2003).

Such lunacy! The statistics cited above are all the result of men "rigging" the situation and sabotaging women's power to the point where they are not representative of their numbers. Someone with that kind of power should not have a problem being a man. But then, that's not really the problem is it?

The problem is not being a man. The problem is accepting the fact that you *are* a man. And while we're sitting around trying to figure it out or "explain" it to anyone who will listen, our women are continuing to move on, alone, and take our children with them.

What We Hath Wrought: Sisters and the Anglo Male

Nothing stays the same. The guy who has the virgin and breaks her in, only to lose her, may regret it when she finds someone else. Although he moves on, he realizes that when he was the first one, the only one that the virgin had in her life and her bed, he had to be the best. She was naïve and had to accept him because there was no standard of comparison. Now she's moved on and the guy left behind may see her and wonder how the new guy(s) in her life are treating her and how they compare with him. It's inevitable, but no one ever talks about it (a problem within itself). Now she's angry and has a dislike for men. As she gets older she may come to the conclusion that she doesn't need a man or if she does find one, he will pay for the transgressions of those who came before.

For centuries, black men had her all to ourselves with only a few ever breaking ranks and going over to the other side for sex and relationships. Now, because of our lack of numbers and a host of other reasons, she is beginning to exercise her power and realize her true beauty and worth. A number of black women are now doing "the white thing."
Oswald (2008) penned an excellent and well-researched article, Why Black Women Are Doing the White Thing." Now true, the sisters she interviewed are not from the United States – but they're still sisters and they still have arguments that I am sure American black women also have and will use in the days ahead. At any rate, I will use Ms. Oswald's findings as the basis of this section of my book, and interject my own views. This is not an attempt to speak for anyone, but because her views are similar to my belief that such relationships are inevitable based upon a number of factors, I feel it is only fair to give her words credit even as I share my own with you, the reader.
The article begins:

> Frustrated with the 'shortage' of 'good' black men, black women
> are expanding their horizons and are dating outside of their race.
> Statistics show that more black women are dating white men
> worldwide, and black female/white male marriages have increased
> by fifty per cent. (Oswald, 2008).

The sister need not "expand her horizons." As men, we are pretty much the same. All that stuff about differences between black men is basically bullshit derived from the days of slavery. Sure, black men are more cool and suave and that kind of thing, better dancers for the most part. Some say better in bed (others say more selfish in the bed). But it's just a matter of time of being ready for the social stigma attached to such a relationship. But the sister can handle it because, as I've clearly shown in this book, she's already stigmatized. If she chooses to date a white man, she is perfectly entitled. And this is coming from a straight-up 'race man' who has always believed in endogamy – marriage and dating within the race.

But times change, and when you become a man, you put away childish things. I've seen and experienced what is going on in this society, and I've been on the front lines of much of it. I don't like seeing black women angry and frustrated all the time, oozing with bitterness because a trust was betrayed. Angry because we black men keep going to jail and keep hustling them instead of giving them all of our love. They don't understand what we have to deal with on a daily basis and maybe they've got their own plates too full to have time to understand it. But at any rate, it's not like we haven't gotten our fair share of the white woman's booty; I already believed that what was "good for the goose is good for the gander."

Because of all this and the "I don't need a man" syndrome, they have defined a man as someone with a job who takes care of the kids (whether they're his or not), pays bills or helps her pay them, and is basically a valet, chauffeur and butler around the house. This is what "love, American style" has come to mean in the black community.

Black male- white female marriages have increased, worldwide, by fifty percent. But those figures, because of the emphasis of this particular article, are probably international stats. Black women here in America haven't started doing it en masse yet, but believe me, it's coming and its going to come soon. And for some reason, it's going to catch a lot of black men totally off guard and by surprise. But again, that's male ego and arrogance; believing its okay for them to glare and stare and flirt and collect phone numbers but when the sister does it, she's got to deal with a lot of attitude. Those days, as they say, are gone.

The article claims that,

> Some argue that this increase in relationships between black women and white men may be attributed to educational attainment. "Some black men will look at you a certain way. They know that you have a lot going on and that they can't play games. Sometimes it's harder to attract black guys when you have a lot going for yourself," says Renea D. Nichols-Nash, author of *Coping With Interracial Dating* (Oswald, 2008).

Really? What I've found is that sisters who have a lot going for themselves" *usually mean that they have a job*. If not that, then they're so deep into the church that they think that they've got a one-way ticket to heaven (but I notice that ain't none of these bitches anxious to die). The job and the church might carry a lot of weight with dudes who are looking for a free meal and somebody whose head they can bump, but I consider that phrase differently.
If you tell *me* or imply that you've got a lot going for yourself, I want to see some plays you've written or some art work; I want to see or hear some language that shows me how you think. I want to see something you've produced other than problems, babies and Bible quotes. I don't want to hear that crap about having it going on *just because you found a white man to adopt you or because you think that you're "saved" and that this means that you've got some kind of intrinsic insight that nobody else has.*

Furthermore, based on what I've observed and experienced, if a sister says she has a lot going on, the average brother is going to assume that she is talking about a job and as a result, is going to try to swoop on her. The fact is, sisters have a sixth sense about certain things, although much of it is rooted in some of the same superficial "checking out" techniques that most women use. They look at the cut of your suit, the condition of your shoes, and the things they basically learned from white women. Older sisters checked to see if a man had his hair combed or if the collar of his shirt was clean. If he treated them well and was polite, then they made a decision based on that – not on whether you wear Armani or off the rack.

Third and most profoundly, what manner of man would be turned off by a woman who has her stuff together? Doesn't *he* have *his* together? Or is he afraid that she might actually have some standards? The guys who sisters believe are afraid of sisters who are organized and together are guys who are doing them a favor by walking away. Because those are the guys who will go off for no reason and end up putting that sister in the hospital. That is because these guys are insecure, have no real talent, and their claim to fame is that they have a job that they don't like, and one that they must ingratiate themselves in order to keep. That leads to a great deal of frustration. Now, pick up a sociology test and look up, "frustration-aggression hypothesis." Once you're finished reading that, I will continue my lecture.

Now that you've been informed, let us continue with the article which reminds us that, "Oscar-winning actress Whoopi Goldberg, who dates white men, found this to be the case. Black men, she says, have a hard time dealing with a black woman with power" (Oswald, 2008).

What is quoted above only proves one thing: that being that even a broken clock is right twice a day. Whoopi Goldberg is as opportunistic as they get, and the stuff she ran on white boys would not work on a brother. Frustrated, unkempt and on welfare, she changes her name to a Jewish surname, comes up with Whoopi, and begins cracking jokes, making fun of her poverty. That's how she made it. Now, she's a source of information about male-female relationships because she won an Oscar playing the role of a witch in "Ghost" – and hasn't made a decent movie since (other than "The Color Purple"). At present she's one of the hosts of ABC's "The View," and dresses like she's a member of a motorcycle gang. Furthermore, Whoopi dates white men because they're white. The black men she comes across in her circle have more money and power than she does, so why would they have a hard time dealing with her. Black men with that kind of money are not going to be physically attracted to Goldberg, and she knows that. Maybe these men prefer white women and don't like Whoopi's locks (hair style).

 At any rate, she not only dates white men, she also marries them and then divorces them after taking them to the cleaners. Again, we have an unreliable source giving her opinion about an issue that she really knows nothing about. The issue is not how much gold digging you can do – it's about falling in love with someone of a different race and making a life for yourself: the way Sidney Portier and Marchia Shimkus have done; the way Minnie Ripperton and her husband did; and so on.

Back to the subject at hand, where the writer states, "Now, rather than sitting around dreaming about the perfect black man, black women are considering the possibility that 'Mr. Right' could be white." He could be. But guess what? That statement is subjective. He could be right for her, but that doesn't mean he's right for anyone else. And in making that decision, he might not be right based on what her mother and father think, either. This situation is not like the other interracial issue involving whites and Asians, whites and Latinos or whites and Native Americans. This is white and black, and one of them is the descendant of enslaved people and the other one is the descendant of the enslaver. White folks might be over it because of guilt, but black parents aren't. so when she finds "Mr. Right," it might be based on her own needs and that might come at the risk of alienating her family.

Oswald comments on the issue thusly: "Casting aside reservations about interracial relationships – for some, due to the atrocities committed during slavery – they are beginning to look past race when choosing a potential mate" (Oswald, 2008).

That is a lot of looking! Sure slavery happened "in the past," but it's still alive and well in America. The benefits that Anglos continue to reap are generated by the vestiges of slavery! The psychological hang-ups and cultural issues that black people are experiencing today are the result of never having been "de-briefed" following a 400-year stint as prisoners of war (which most of you call slavery). So the impact is still here and the decision for a mate from the oppressor class, like the decision to marry the descendant of the enslaved, are issues that do not over-ride slavery; they merely are an extension of it.

Remember, if you will, that there were white women and men willing to risk it all to have sex with black people. Remember that there were well-meaning whites who also risked their lives to combat slavery. That is the same mentality that is in play when a white male decides to marry a black woman; he loves her despite what his peers are saying and what his cultural super-ego is telling him. The impact of slavery still exists for both the white male and his black female girlfriend or wife; if they think they are ignoring it just because they say they are, then they are ignorant of the impact of slavery and the significance of history (again, the latter does not only record the past; it also coordinates the present and projects the future).

Oswald's article continues:

> "I'm not saying that white men are the answer to all our problems," 35-year-old Chantelle Perry says. "I'm just saying that they offer a different solution." Many black women, who are becoming

increasingly frustrated as the field of marriageable black men
narrows, share Perry's view (Oswald, 2008).

Two points here. First of all, is this woman saying that women seek husbands just so they can address their problems? What's this about a man offering a "solution"? The solution is supposed to be the decision to get married because you care about somebody because that person is someone you can relate to. This thing about marrying somebody because you've got bills or a dead end job and that person can supplement your income – man, that's why people end up in divorce court. No man wants to be used that way! If these women are so "liberated" and independent, what is all this stuff about the man coming along as a "problem solving"? Methinks the woman wants her cake and wants to eat it, too!

Secondly, the preceding excerpt says sisters are becoming frustrated as the field of marriageable black men narrows. This is the kind of thing that leads to mistakes. You can't become frustrated and then think that the person you finally found is the "answer"!

I recall a quote from Eric Hoffer who once said, *"Our frustration is greater when we have much and want more than when we have nothing and want some. We are less dissatisfied when we lack many things than when we seem to lack but one thing."* The black woman is frustrated because, as a black woman, she already has it all (but may not realize it). That is why her frustration is so intense and immense, because having it all, she should attract people who also have it all. Or, at very least, attract people who appreciate her so much that they are willing to do whatever it takes to be associated with one so blessed. By that not being the reality, she is frustrated and in many cases, depressed. And this makes her angry and as a result, she turns her back on black men.

This explains, or at least I believe it explains, why she is now willing to move to marry outside of the race. She sees others doing it. And she knows what's going on around her. Oswald (2008) provides additional insights:

> Black men are nearly seven times more likely to be incarcerated than white men, and more than twice as likely to be unemployed. Another arguable reason for black women opting for white men is social environment. Race doesn't matter to Paul Kennedy and Michelle Clarke. Best friends since primary school, they are now in a relationship together. Kennedy is white and Clarke is black. "People are finding people with common interests and common perspectives and are putting race aside," says Clarke, 26, a Middlesex University graduate who works at Barclay's Bank (Oswald, 2008).

That's what it's about; finding somebody you have something in common with. And as long as black men keep acting up the way that we do, or as long as we keep on chasing other women, then sisters are going to do what they have to do. Why? Oswald provides some semblance of an answer in the following paragraph:

> Clarke and her friends are among the new generation of black females that are opting to date outside of their race due to their social environment. Like Clarke, the majority of young people have friends or acquaintances of different races and nationalities, and are seen as more tolerant and open-minded than previous generations. Unlike their parents and grandparents, today's teens and twenty-somethings have grown up hearing the buzzwords 'diversity,' 'multicultural' and 'inclusion', and are used to seeing interracial friendship and romance portrayed in films and on TV – especially in soap operas and adverts.

I agree with the point of this generation has more friends and acquaintances of different races than previous generations did – a point I made earlier in this book. And in America, that is a good thing since sooner or later, white folks are going to have to learn to interact. But let us not forget that this is a "system" and no matter how much individual actions may change, this "system" is racist to its very core. People may learn to love and interact and marry, but this system is always going to find ways to place obstacles in their paths. Buzzwords are not the kinds of facts or foundations on which to build a truly egalitarian society.

And to show how omniscient this system is, even when people want to do good or do the right thing, their collective ignorance – spurred on by a system concocted and maintained by the ignorant – always comes to surface. Witness, for instance, the following statement:

> "I don't see colour as an issue," states Clarke. "We have been very happy together and apart from a few isolated incidents, we have not experienced any open hostility towards our relationship" (Oswald, 2008).

Clarke lies when she says she doesn't see color as an issue. Her whole commentary has been about color. What she means is that she doesn't see color as an issue that is going to prevent her from being happy. These are two totally different concepts.

To not see color is a foolish comment that you hear made by these liberals who want to act as if they are not racist. *To be "colorblind" in a society filled with people of color means that you see them as white people.* It also means that you don't care enough to get to know them despite their difference in color – you are so arrogant and racist that you refuse to acknowledge that black people are not well-tanned Europeans, Latinos are not browned Caucasians and Asians are not white folks with jaundice. To be "colorblind" is to be a true racist, in my book. The key is to see and acknowledge color (cultural relativity) and to nevertheless have a concern about that other person.

Now we get to that issue of "selfishness versus what your people think" argument that I raised earlier:

> Admitting that at first her parents disapproved – she was told while growing up never to come home with a white man – Clarke explains that her parents have come to accept her relationship decision because she would not back down, and Kennedy has proved his commitment to her and, most importantly, her family. "I come from a stereotypical Caribbean black family and I am the first Clarke to date a white person," she says. "At first my parents were dead against my relationship with Paul, but our commitment towards one another has outshined any doubts" (Oswald, 2008).

Brothers and sisters from the Caribbean are, in my opinion, more likely to fall for white folks than we are. They've got this mentality about America and they've got a trust and love for Europeans that dates back to the days of Toussaint L'Oueverture, a brilliant black military man who trusted the white folks, took their word, and ended up being locked away in a dungeon for life. I am not shocked at all that Ms. Clarke hails from a Caribbean family and then comes to America and falls in love with a white man. This falls right in line with that "American Dream" myth that immigrants have about this place; latching onto a white man translates to mean "smooth sailing ahead" to them just like finding a well-to-do white woman means to a lot of brothers from the hood.

Furthermore, I am not surprised that a white man would fall for a Caribbean woman because, in addition to their beauty, they have that European accent (read: "exoticism") that drives white Americans and Black Americans alike out of our collective minds. I mean, after all, it's not like they're "real niggers" like the ones in this country. That's why these crackers can spend their vacation money in the Caribbean, surrounded by black people while hating the black people right here in the states. To them, there's a difference; It's all part of the process of assimilation that we've had forced down our throats by the media and by various American and Euro American institutions.

Most Caribbean people are honest and will tell you what's on their minds. What Ms. Clarke is describing is love based on familiarity:

> Clarke, who lives with her parents, says that her three-year
> relationship with her present partner is no different to previous
> ones with black men. "I don't believe being with Paul is any
> different from any of my past relationships. Being with Paul feels
> so natural because we have known each other for years, and I do
> believe that one of the secrets to a successful relationship is
> friendship." Asked whether sex is different, Clarke says: "No!
> Why should it be?" (Oswald, 2008).

If she lives with her parents, then he knew her financial and social status and she knew his. She shared this with her parents and they watched him "date" her (translation: spend money on her). Because the world knows the power of white people in America, the parents want what is best for their daughter. If she marries a white man, at very least she will be taken care of financially. These are factors that the article won't mention, but they are facts that exist in the real world, the American dating world, the world where "there can't be no romance without finance." The world of *today*.

But check out the next sister, from London, but honest to a fault:

> However, 25 year-old Simone Thomas from southwest London
> found it difficult to enjoy an intimate relationship with dates of a
> different race from her own. "Believe it or not I have tried to have
> a physical relationship with several white men, but when it came
> down to the bedroom action I could not see it through." "I know it
> sounds crazy saying it out loud. Trust me, I'm an educated woman,
> but whenever I saw their private parts I was totally put off sleeping
> with them." Asked if it had anything to do with size, Thomas
> responds: "No, not really. It was just the colour, and all the black
> men I have dated have been circumcised and the white men were
> not." (Oswald, 2008).

Such honesty! But sisters in America, they know about the stereotype. They know that if they want oral sex performed on them, a white man is more apt to do it than a black man. And some sisters are into that kind of thing. But nobody wants to write about it and nobody wants to discuss it in those male-female relationship forums that we're so fond of having (usually during Black History Month, the shortest month of the year).

Then there are the dyed-in-the-wood sisters, the ones who came up during the 1960s usually, who haven't forgotten those glory days or what they learned about their own history and culture. Though few and far between in this day of black art on the walls taking the place of true consciousness and commitment, some still remain. Check out the following sister, also from London:

> Cultural differences and religious beliefs are some of the reasons why numerous black women are reluctant to date outside their race. "Life is hard enough without having to add any unnecessary stress. I just want a man that I can relate to," declares Charlene Clifford from north London. "A man that will know and understand me, and vice versa. Dating a white man would just be too complicated." (Oswald, 2008).

What beautiful words: "I just want a man I can relate to." And in the final analysis, we all want someone in our like that. The problem is finding such a person in a society that is so full of people who are shallow, banal and sophomoric. And here's some data that shows why sisters may be about to flip the script on black men:

> Historically within the black community, people are more used to seeing black men dating white women. Black men as a group are three times more likely to date and marry white women. But black women are now exercising their options like their brothers. "Race is becoming less of a deal in dating. People want to explore their choices," says Adam White, author of *The Interracial Dating Book for Black Women Who Want to Date White Men* and *The White Man's Guide To Dating Black Women*. (Oswald, 2008)

Bullshit. Race is still a factor except now the stereotypes have come full circle. Now that the laws and social mores have been relaxed, the black woman is still considered a hyper-sexed creature and the black man is still viewed as a walking phallic symbol – but now it's alright for them to date us. That's the only thing that's changed when all is said and done.

Furthermore, where did those figures come from that lead to the conclusion that a black man is "Three times more likely" to date and marry white women? More likely to do what? Three times more likely than to marry a sister, three times more likely to marry a white woman after divorcing a black woman? These people have to write as if they care about imparting information. Furthermore, I doubt those figures: I'd say it is 20 times more likely that a black man will marry a white woman and not just date her because she's got the best chance of having a job and keeping one. And, as I've said, the chickens have come home to roost, and the black man can't take it. What few black men there are, that is:

> "As scary as this may sound, there are more black women than there are black men, which means there are a lot fewer black men available for relationships," White adds. "This is mainly due to

> early deaths, prolonged incarceration, homosexuality, unemployment and marriage to white women or other races. It is a common refrain to hear black women complain that there are 'no good Black men' in their social universes. *"Black women are fed up of waiting for a black Mr. Right to come along* and now want to explore dating outside their racial box. Black women are … exploring their options (Oswald, 2008 – emphasis added).

And on that note, I think I'll put this section on reasons why black women act and feel as if they don't need a man, and deal with yet another reason why that might be the case: "down-low"= brothers, who in many cases are actually married to black women but who, for some reason, sneak down the street or down to the club and engage in sex with other men. They claim they're not gay. That's bullshit. Either you like pussy or you like balls slamming into your chin. Take your pick.

THE DOWN LOW ON "THE DOWN-LOW"

Normally, "double indemnity" refers to a clause in a life insurance or accident insurance policy providing for payment of twice the value of the policy in event of accidental death. *In this case, the beneficiary of the double payment is the Anglo-American system itself.* They get to use a black man to assist in the destruction of black women through AIDS, they get to blame homosexual behavior as the cause for AIDS while, at the same time, promoting the concept of "bisexuality" as something normal and quite acceptable for anyone who is gullible enough to believe it. *Double indemnity.*

The fact is, with such sexual confusion going on, no sane race of people can survive for long. Other than black male workers, however, those in power have no need for the black female, but she can be easily exploited because she is the backbone of the family. An angry backbone, but a backbone nonetheless. Almost five years ago, the following information gave rise to yet one more nail in the coffin of sisters everywhere. The concept of "the down low" finally crawled out of the quiet of the closet and hit the mainstream. One report from a July 2004 document put it this way:

Men who have sex with men *and* women are a "significant bridge for HIV to women," the CDC's … data suggest. The findings come in a presentation to the XV International AIDS Conference in Bangkok by CDC researcher Linda Valleroy, PhD. The CDC's Young Men's Survey shows that about one in 10 men reporting sex with men also has sex with women. And more than one in four of these bisexual men has unsafe sex with both kinds of partners (DeNoon & Smith, 2004).

So when I write about black women, and the fact that they have been endangered, I know what I am talking about. I also know that they are very angry and why not? What is more humiliating than knowing that *the male of your own species is killing you off by having sex with other males and then bringing disease home to you?* Wasn't it bad enough when he was screwing women down the block and then giving you some STD or a yeast infection? Continuing:

> "Men who also had sex with women had similar levels of HIV and STDs [as exclusively homosexual men] and higher levels of many risk behaviors … Another study presented at the AIDS conference -- based on interviews with nearly 2,500 bisexual men by the San Francisco Department of Health -- shows that 14% of men who have sex with men also has sex with women. But the study, led by Willi McFarland, MD, PhD, suggests that these men may have fewer risk behaviors than exclusively homosexual men (DeNoon & Smith, 2004).

What is a "bi-sexual," anyway? I'm not here to argue one side or the other, but I will say this: if you're a man, either you like sex with women or you like nuts slamming against your forehead. I can't see a situation where you could dig both. Maybe I'm just old school, but that's how I view it. And for that reason, I view this "bi-sexual" thing as just one more fad that we followed the Anglo off into – along with wife-swapping, shacking up, and a host of other sexual tendencies that we, today, simply pawn off as "the American way of life."

We are in trouble. Younge (2004) sums things up as he cogently contends that, "The situation, some argue, is compounded by an apparent scarcity of potential black male partners, particularly among the middle classes, which can contribute to black men having a higher turnover of relationships. It also puts more pressure on women to have unprotected sex. … Many of the women on campus are panic stricken because of the feeling of scarcity," … "I see a lot of problematic sexual decision-making among black women across class and age lines."

It's not only on campus: black women are panic stricken because there is definite scarcity of black males in the society at large! And even with that scarcity we still have some black men who have such serious psychological issues that they are leaving the warm confines of a home with a beautiful black woman and walking down to the corner to get their knob slobbed on by a dude???How could a black man who already has the benefit of being outnumbered by sisters sometimes ten to one in our major cities, still want to have sex with a man? If you have those kinds of yearnings, I don't care what you say, how many women you've got or what kind of excuse you make: *you're gay in my book.*
What else could you be? Moving right along:

> Black men call it the DL: the down low. Fearing loss of
> community support, men living this lifestyle keep their bisexuality
> -- and their sexual relationships with other men -- secret from their
> female partners. Whether they call it the DL or not, many white
> and Latino men also keep their sexual affairs with men secret from
> their female sex partners. "Most people believe this is only
> something happening with black men," CDC scientist Greg Millet,
> MPH, tells WebMD. "We see it in Latino and white men, too.
> They say they are heterosexual but report sex with other men in the
> last three months, in the last year, in the last five years. Sexual
> identity is not destiny" (DeNoon & Smith, 2004).

I know what I think about it. I think that a whole lot of men have had these feelings for a long time and those feelings scared the hell out of them. With the coming of sex role socialization, it was even more imperative to hide your feelings of homosexuality. Every male-dominated culture saw a man as acting one way when it came to sex and sexuality, and the Anglo didn't want to feel left out, so he had to "out-macho" everybody else; hence, his proclivity for killing, for guns and especially the hand-held pistol that looks a lot like the male penis – and so on. And the key, of course, to showing total control by all men it seems is to inferiorize the female. More on this later.

One article quotes an expert on the subject:

> John Peterson, PhD, professor of psychology at Atlanta's Georgia
> State University, has studied the issue for a long time. "The DL is a
> new name for an old issue," Peterson tells WebMD. "Bisexual men
> not telling their female partners about their male relationships
> takes place across all races and ethnicities. But what we really
> don't know is how these men behave when they have primary male
> or female partners." (DeNoon & Smith, 2004).

So it's becoming even more difficult to know who the players are. And the sister is caught in both the middle while at the same time occupying a position somewhere on the fringe. She's watching her man chase after every other woman on earth, and now she's got to even be cognizant of his chasing after other dudes! But as the article points out, "Secret affairs put the unwary partner at risk of HIV and STDs. But there are different levels of risk. Not all sex behaviors carry the same risk of spreading HIV … We found a long time ago that two-thirds of the time, the female was not aware of the extracurricular sex the behaviorally bisexual man was doing," Stokes tells WebMD.

What I am finding out from the streets and the sisters who confide in me is that these black men are the very ones who have to define their manhood in ways that put them above suspicion. I recently saw an episode of Law and Order SVU where the issue was black men on the down low. What that episode pointed out were these macho football players who were well-to-do and, once a week, they'd go to one guy's house to "play cards." Of course, you know what they were really doing with each other. I don't know that much about these rump roasters and switch hitters. All I know is that this country has polluted the morals of almost all of its citizens, and the Catholic Church, the most powerful and richest of them all, is but one prime example. And it seems to trickle down from there.

Look at how money and conspicuous consumption drives black folks mad. They become sexually locked into all kinds of freakishness. Of course the people who control the Hollywood casting couch may be bisexual themselves, and the people who get the roles might just be going along in order to get along. A lot of the wealthy brothers and sisters are still in the closet because they know that such behavior still carries a stigma in the eyes of their parents and the church they might still attend. But most of us know who's a bone collector and who's not.

But the key is that this down low behavior is contributing to the rise of AIDS among black folk. That includes, of course, black women:

> Most black women with HIV say they were infected through heterosexual contact, but it isn't known how their male partners were infected -- by sex with other men, or by using contaminated needles to inject drugs. "We need to take a step back when we look at the down-low phenomenon," said Gregg Millett, a behavioral scientist with the CDC division on HIV/AIDS. "There's very little that is known." The definition of down low depends on who does the defining. The term comes from the world of hip-hop and R&B music, where it means an illicit relationship. As adapted by a subculture of black men, being on the down low describes men who have sex with other men but appear straight, have relationships with women, and don't acknowledge being gay or even bisexual. (DeNoon & Smith, 2004).

The term doesn't come from hip-hop, either. The application of the term does. For instance, the term "pig" refers to an animal, but it wasn't until Bobby Seale's attorney, Beverly Axelrod, used the term in reference to Oakland cops that it caught on. In like manner, the "down low always meant keeping something quiet, on the hush-hush. The hip-hop generation, getting things ass backwards as is their legacy it appears, took the term and gave it the application that we are now discussion: referring to black men who have sex with other men.

Again, we find that the black man is aiding and abetting in the proliferation of the problem; his ego is at stake and he's infected but not willing to tell anyone. Johnson (2005) capsulizes the situation rather nicely when he writes,

Many down low men find it difficult to see themselves as gay because of the stigma attached to homosexuality in the black community, said Phil Wilson, executive director of the Black AIDS Institute in Los Angeles. Being gay risks rejection by family and friends. They don't identify with gay culture, which they see as white and effeminate. And when they do venture into gay communities like San Francisco's, which are predominantly white, they feel unwelcome, according to several studies of gay men of color. Because these men have so much at stake in keeping their sexual activity secret, it is unknown how many there are and it is difficult to trace the sexual history of their female partners. The longer these men lead double lives, health officials say, the higher the risk for their partners.

This doesn't make sense to me. To begin with, these DL men claim to find it difficult to see themselves as gay because of the stigma attached to homosexuality. So then, if there was no stigma would these guys still find it difficult? This is the kind of "if-she-don't-know-it-won't-hurt-her" bullshit that is killing black women; he's afraid for HIS reputation and feelings, but that doesn't stop him from playing hide the baloney pony with his buddy down the street or "around the world in 80 ways" with some guy he barely knows. Absurd!

Moreover, the preceding passage says, "being gay risks rejection by family and friends." Maybe so, but that's a risk that a real man ought to be able to take. If people don't accept you, then that says more about them than it does about you – they prove, by their response and actions, that they never were friends in the first place. Perhaps this is easier said than done, but I have found that it is always better to work with hard facts than to play with pleasant, but unproductive, dreams.

The excerpt claims that DL men have "so much at stake in keeping their sexual activity a secret." So then they keep it a secret and place all that pressure on the back of the unwary black woman. What cowards! The inability to deal with personal issues (while opting to lead out in public, and talk into any microphone that gets poked in your face), is one reason why black women are endangered from the outside and, apparently with this HIV/AIDS crap going on, also being threatened by their own racial mate. Take note of the following series of copouts by so-called "black men:"

> "And what benefit do men have for disclosing their bisexuality in a society where positive support and affirming resources for bisexual men are all but non-existent, and negative stereotypes prevail? This is another example of an ongoing debate between public health and public morality. Sexual risk behavior is a public health issue; disclosure of sexual behavior is, in large part, a personal and moral issue" … [B]lack bisexual men have been largely blamed for the high rates of HIV among heterosexual black women. "There are bisexually active black men who are contributing to the epidemic

in the black community, but there are also heterosexual men and women, and homosexual men who are contributing." (Dodge, 2008).

The on-going debate should be taking place between those black men and the nearest psychologist, first of all! If you want to get some head from another guy, why involve the sister? Tell her up front that you're a rump roaster, a peter puffer or a cock-jockey, and be done with it! According to Dodge, in 2001, the CDC issued a report citing rising rates of HIV and AIDS among gay black and Latino men. The agency then found signs the disease was spreading more broadly among male and female blacks:

> -- In 2002, African Americans accounted for more than half of new HIV cases reported in the United States, though they are only 13 percent of the population.
> -- In 2003, African American men accounted for 44 percent of new AIDS cases among all men.
> -- In 2003, African American women accounted for two-thirds of new AIDS cases among all women. White women accounted for 15 percent and Latinas 16 percent.
> -- The rate of HIV and AIDS was 58.2 cases per 100,000 black women, and only 2.9 per 100,000 white women. The rate for Latinas was 8.1 per 100,000.
> -- The leading cause of HIV infection among African American women in 2002 was heterosexual contact, followed by injection drug use, according to the Centers for Disease Control and Prevention.

The black man needs to get his life together and stop trying to adapt to everyone except for the black woman. If a black man wants to live his life as an ass wrangler, a pole smoker or a fudge packer, then he should just go ahead and do it. Why jeopardize someone's mother, someone's sister, someone's grandmother or aunt? Why spread that stuff all over a community that is already dying from more preventable diseases and afflictions than any other race? Why man, why???

MALE NEGLECT CREATES STOICISM

"You bitches don't seem to realize how important my time is. Now come on! I wanna see some asses wigglin' – I want some perfection!
--Morris Day to Vanity 6 in the movie,
"Purple Rain" (1984).

The opposite of love is not "hate." Hate involves passion, so the thing or person that you think you hate, you remain emotionally tied to because of the intensity of the emotion; hate, then, could be viewed as the flip side of love. *The opposite of love is indifference*, meaning that when you get to the point of not caring, that is the opposite of love, an emotion that involves so much caring. Stoicism is a form of indifference, and our children are becoming increasingly "indifferent" about the direction and quality of their lives. And as such, they find it difficult to understand how they view pain and pleasure and, for that matter, what pain and pleasure really are as they relate to the future of the race.

There was a time when young people acted like young people, and stoicism on the part of a young teenager would not even be a part of our discussion. But look at how times have changed. We, the baby boomers, raised our children to have more than we had and, in the process we spoiled them. Unfortunately, part of that trust included turning them over to the media and they grew up watching television, going to the movies, and using technology to learn more about soft porn that we ever dreamed of learning. As a result, we have successfully raised a generation of teen-aged adults who have the bodies but not the brains to know that if you ask for something too much, you might get it. They want to be grown and as a result, they have adopted grown folks problems and tendencies. Stoicism – indifference about pain, pleasure and life to an extent – is one of those tendencies. It's nothing new: say it or do it enough and young people will mimic it. In education circles it's known as "reinforcement through repetition." As far as the media and its mission are concerned, imposing and pounding in stoicism in the minds of our young people is key. Stoicism, succinctly defined, is "an indifference to pleasure or pain." Like zombies our kids play video games and worse, watch on television as our young women parade around butt naked, breasts pumping to the music, while young boys lust after them and treat them like, well, you know – hos.

I want to deal with stoicism and the image of the young black male, but I want to use a contextual and comparative analysis. What I want to do is take the issue and then show the thinking (or lack thereof) of those who are supposed to know better, those blacks that most of us would consider, and "in the know." And remember: if you're stoic when you're young, then there's a good chance that you're going to have that tendency when you get older.

The following story comes from a September 2003 issue of *The Final Call* newspaper, and covers an event sponsored by the Congressional Black Caucus. Let's take a glance and we'll teach more about the CBC, about young black women, television imagery and what I view is the growing "stoicism" among black youth.

The article begins, thusly:

> From singer Beyonce Knowles to Iraqi war hero Spc. Shoshana
> Johnson, the images of Black women in the media have reached an
> all time low ranging from "sexually seductive and available to any"
> to "be all you can be" but few, if any, will care. How the world
> sees Black women, and more importantly how America sees Black
> women, is shaped and fashioned each day in executive suites and
> then spoon-fed like pabulum to the American public who
> unquestionably laps it up while developing an appetite for more
> (Muhammad, 2003).

While the preceding appears to be about black women, it is really about black men. When women are prompted to "be all that you can be" and the images that are fashioned in those suites are, today, geared toward making them independent of and in some cases hateful of, menfolk. They have a choice and it is my belief that increasing numbers are choosing the latter over the former – especially when it comes to black men.

Because of the global economy and the international community that has evolved due to technological advances, it is indeed more important how the world views black men than the American perception. I say this because the American perception may not ever change because of tradition and acceptance. But the world, because of so many of its members are people of color, could alter their perceptions of black men and in doing so, also better understand how cold and callous America's media is for presenting such negative and untrue imagery in the first place. The black man today, other than the athletes or entertainer, is the bane of the world when it comes to relationships and family. That is yet another reason why black men and women are so divided.

The idea of providing images of women does not mean that the people in the executive suites accept these images as true. They are peddling what they view as being compatible with what society wants. If society wants sex, give them the woman with the most curves, and that would be black women; if America likes color in the skin, the sister has it naturally. If the public wants attitude, conviction and assertiveness, the sister can provide it. And in most of these images the black man's image is totally ignored as the women of color get lighter and lighter, thinner and thinner and more and more Caucasian in appearance.

To alienate the black man and make him stoic is to create an image that is undesirable. So much of what is presented is rooted in some truth. The problem is those who create the images deal in caricature and exaggeration. All of a sudden a full set of lips have to droop; a wide nose has to have a bone in it; when it comes to the black woman sexy curves have to be exaggerated so the sister comes out looking like Shirley Hemphill or that exaggerated woman Medea that has made Tyler Perry a millionaire. These people may exist, but they are not in the majority nor are they in the vanguard of any social movements. The white man puts his most virile, energetic and color-less on the screen to drive home points for his racial grouping; when it comes to everyone else, it has to be an image that he can accept. Handsome black men, virile Latinos and confrontative Asians ala Bruce Lee need not apply.

Video is replacing film and its big time on television. Corporatists have taken music and video and combined them into a genre that fits into hip-hop culture quite well. The only problem is that the imagery associated with what is produced is paving the way for deviant behavior on the part of those who witness it. Muhammad (2003) writes that,

> Mention the vileness of videos or the lewd and lascivious lyrics and most will say it's the beat that draws them and the images are meaningless. Sister 2 Sister magazine publisher Jamie Foster Brown disagrees. "The images are horrible. They are soft porn. My son told me, 'The videos are programming me below my navel.' We're breastfeeding our children on sex and violence." As if once was not enough to make her point, she repeated, "We are breastfeeding our children on sex and violence. The guys have on more clothes and the girls have on less. The girls must look like a '10' while the men can look like they chew roaches and it doesn't matter."

If the black woman has a cold when it comes to these images, the black man has pneumonia. He may drool over these kinds of women but the relationships that he pursues won't last. He is viewed as a player and a leech because he can't find a job (and the jobs he has are on soft money or at the behest of his white master), or he is viewed as someone with no dreams or vision.

The latter point made is important because black male youth are of the mind that they can do whatever they want, vision or not, dress whatever they want and say whatever they want and still "get the girl." Remember back in the day when brothers would actually get dressed up to "call on" a girl? Remember the courting and wooing that took place? I can't remember us wearing tennis shoes to go out on a date. And yet these young males today wear pants that sag and anything else they feel like wearing, including baseball caps turned backwards. And what is so painful is that the black girls *accept it*. In accepting it, they are condoning it and saying, in essence, "you can treat me any way you want to, and it's alright. I don't deserve better."

Check out the following point:

> "What we need is a Rosa Parks in the music industry," said Yemi Toure, the director of the Center on Blacks in the Media, a media-

> monitoring group. "We need her to come forward and sit down in the middle of a video shoot and say enough is enough. We need to start a new movement just like Rosa Parks did," he told The Final Call. (Muhammad, 2003)

I know Bro. Yemi from back in the day and his great presentations at the 1977 "State of the Race" conference. So my question is: why doesn't he sit HIS ass down in the middle of a video shoot and not rely on some old sister to stagger in from the cold and do it for him? Isn't that the problem now – black men expecting black women to come in and do all the work? Isn't that why her endangered status is going on, unabated, to the point where she is now targeted for extinction? Isn't that why black men – and women for that matter – are becoming increasingly stoic?

Now, take note of the following, because it has the same shallow tendency that far too much of what we say, do and write tends to have. I'll explain on the other side. Muhammad writes that,

> Ashanti, Lil Kim and Maya may be the standard in music videos, but on dramatic television shows Black women fare a little better. Tisha Campbell-Martin plays the loving wife and mother on "My Wife and Kids." She's educated, presents well and is totally clothed. On "CSI-Miami," Khandi Alexander plays the "no nonsense" coroner Alexx Woods and Garcelle Beauvais-Nilon plays the intelligent assistant district attorney Valerie Haywood on "NYPD Blue." (Muhammad, 2003)

This is what I mean when I say that much of what we write is shallow. There is no depth. While on the surface, Muhammad (a woman) seems to know what she is talking about, we have to remember that an image is more than just what we see; it is also assessed and evaluated by the impact it has. Every woman mentioned has an image or gives the impression that unless a black man is making major money, he doesn't have a chance with her.

For instance, Tisha Campbell-Martin's character on "My Wife and Kids" was not a positive one. She was a set of reactions to a husband who was "humorously cruel." Damon Wayans used her as a sperm spittoon even though she was his wife, and she whined a lot. She might have been totally clothed, but she was married – that is the way married women are viewed. Look at her role in Spike Lee's "School Daze" or 1990s "House Party" – check out her imagery in THOSE roles. And her male counterpart, in the roles she plays, are as clueless and stoic as they come

As for Khandi Alexander, she is a lovely chocolate sister who does her job on CSI-Miami, true enough. But I remember seeing her in "CB3," and she was dressed just like those "hootchies" that appear in the videos today. And what was her advice to the young hootchies: get a car and some money from a rapper because if you don't, you're not doing good business, you're just being a "ho." Garcelle Beauvais-Nilon became an "intelligent district attorney," alright ("NYPD Blue"), but it was after she starred on "The Jamie Foxx Show" with emphasis on her micro-skirts, long legs and low-cut blouses.

So images on TV meaning little if they are not consistent. These three women, when all is said and done, are no better than Li'l Kim, Maya or Ashanti: at least those young girls are *consistently* (as opposed to selectively, depending on the paycheck) *sluttish.* Black men are therefore programmed to not give a shit (or pretend that they don't) about women like these because they (the black men) don't believe that they can retain the attention of these women for very long. Essentially, they (black men) become tricks who pay women like these for their attention.

Now would be as good a time as any to show how all this stigma, stereotyping and image control feeds into the "stoicism" that seems to permeate the thinking of our young males as well as those who are older. Braithwaite discusses the concept of "stoicism" as a possible explanation of why black men are disconnected from the American healthcare system and are reluctant to participate in health-related activities. The theory of stoicism suggest that black men become "indifferent to pain or discomfort and do not seek healthcare services until absolutely necessary, and then most often in the emergency room." Braithwaite (2001) suggests that Black males "learn pathological levels of stoic tolerance" to symptoms of distress and illness in order to mask any semblance of weakness (p. 63).

Just as black males are found to exhibit "stoic tolerance" when it comes to masking weakness, this also pertains to "stoic coolness" or "stoic distance" when it comes to anything emotional. These young males don't exhibit anything other than hateful glares, loud voices, curse words and every now and then an occasional scowl. They associate anything that is emotional or honest with being "soft." Like convicts, they seem to measure their worth and all that is of value by how much pain something can inflict. This applies to guns, a prospective scam or crime or to another brother down the street who gets "mad props" because he killed more than one person.

Not only that, but many of them are "mama's boys" behind closed doors. They beg for money, they ask for their clothes to be washed and ironed and they don't pick up behind themselves. They are stoic in the sense that they show a "stoic intolerance" to being responsible. And with that out of the way, and knowing that this is the quality and caliber of black male that is out there, let's see how stoicism impacts and affects the young sister.

To begin with, stoicism is a tool that a great many women use to hide certain problematic concerns. And this impacts on and is also affected by the black male. According to Kumea Shorter-Gooden, a clinical psychologist and author, a lot of woman particularly the blacks in America, are emotional overeater's who try to mask their depression with food … She claims that the black women mask the signs of depression by becoming stoic overachievers. She claims she has never known a group that sleeps less than black women. Others she feels tend to get too involved with their job, feeling that involvement can mask their depressed feelings, or others simply go for "Binge eating" to hide their feelings. (Bio-Medicine, 2008).

I know a woman who immerses herself in her work, her grandchildren and, supposedly, the church. I say "supposedly" because depending on how her love life is going, that can serve to supplant some of the stoicism and then she reverts back to "worldly ways." At any rate, the point is that the stoicism – the indifference toward pain and pleasure – is a characteristic of a great many Americans because of the culture that we live in and because *pain* is so closely tied to love under such conditions. If you're depressed and getting fat, then you become more desperate when it comes to a relationship with a man. And with desperation, in most cases, come foolish decisions.

In their 2003 book, *Shifting,* that Shorter-Gooden penned along with Charisse Jones, Shorter-Gooden writes about "Shifting." It's essentially what all women do, but these sisters think that such "adapting" is something unique to black woman. Maybe it is by degree, but because all men are screwed up – not just black men – I have a feeling that white women, Asian women, Latinas and Native sisters are all doing some "shifting." But that is a story for another time and context.

What Jones and Shorter-Gooden write about shifting, at least in part, contributes to our understanding of the "stoicism" that a lot of people see black women exhibiting, and yet still don't understand or want to acknowledge. The authors write,

> Our research shows that a large number of Black women in
> America feel pressured to present a face to the world that is
> acceptable to others even though it may be completely at odds with
> their true selves … The women we interviewed use a variety of
> images to describe the shifting process, referring to the "mask"
> they wear, the "Chameleon" they have become, having to
> constantly "bend" what they do and who they are to please others
>
> …

Furthermore,

> In some cases, black women shift in ways that are less conspicuous to others … Some women say that they constantly mull over much of what they say and do. They become hyper-alert, endlessly on patrol. Scanning the environment for danger and ever prepared to respond. *Others erect a wall of stoicism* to protect themselves from the profound emotional pain that they would otherwise feel (Jones & Shorter-Gooden, pp. 61-62—emphasis added).

And so it goes. But this "shifting" originated with black men who, in my view, set the standard with the "uncle tom" role. There is no doubt that the black man wanted to kick the white man's ass thousands of times but instead, curried favor, carried water and scratched when didn't nothing itch. Women may be "shifting" now, but black people as a group, have been doing it as a survival mechanism. And with such individualism and stoicism, the seeds are sown for conflict, struggle and various forms of violence.

Now we move into the 21st century and, to all that stereotyping and stigmatizing, we interject a major social taboo: interracial dating and marriage. Why? Because this generation, male and female, more than perhaps any other, is going to be actively engaged in it, they believe in it, and their music brings them together in perhaps most social and cultural venues than any other generation before them. I want to provide background, viewpoints and research on the stoicism of the black man and how it might manifest itself when increasing numbers of black boys and men date and marry out of the race. And furthermore, what the options of the black woman might be.

Body Image Issues

Black women have a lot of reasons to have pent-up frustration and disdain. One of them is the body-issue reality that few people want to talk about for fear of getting their asses kicked or having to watch her put her hands on her hips, engage in chicken-necking, and shout out, "Oh no you di-int," or "what did you say, muthafucka?" You've seen it and heard it; most people are bad at taking constructive criticism and of that group, black women are among the worst.

For the most part, discussions of "body image issues" are confined to young girls and how they are engaging in self-starvation so that they can lose weight, or how the magazines and television are providing them with images that are unattainable. That's all fine and good. But what about these grown ass women who have issues, hailing back to when "daddy left mama" and then after that, their first boyfriend screwed them and then dumped them. They retain this stuff, and along with the body images is a hatred of all that is male. When combined, you find women doing a lot of things so that they can "feel cute;" I don't think it's about looking good for men, but looking good for themselves and for other women. They need acceptance from *somebody;* it doesn't matter if it's a male or a female. Let's call it like it is: some of these bitches are just plain fat. The tendency around the nation is to refer to it as "having curves." As far as I'm concerned, those curves were created by one too many mayonnaise sandwiches and too much time spent sittin' on their ass watching "Dynasty" and, more recently, "The Real Housewives of Atlanta" or VH-1. The day of "more cushion for the cushion" and "the more fat, the tighter the cat" does not apply to the women of today. They are not large and in shape from hard work; they are large, lazy, out of shape and trying to pretend that the fat doesn't exist. This, in turn, makes them even fatter. This is the main body issue, but it ain't the only one.

Everything is about a cover-up. So if they don't want to wear their own hair, what little they've got, then it's down to the shop to splice on the hair of some Indian bitch that got paid to have her shit cut and sold in a shop that is usually located in some U.S. ghetto. And if it was just the hair, that would be bad enough. But check this out: remember how we used to see them, on TV, flipping their hair out of their eyes or using the left and right hand to brush it out of their face as they talked. These sisters today have this down to an art: (1) they've duped themselves into believing that the hair is the hair they were born with and (2) that having it in their face and eyes are something they don't like when, in reality, they planned it. Body image issues are "repaired" or "mended" but never adequately addressed. What happens is that these women look in the mirror and they don't like what they see. So instead of dealing with the ugliness, they break the mirror. And in all that melodrama, they have not eliminated the thing that made them ugly in the first place. Look at some examples of what they go through to modify that pent-up aggression and anger that permeates their very being.

Hair extensions? – What's up with three or four feet of hair extensions from the head of women in faraway India? Who are these women trying to fool? It doesn't match their natural hair in most cases and in many cases it's a totally different color which brings even more attention to how fake they are. The braid it and then, like the white woman, spend inordinate amounts of time brushing it out of their eyes. This is straight-up assimilation and it affects the way they live their lives: there are certain things they can't do, they can't do a lot of sweating, they refuse to get it dirty and when they do, they have to wash it a certain way. All this and for what? So they can look cute – for themselves.

How about false eyelashes? Are these supposed to add to attractiveness of the appearance of health? Are they supposed to make your eyes appear "more mysterious"? I think they make women look like sluts, pure and simple. Many of these women cannot even glue them on right and that makes it look even worse. But they think they're cute, and for whom? Themselves.

"Tainted contact lenses" – Every now and then you'll come across some black woman with hazel green eyes, sometimes even blue, that you know are not her own. They've been asked this question so much that they have the same answer that they have when their hair grows from one inch to down to their waist overnight: "yeah, it's mine – I paid for it! What possesses a person to want to alter their physical appearance to such a degree? So that they can look cute – for themselves.

Fake fingernails – You've seen them. And just as is the case with the hair extensions and the wigs, the "beautification process" is almost totally controlled by Asian women. They have seen how shallow black women have become and they exploit it. The same Asian women that do nails to not wear them themselves; the same Asian women who sell the hair off the heads of Indian women (from India) do not (and do not have to) wear that hair. They direct it at black women and they hunker down in inner cities, hang a shingle and make huge amounts of money. And for what? So their finger nails can be "cute." For what? Does it make them type any faster? Is it a look that you can wear in the corporate boardroom? No. It's for ego gratification, nothing more or nothing less.

Low-cut blouses: Breasts as an attention-getter – The new trend among black and white women, is to wear a blouse cut as low as the law will allow. Where possible, add that to the push-up bra that I deal with later on. Many of them have such little respect for their spouses or boyfriends, that they wear them anywhere they want. Why? To be acceptable by strangers and to appear sexy because they don't really feel that way when it comes down to it.

New-wave girdles and under-alls – These hold the stomach in and also push the ass up so that its rounder and more developed looking. This might look good in a skirt or some slacks, but what happens when she takes this stuff off? It's like an inflatable raft: the girdle does the job and the skin tight jeans serve as an external girdle. That figure disappears, the ass sags and that small waste line becomes the "gut" that it naturally is. They don't care what you think: they look in the mirror and find a way to be "pleased" with the way they look. It's all about how THEY see themselves physically.

Push-up bras – Related to the "Breasts as an attention-getter" allegation launched earlier, this is for those women whose breasts sag as they age and for those whose breasts are so small that they are about 80% nipple.

Body image issues are psychological as well as physical. In both instances, body image issues contribute to pent-up defensiveness, and this explains why so many black women are bitter.

Deep-Seated Hatred of Interracial Relationships

Black women have a love-hate relationship with white women. On the one hand they love them and seek to imitate them because they have "white privilege" working for them and they are the prototype of how to "marry well" and then use men and their vaginas to get what they want. They've done it throughout history while pretending to be the "weaker sex," there is little doubt that white women will fuck anything to get power and security.

Then there is the hatred that black women feel, much of it rooted in jealousy, where they see how black men react when they see one of these snow bunnies walking down the street or on the television. Black women can feel the lust that black men harbor for long hair, pale skin and small breasts. This is what most white women bring to the table, in addition to the fact that they will perform fellatio much sooner in a relationship than most black women will.

As I see it, when the rich and white marry across racial lines, the person of color they marry is a paragon of beauty or success – someone who is palatable and aesthetically compatible with what white people view as "beautiful." When black men and women marry, the other person may or may not have celebrity but they bring something to the table which appears to be not only a novelty but also a necessity: white skin. This is what young people see among those blacks that have "made it;" many of them will, inevitably, consider the action as "socially approved" and may seek to emulate it. Combined with an indifference to pain and pleasure, the way has been paved for no longer caring about much of anything. If black women adopt the attitude of not caring, the race will then truly be doomed.

Many believe that when a black person "makes it," they have an obligation to do for those who are locked out. This is what I believe as well. Unfortunately, those who "make it" are either forced to be apolitical or ordered into a suburb where they are out of tune with the masses of black people.
At any rate, having a white wife certainly exacerbates the alienation that these individuals already live with. It appears to me that at both the celebrity as well as "grass roots" levels, when the woman is black and the husband is white, he is usually a businessman or someone well-to-do in another profession – it's about money and marrying upward. When it's the white woman, there appears to be more subjective reasoning – "love" or something along those lines. She is the one who "marries up."

Perhaps Frantz Fanon, sounding a great deal like Eldridge Cleaver who is quoted later on, summed it up his own version of what I call "white wanderlust" in the following poem:

Out of the blackest part of my soul,

Across the zebra striping of my mind,
Surges this desire to be suddenly white.
By loving me [the white woman]
Proves that I am worthy of white love.
I am loved like a white man.
I am a white man.
Her love takes me onto the noble
Road that leads to total realization.
I marry white culture, white beauty
White whiteness.
When my restless hands caress those
White breasts, they grasp white civilization
And dignity and make them mine.

--*Frantz Fanon*

I have probably read close to thirty thousand books in my time and I have yet to read a poem where a black woman writes a love poem about a white man. This is not to say that there is not that kind of feeling out there; but when you commit it to writing and then proceed to publish it, that says a great deal about the depth of your love. Maybe they do write about white men and leave out the racial aspects. But it is clear that Fanon, one of our deepest thinkers and scholars, did not.

Nor does a 2012 television commercial for Palmer Cocoa Butter Body and Face Lotion. Identical twins, African-American and ripped, dressed in football muscle t-shirts walk toward the camera and talk about how smooth their skin is. As they walk, football gear clad individuals, replete with helmets and pads, bounce off their rock hard bodies. As the commercial is about to conclude, the narrator tells viewers, "Perfect formula." And the twins add, "Extraordinary results" at which time two white cheerleaders, once blonde and one brunette, fall into the arms of each of the two men. Translation*: use this and you can latch on to a white woman no matter how dark your skin is.*

I chose to narrow my inclusion of this topic down to celebrities because the cases are easier for many people to recall and, as a result, to relate to. Our parents and their parents recall the feelings they had when they heard about this black man dating this white woman, or how this white woman said something nice about this black man. That is the way the racial situation was back in the day. It was taboo, but there were always people who were willing to engage in such relationships anyway.

Today, such relationships are not a major shock for most of us, and surely not for our children. My file system, some 37,000 strong, contains two very thick folders under the heading, "miscegenation." The sources I cite in this chapter will establish that I've been clipping such articles and saving them for quite a while.

As a result, it would be the height of redundancy to even attempt to discuss "successful" blacks and the tendency for a disproportionate number of them to marry out of the race. Such exogamous practices have been taking place ever since legal barriers were relaxed, and many took place even before that (e.g., Jack Johnson, Scatman Crothers, Lena Horne, etc.) The tendency continues, and these "case studies" are examples of this cross-racial proliferation.

Speaking of Lena Horne, she confessed to *Ebony* magazine that her marriage in 1947 to Lennie Hayton, a prominent white music personality, was not as much the result of love as it was a ticket to professional success. She says she eventually fell in love with her husband and they had a long marriage until his death in 1971. (Ebony, 1982: 79-80)

If mega-millions of dollars constitute celebrity status, then let us begin with former TLC president Reginald Lewis, a major wheeler and dealer of TLC Beatrice International Holdings. He was the company's chairman and largest stockholder, but died from brain cancer in 1993. (Stodghill, 1994: 38) His posthumous autobiography is called *Why Should White Guys Have All the Fun?* But guess who inherited the $1.6 billion food conglomerate? His *Asian wife* of 24 years, Loida Nicolas Lewis.

When Sammy Davis Jr. fell in love with and married May Britt, American society went wild. The question on the signs outside of many of Davis' appearances would read, "What's wrong Sammy? Can't You Find a Negro Girl?" Sammy himself was the poster child for the "successful Negro" during his days of conspicuous consumption, and *Ebony* magazine was pushing interracialism and integration even before either was in vogue.

For instance, in June 1981, *Ebony* contains a feature titled, "Sammy's Kitchen: For Down Home Cooking, Sammy Davis Builds a $95,000 Kitchen." In July of 1989, an article with Sammy, Frank Sinatra and Liza Minnelli above it is titled, "Sammy Davis Jr. Faces Life, Aging and Cocaine." As his live wound down, it was again *Ebony* that wrote in its February 1990 edition, "Hollywood's Biggest Tribute: To Sammy With Love," and five months later, after Sammy's death of throat cancer, *Ebony* devoted more than 10 pages to the superstar entitled, "The Legacy of the World's Greatest Entertainer."

Sammy's obsession with material things and conspicuous consumption are well documented in my book, *Feets Don't Fail Me Now*. However, for the purpose of this paper, let it be known that Sammy was "friends" with such white female celebrities as Ava Gardner and Kim Novak – and caught hell from the white press. An infuriated Harry Cohn, then head of Columbia Pictures, which had the popular Novak under contract, reportedly said, "I could understand Belafonte, but him!" (Bogle, 1990: 75)

This didn't stop Sammy. Not only did he convert to Judaism, but in 1960 he married blonde Swedish actress Mai Britt. The two had a daughter, Tracey, who grew and also decided to marry out of the race. Bogle observes that, "the marriage, however, made it look even more as if he were a black man in flight from his ethnic identity." (Bogle, 1990: 75) Sammy opened doors and set precedents in more ways than just his entertaining. He was, perhaps, Hollywood's first "white girl chaser," or at least, he was the first one to flaunt it, get away with it and get the blessing of the white establishment!

If you're going to cross racial lines in Hollywood – and survive – you've got to keep a low profile. Take the case of Sidney Portier.

It was 1975 when Sidney Portier married Joanna Shimkus, and the relationship was the talk of the town in the Black community. Although Portier was admired by blacks for his acting, he was always considered to be somewhat of an Uncle Tom. At any rate, in September of 1985, writer Jackie Collins ("Hollywood Wives,""The Bitch,""Lucky") said that Portier and Shimkus have one of the few marriages that has been able to withstand the trials and tribulations of Hollywood. (Jet, 1985; Redbook, 1992: 90)

The key is simple: Portier and Shimkus don't attend a whole bunch of parties or wear that "everybody kiss each other" label on their sleeves. They keep a low profile and, as a result, they have been able to survive. The same goes for Gregory Hines – very few people know that he is married to a white woman.

Another black man whose white wife serves as his manager is Dorian Harewood. He is famous for his roles in "The Jesse Owens Story,""Against All Odds,""Beulahland" and his role as Simon Haley in "Roots: The Next Generation."

His wife, Ann Curry, share something in common with Portier and Shimkus. According to the July 1984 edition of *Ebony*, "Although he has been in the acting profession some ten years, he shuns the glitter and glamour that usually accompanies the Hollywood lifestyle, preferring a simple life in a relatively modest home in West Hollywood." (Ebony, 1984: 60) But Harewood keeps a low profile and, like Portier and Hines, is able to survive and land some key roles every now and then.

Quincy Jones' marriage to Peggy Lipton while the both of them were on the set of the 1960s flick, "The Mod Squad" (Jones as the music director and Lipton as one of the co-stars) turned a lot of heads and then, after being married to her, he married another white woman, Verna Harrah. (Redbook, 1992: 90) Tyne Daly ("Cagney and Lacy") and Georg Stafford Brown ("The Rookies,""Silver Streak") had three kids and were married for 24 years before they were divorced. (Redbook, 1992: 90)

Another famous black man, this one a dancer and actor, is Ben Vereen, famous for his TV show, "Tenspeed and Brownshoe" and a host of roles including Chicken George from the TV miniseries, "Roots." He is married to a blonde haired, blue eyed white woman named Nancy and they have three children: Benji (33), Naja (27) and Mikikia (28). (Jet, 1985: 45)

Other brothers who have achieved status and opted to marry white women include Supreme Court Justice Clarence Thomas, actor/dancer Gregory Hines, former football great Mike Singletary and basketball star (and the world's tallest Uncle Tom) Charles Barkley.

In October of 1993, Whoopi Goldberg and Ted Danson made the news after they appeared at the Friar's Club together, Danson in blackface with white lips and Goldberg on stage assisting him while he cracked "nigger jokes." On Black Entertainment Television, Danson said, "First I'm a nigger love, now I'm a racist." (Collins, 1993: C-5)

Lisa Collins, a sister out of Los Angeles who writes a celebrity column and who I got to know when I was editor of the Courier, sheepishly claimed that the very fact that Danson appeared on BET shows that he is neither a nigger lover or a racist. Goldberg, who many black people despise – including me – said, The reaction of Black folks to the controversy has not surprised me. My relationship with us (Blacks) has always been somewhat checkered," she said. (Collins, 1993: C-5; St. John, 1994: A-8)

It is my belief that Ted Danson is a racist. After all, "Cheers" was one of the most popular shows in the history of television and stayed on for over seven years, and yet very few blacks ever appeared during that time. Did Danson complain? No. The city where the bar Cheers is located is Boston, one of the most racist cities in the nation. And when the Boston Celtics were featured from time to time, who was it? Kevin McHale and Larry Bird, not any of the black team members, and yet the NBA is 80% African-American. There was never any mention of the black community of Roxbury, which is in the heart of Boston, no mention of the racial problems and the fight against busing. No mention of the segregation. Did Danson use his awesome power as the key character in the show and launch any complaints? No.

The two of them met during the making of the movie, "Made in America," which was racist in its own right. Will Smith made his acting debut in this movie, which was about Goldberg's daughter (played by Nia Long) becoming curious about who her father was. She discovers that she came from a sperm bank, goes there and finds out that her father is Danson, a used car salesman. In the end they all get together, one happy, multiracial family – without incident.

This brings us to another interracial couple. At the Friar's banquet, when Danson appeared in blackface, talk show host Montel Williams and his white wife walked out. Montel immediately contacted the media and said that "as a black man," he was insulted. It is interesting how "black" these people become when they find out that they are not above being racially insulted. At the press conference Goldberg responded that "maybe Montel is angry because his talk show isn't doing all that well." His wife works as his "manager" and, even now he is directing a movie in which she stars.

Along the same lines as Williams is Cuba Gooding, Jr. One would think that having made the movie "Boyz in the Hood," where he played the role of Trey Styles, the son of "Furious Styles" (Laurence Fishburne), a militant, that Gooding would be conscious. But nothing could be further from the truth. His father is Cuba Gooding Sr., the former lead singer of the group The Main Ingredient. He was born in New York's South Bronx and raised in southern California, and is married to a blonde haired, blue eyed woman he's known since high school. (Gregory, 1993: 42)

And he's had some roles which reflect his tommishness. For the HBO Showcase he made "Daybreak," and starred as a young man who was in love with a white girl when both contracted a deadly disease. He was in "Judgment Night" a movie where, in the opening scene, he parks his Corvette across the street from best friend Emilio Estevez's house and runs to catch up with a blonde white girl who is walking her dog; But the really degrading movie was "Lighting Jack," where he starred opposite Crocodile Dundee star Paul Hogan. He plays a deaf mute named Ben who is silly and a virgin. This sets the stage for the kinds of racist hijinks one can expect. The lily-white written Video Hounds Golden Movie Retriever for 1997 was even upset. They wrote in their analysis, "Mute store clerk Ben (Gooding) winds up as his partner in crime, while barely eluding criticisms of Stepin Fetchitism." (p. 445) In all fairness to Cuba, however, he has taken more serious roles, including the movies "A Murder of Crows," "Men of Honor," and the classic, "Jerry McGuire," for which he won an Oscar for Best Supporting Actor. And his most recent work, "Gifted Hands: The Ben Carson Story," is a masterpiece for the ages.
But Black newspapers, for the most part, praise him and simply remind the audience that he won an NAACP Image Award nomination as Outstanding Actor in "Boyz N the Hood." (The Columbus Times, 1994: C1)

What about the beautiful Alfre Woodard, one of the most beautiful women in Hollywood? Famous for her roles as Isaiah Thomas' mother (The Mary Thomas Story"), and as Winnie Mandela ("Mandela"), Woodard says of herself that, "I am a very African-looking woman." (Collier, 1990: 52) She might be African-looking, but when she gave her heart it was to Anglo actor Roderick Spencer, whom she married in 1983.

What about Janet Jackson and her former boyfriends – one was Italian and the other one Latino), sister LaToya (who married her Italian manager and then got beat up by him when she tried to leave), and Grace Jones and her long-time relationship with blonde Swede Dolph Lundgren? What about disco diva Donna Summer, former model and actress Sheila DeWindt, Shari Belafonte and Toukie Smith. Who is Toukie Smith, you ask?

She has been Robert DeNiro's "longtime companion," as the newspapers call her. Not only is the sister of the world-renowned designer Willie Smith (this gay dude who died of AIDS), but also she is a former model and has appeared on a number of TV shows such as "Miami Vice" and "227." While DeNiro hasn't married her, they remain close and she miscarried with their child in June of 1988. (Randolph, 1990: 52-53)

Ruth Pointer of the Pointer Sisters is married and gave birth to twins at 47 years of age. She is married to Michael Sayles, a real estate developer. An article in the integration-pushing publication Ebony documents that, "Shortly after meeting her 36 year old husband in Los Angeles four years ago, Pointer felt Sayles was the kind of man she would like to have children with. "He is such a traditional kind of guy," she says. "I need that kind of grounding." (Ebony, 1993: 122)

Speaking of "extraordinary canaries," what about songstress Mariah Carey? The black women say she's a white girl, but that is because of jealousy: her father is black and that makes her black, no matter what she says and no matter what some of her ignorant fans say. A talented "sister" who wrote "Vision of Love" and most of the other songs she's made into hits (Norment, 1991: 56-57), Carey was married to a white man who was her manager and, since their divorce, has been seen around with several other white men.

When talking of a string of white men, one has to address the lifestyle of Diana Ross, formerly of the Brewster Projects in Detroit. She's been married to at least three white men, one of them being shipping magnate Arne Naess in 1985.

Rae Dawn Chong, the daughter of comedian Tommy Chong (of Cheech and Chong fame) is a beauty whose career is permeated with whiteness. She was the girlfriend of a white boy who pretended he was black in "Soul Man" (she eventually married the man, C. Thomas Howell); she was Arnold Schwarzenegger's "girl pal" in the movie "Commando;" and she was the lone black in the bomb "Quest for Fire." Before marrying Howell she was married to stockbroker Owen Baylis. (Johnson, 1982: 131)

Even conservative black scholar Shelby Steele may be better understanding the issue of race. Steele, who is married to a white woman, published the book, *The Content of Our Character,* which I reviewed back in 1991 for the Milwaukee Courier. A staunch conservative anti-affirmative action, Steele said in the March 1, 1995 issue of the New York Times that he is now troubled to see the demise of affirmative action and how "glib' politicians are who oppose it. (New York Times, 1995: 19)

A black man no less than the late Dr. Martin Luther King Jr. was in love with a white woman and was going to marry her while he attended Boston Theological Seminary. A close friend, a minister, talked him out of it and those closest to him went out and "found" Coretta Scott, a light skinned black woman. And that is who King ended up marrying.

And yet, it is Dr. King -- quoted by Myra (1994) in response to a woman who rejected interracial marriage – who makes the statement that -- "She failed to see that implicit in her rejection was the feeling that her daughter had some pure, superior nature that should not be contaminated by the impure, inferior nature of the Negro … The question of intermarriage is never raised in a society cured of the disease of racism." (p. 13)

This shows that Dr. King was a hypocrite. While he was lecturing someone else on the issue, he could have personalized it and come clean and admitted that he, too, had once come close to marrying across racial lines. But he didn't because he knew that the words that he said about the nature of the Negro being impure was right on time. He felt impure and perhaps felt that anything "light" was better. On the other hand, he says that "the question of intermarriage is never raised in a society cured of the disease of racism," so this was his way of not raising the issue!

And the idea of interracial liaisons affects Africans as well. Leopold Senghor, the author of a beautiful poem about the black woman nonetheless married a blonde, blue-eyed white woman. The late King Hussein of Jordan, whom I consider to be a man of color, is married to a blonde, white woman. Several instructors in this very department have taught Black Studies while going home to white female mates.

Let's not leave the athletes out. We can cite the likes of Mike Singletary who I mentioned earlier, but who shocked me in his book *Samurai* when he said that when he saw the white woman who would eventually be his wife, he knew she was the one. He went through all kinds of changes with her parents, but this woman knew this man was going to turn professional. Now they live happy Christian lives in their little suburb outside of Chicago.

What about Kareem Abdul Jabbar, one of the most conscious brothers on the college campuses during the 1960s, but who now lives with a white woman now that he's retired? What about former Celtic star Robert Parrish who allows the entire city of Boston to call him "Chief"? Then there's Marcus Allen, whose wife is a clone for O.J. Simpson's late wife who, by the way, Allen also had an affair with.

Ebony makes a silly claim as one justification for dedicating yet another article to black men and white women in its opening paragraph:

In the midst of all of O.J. Simpson's legal and career problems, what seems to bother Black women the most is the fact that Nicole Brown Simpson was White. And quite a few Black women were appalled that handsome hunk Barry Bonds, who has a $43 million, six-year contract with the San Francisco Giants, was ordered by the court to pay his estranged White wife $30,000 a month. (Norment, 1994)

It appears that State Senator Ernest Chambers was correct in what he said about the black athlete and the white woman. According to the state's only black solon, the white man cannot afford to pay the white athlete as much because the white athlete is not as good. But what he can do if he has to pay the black athlete all those millions is promote or condone relationships with white women and then he (the white man) can get the money back *through her.*

The media. Celebrity role models. Black men dating and marrying white women and pawning it off as a "preference." And then you have the black woman, exhibiting a stoic façade to hide her pain. Then the media, on the back end, records the pain and further exploits it by pawning her off as "indifferent" to what's going on around her.

The 1960s "liberated" this country's sexuality and freed up some jobs for black people. But since that time, we seem to have lost our collective minds. We have ignored our families and watched as our divorce rates have skyrocketed. Black men have been arrested at a heretofore unheard of rate, and we have more black homosexuals, bisexuals, transsexuals and tri-sexuals (a "tri-sexual," according to Cheech Marin, is somebody who will "try" anything once!) than ever before in our history. Is there any wonder black women are turning to single lives, lesbianism and the kind of stoic immersion into their jobs and grandchildren to hide their anger, shame and pain?

Speaking of the 1960s, let's now take a look at the "movements" that this nation has undergone, and how the sister was treated at a time when we, as black people, were at our most aware, our most conscious. It seems that that these are the time periods where we can assess and test just how much we love her, how deep our love goes. *What I found was that no matter astute we are artistically, profound we become politically, or how collected we act consciousness-wise, the black woman continued to get shoved to the side.*

Chilling Effect: Handcuffed by His Church

A **chilling effect** is a term in law and communication which describes a situation where speech or conduct is suppressed by fear of penalization at the interests of an individual or group. In other words, the speech might cause a riot or a negative reaction by a group of people. But that is not exactly how I mean it in this instance. Women don't like to be told to "shut up" – unless it's by a man who claims to be a priest, a minister or a preacher.

In essence, the "chilling effect" is about conduct. It is about an institution, such as the church, that has violated the interests of a group with its words, actions and attitudes. The anti-female dogma of its religious documents and focus make it clear that women cannot rise into power or that "man" has to be at the head of the institution. This is a situation where conduct is negative and could cause harm, but nobody has the GUTS to suppress it or penalize those who practice and promote it. But it nevertheless has a chilling effect on those of us who have a conscious and believe that "what's right is right," and who also believe that, "just because a man says it, doesn't make it so."

The old folks used to have a saying that, "His mouth ain't no prayer book just because it opens and shuts." This is the kind of homage that we have always paid to the Bible and to the Christian faith; hell, black people created the concept of Christianity. But that's a story for another time. We have to deal with the present day and how it is applied and practiced in the hands of the people that we are living with and dealing with daily. We have to deal with things as they are, not as we imagine them to be. And that is why I wish these incredible black women would take some of those blessings that they have had bestowed upon them and use that power to transform the church into what it has the potential to be; do away with, "melt down" if you will, that "chilling effect."

When I say "church," what I mean are religious institutions, period. It could be a Mosque, a Masjed, a Jewish Temple or Synagogue. In my book the religious documents make women into second-class citizens and then it's up to the various institutional arrangements to support that reality. The men are at the top (and on top, hence the term "missionary position" as it relates to the sex act), and the women bring up the rear. And then we wonder why they are always so pissed off: when "God" is against you, what kind of chance can you have in life?
What the Bible lays out and makes clear in regard to the "second class status" of women is reinforced by the hard-core day-to-day realities of the church here in the 21st century – and beyond.

You would think that since black women have been endangered for centuries, and since the black church is majority female, that it would be this institution that would have a vanguard role in protecting our sisters. Right? Wrong. A book titled *Righteous Discontent: The Women's Movement in the Black Baptist Church, 18880-1920* comes to a conclusion about that period that still exists today. The author, Evelyn Brooks Higginbotham, makes telling points outlined below by reviewer, Michael R. Walker:

Higginbotham convincingly demonstrates the long-neglected but important role of black Baptist women in both the racial uplift of blacks and the fight for gender equality from the 1880's to the 1920's. She skillfully weaves together the complicated factors of gender- and race-consciousness. These factors all surround the theme recurring throughout the book: "Black women found themselves in the unique position of being at once separate from and allied with black men in the struggle for racial advancement while separate and allied with white women in the struggle for gender equality."

To begin with, every Baptist preacher should be required to read the Higginbotham book. I did and found it fascinating. The fact that the role of women has been long-neglected is not news; what is news is how these Christians can allow black women to continue to be abused in this manner. Of course, these individuals allow a lot of things to go on in their church and they stand by and do nothing. It works in their favor for the black family to be divided; in that way they (ministers) can step in and take over the role as husband, lover and father. Not in a financial sense, but in a sexual sense. And that is exactly what they do.

Remember the Rev. Lyons case? I was personally involved with the woman that helped bring him down, and I can say that she was the type that you could see was trouble. Her name was Bernice Jones at the time, but after she got busted with Lyons, it was discovered that she was going by the name Bernice Edwards. She was, at one time, the wife of the brother of the man who owned the radio station and newspaper that I worked for.

This woman ran scams up and down Milwaukee, including ripping off the Milwaukee Public Schools. In fact, I wrote one of the grants that enabled her to land a contract with MPS. But that is about all I knew about her until I read about her seduction of Lyons a few years later, got herself a new house out of the deal, and then he is "outed" by the church.

The point to be made here is simply that the Baptist church keeps women out of power when it is the men who are screwing up, nationally and locally. This is not gossip. These are facts that these Baptists intentionally ignore or deny. They do all this while also denying women a chance to share power in the upper echelons of the church. These kinds of actions rank as "sins" in my book. And these actions divided black men and women based on "religious affiliation and commitment" (translation: who's putting money in the collection plate and who is not) as well as gender. Division in the ranks being fostered by an institution that most black people view as a guide and a moral leader. That is why the scams emanating from these churches are so successful.

According to another writer (Briggs, 2008),

> Black women activists say change is long overdue in their struggle
> for equal opportunities in their church. They can be trustees and
> teachers and can even be ordained as deacons and ministers in
> some black churches. But like many evangelical churches, many
> individual black congregations still ban female clergy. And even
> among churches that accept women ministers, it is rare for a
> woman to be a senior pastor.

Why does it take "activists" to have to address what is obviously a gender bias? The Baptist church is probably 65-70% women, so doesn't it occur to anyone that something is wrong when a man is up front, preaching about how God says this and God says that, eats all the chicken and cake that the "sisters" in the church can muster up, receives thousands of dollars in donations ("offerings") each Sunday and a special collection on Ministers' Day, and knows everybody's business?

Not only that, but you've already read about some of the things that the Bible says about women. So here is a man in front of a female-based congregation, talking about how wonderful God is and how men should do this and that and how women are supposed to take care of the man. This is the basic message from the Bible: he's the head of the house and she does everything else. You've seen and heard the quotes before – every sexist and misogynist knows these quotes by heart. Briggs writes that,

> Tradition and a literal interpretation of biblical texts urging women
> to be silent are part of the reason women have been kept from the
> front of the black church, observers say. There are concerns that
> women clergy could undermine the historic role of pastors as
> important leadership models for black men. The issue also is about
> power and sexism, some women insist (Briggs, 2008).

Of course it's about power and sexism. But these are generic charges. The specific problems posed by the black church are much more sinister and diabolical; and they are also calculated and designed.

For instance, if the man is "ordained" to be on top, then that makes the woman a set of reactions to him. If this applies to the white man and his mate, what does that leave for the black man, who is already a flunky for the white man? What it does is that it takes a "slave" (the black man) and then that makes the black woman the "slave of a slave."

According to this same article, black women are tired of it and these actions by Baptist churches are creating unnecessary hostility – and rebellion:

Many black male clergy keep women from the pulpit based on Bible passages that emphasize female submission. This has led many black women to turn to predominantly white mainline churches such as the United Church of Christ and the Presbyterian Church (USA) ... substantial numbers of black women seminary graduates have switched to white denominations. More than half of the 380 ordained black women in one study turned to white denominations. Mamiya noted the number is declining slightly with the opening of opportunities in historically black denominations such as the African Methodist Episcopal Church. "However, denominational switching still remains a significant factor for black women in ministry, and black church denominations are losing," he reported (Briggs, 2008).

Denominational switching is just a degree below "spousal switching" in my book. I've already pointed out what sisters are doing in response to their body image issues and they also have abandonment issues: first the daddy leaves, then their first boyfriend messes around behind their back, then they get married and their husband gets sick of them. This frustration has many of them turning to the church and what do they find: even the Bible hates their guts! It's only logical that they would switch denominations (and partners) if they ain't getting what they should be getting!

According to Lowen, "Although gender inequity may not be of concern to many women in the black church, it is apparent to the men who preach from its pulpit." In an article entitled "Practicing Liberation in the Black Church" in the *Christian Century*, James Henry Harris, pastor of Mount Pleasant Baptist Church in Norfolk, Virginia, and adjunct assistant professor of philosophy at Old Dominion University, writes:

Sexism against black women should...be addressed by black theology and the black church. Women in black churches outnumber men by more than two to one; yet in positions of authority and responsibility the ratio is reversed. Though women are gradually entering ministry as bishops, pastors, deacons and elders, many men and women still resist and fear that development. When our church licensed a woman to the preaching ministry over a decade ago, almost all the male deacons and many women members opposed the action by appealing to tradition and selected Scripture passages. Black theology and the black church must deal with the double bondage of black women in church and society (Briggs, 2008).

Can the Baptist church – and the others – reverse their discriminatory trends? If the Bible was divinely inspired, then does this mean that God is a racist and a misogynist? Why must the church condone this kind of activity when it is clear that women, especially black women, are already catching hell at the hands of society at large? Black women are frustrated, pissed and suffer from feeling s of low self-esteem and rejection. What's a girl to do?

And then there are the Catholics. Why can't women be priests? Richert (2008) answers the question as follows:

> Among the most vocal controversies in the Catholic Church in the late 20th century and early 21st has been the question of the ordination of women. As more Protestant denominations, including the Church of England, have begun ordaining women, the Catholic Church's teaching on the all-male priesthood has come under attack, with some claiming that the ordination of women is simply a matter of justice, and the lack of such ordination is proof that the Catholic Church does not value women. The Church's teaching on this matter, however, cannot change.

At least the Catholic Church *admits* that it cannot change. On the other hand Baptists, especially black ones, area always endorsing the concept of change, particularly when that change is social. It is an institution that backs civil rights, supports black politicians and claims to care about the black community. Why then, can it not support "change" when that change is about bringing together the male-female unit? Because if it did, it would upset the proverbial apple cart of humankind, that's why! All religions treat women like shit and therefore if Christianity is going to remain number one in the world, it must continue to "out-sexist" the other religions, simple as that!

What the Baptists and Catholics have in common is the whole "men and women are different" issue. And when they talk about being different, that means that *somebody* is going to be *deficient.* Here's how a Catholic scholar explains it in Catholic terms:

> Christ, of course, was a man; but some who argue for the ordination of women insist that His sex is irrelevant, that a woman can act in the person of Christ as well as a man can. This is a misunderstanding of Catholic teaching on the differences between men and women, which the Church insists are irreducible; men and women, by their natures, are suited to different, yet complementary, roles and functions (Richert, 2008).

Where is the evidence that Christ was a man? In the Bible, of course. And who wrote the Bible? Men. And oh yeah, we can't forget that the Bible is the book where a man gave birth to – of course, a woman. And it gets worse from there as I've established elsewhere in this book. But there is no logic in stating that the same species that starts wars, spreads disease, hates people on the basis of race, ethnicity, gender and geography, and who has basically blasphemed the Supreme Being more than any other racial group on earth, should be "the head" of the church.

The Catholics say that Christ ordered things to be this way:

> Yet even if we disregard the differences between the sexes, as many advocates of women's ordination do, we have to face the fact that the ordination of men is an unbroken tradition that goes back not only to the Apostles but to Christ Himself. As the Catechism of the Catholic Church (para. 1577) states: "Only a baptized man (*vir*) validly receives sacred ordination." The Lord Jesus chose men (*viri*) to form the college of the twelve apostles, and the apostles did the same when they chose collaborators to succeed them in their ministry. The college of bishops, with whom the priests are united in the priesthood, makes the college of the twelve an ever-present and ever-active reality until Christ's return. The Church recognizes herself to be bound by this choice made by the Lord himself. For this reason the ordination of women is not possible (Richert, 2008).

The Baptist ministers and their advocates say that preachers are "called" to preach and are ordained by God to do so. The Catholics have a similar modus operandi:

> Still, the argument continues, some traditions are made to be broken. But again, that misunderstands the nature of the priesthood. Ordination does not simply give a man permission to *perform the functions* of a priest; it imparts to him an indelible (permanent) spiritual character that *makes* him a priest, and since Christ and His Apostles chose only men to be priests, only men can validly become priests (Richert, 2008 – emphasis original).

Wow. A man can be made a priest by another man. And the question, once again, remains: where are the women? And can you now see more reasons why the black woman is frustrated and shackled to a situation where even the most moral and holy of institutions relegates her to second-class citizenship?

Black people have worked to try to "humanize" the Catholic Church. But the National Black Catholic Congress is basically a good idea, but its simply traditional Catholicism in blackface. No juice and no real power.

The Koran cuts the sister a little bit more slack, or so it would appear. When it comes to marriage and divorce, for instance, The Book of Women 4:3 reads, "And if you fear that you cannot act equitably towards orphans, then marry such women as seem good to you, two and three and four; but if you fear that you will not do justice (between them), then (marry) only one or what your right hands possess; this is more proper...." (English translation by M.H. Shakir). In all the religions I've studied, the man has the power and the woman is just there.

The Book of Women 4.34 says,

> "Men are the protectors and maintainers of women, because Allah
> has given the one more (strength) than the other, and because they
> support them from their means. Therefore the righteous women are
> devoutly obedient, and guard in (the husband's) absence what
> Allah would have them guard. As to those women on whose part
> ye fear disloyalty and ill-conduct, admonish them (first), (next),
> refuse to share their beds, (and last) beat them (lightly); but if they
> return to obedience, seek not against them means (of annoyance):...
> "

The Bible is not alone in fostering anti-female bullshit. Do you know the Quran is equally full of this. In that book they're not called "chapters," but they're called "Surahs." And the books have different names as well. So let's just pick one up, as I did, and take a glimpse at what we find.
Women have to be "obedient" to men, admonished by men and lightly beaten? What about the men? But at least the woman has some semblance of recourse: "If a woman fears cruelty or desertion on her husband's part, there is no blame on them if they arrange an amicable settlement between themselves; and such settlement is best; even though men's souls are swayed by greed.... " (*The Book of Women 4:128*).

And in the Surah there is a *Book of the Heifer,* where in 2:229 it is read: "Divorce may be retracted twice. The divorced woman shall be allowed to live in the same home amicably, or leave it amicably. It is not lawful for the husband to take back anything he had given her.... "

While still biased, at least this is a book that gives the woman some recourse; but it is akin to allowing an enslaved group of people to "go out on the town on the weekend, drink and have a good time." It is a reprieve and as soon as it's over, you go back into a system that is anti-human and treats you like chattel.

And surely you've been on college campuses or on the street and seen some

Muslim sisters clad in floor-length clothing and when you look at them, they immediately look at the ground. It's not you – it's the way that they, like a lot of Christian women, have been programmed. Check out what it says in *The Book of Light,* 24:31:

> "And say to the believing women that they should lower their gaze and guard their modesty; that they should not display their beauty and ornaments except what (must ordinarily) appear thereof; that they should draw their veils over their bosoms and not display their beauty except to their husbands, their fathers, their husband's fathers, their sons, their husbands' sons, their brothers or their brothers' sons, or their sisters' sons, or their women, or the slaves whom their right hands possess, or male servants free of physical needs, or small children who have no sense of the shame of sex; and that they should not strike their feet in order to draw attention to their hidden ornaments.... "

What a chilling effect such a belief system has to have had on women all over the world, but especially women of color. I say this because most of them are already oppressed by the system, and then they now have to endure a similar "dogging" under the aegis of religion!

Jewish dogma, synagogues, documents and scripture give the woman a little more leeway (despite their sexist core). Hauptman, for one, asks the question, "sexual arousal: whose fault?"

> While statements in the Mishnah describe the woman as the evil temptress and as easy to seduce, much anecdotal material that follows often suggests just the opposite: that it is men who are easily aroused and single-minded in pursuing release. One particular anecdote … mocks the complacency of men who believe that their involvement in Torah study places them above all temptation. Here, too, the disguise of a woman, brings home the point.

Women are damned if they do and damned if they don't. If moral documents condemn them in such a way, what is a woman supposed to think of herself. Why shouldn't she be pissed off?

So here we are: on the one hand, a Bible that implies that women are evil, lascivious temptresses and that man must avoid their allure, and a Jewish document that teaches that the man is the one who is out of control. Let us also not forget how Islam forces women to "cover up" lest they "tempt" men. But in any case, it is the woman who has to pay; in the former case, with her reputation and sometimes with her life and in the latter instance, paying by having to cover up and stay outside of and beyond the lustful advances of the male.

DOMESTIC VIOLENCE AGAINST MEN

Before you can understand the act you have to understand the way the mind functions and the impact that the media, peer pressure and other institutional arrangements have on their subtle and not-so-subtle endorsement of domestic violence against men. It is not something that you see taking place very often because that is the way it is supposed to be. But it happens on a number of levels and has been taking place since the inception of this country. When the white man brought his sexism from Europe to America and created that "woman's place is in the kitchen and the bedroom," she went to work incorporating power into those roles and using them to slowly but surely etch a niche into the family power relations to the point where she now calls the shots.

But let us focus on America. You can watch an old movie made in the 1930s and see how white women are viewed calling the shots. There were images of them slapping the shit out of men and the man standing there just taking it. Early movies depicted women in the old west, the "gay '90s," Prohibition days, riding as molls with gangsters, and sitting on the control deck on space ships headed to other galaxies working with her man to find other planets to colonize. She's always been right there and she's been watching and waiting. She never said "stop all this white supremacy bullshit"; she simply said, "scoot over and let me rule those other people at your side."

The fact of the matter is, until recently, catching your wife in bed with a lover was a defense for murder in some places. Jealousy, possessiveness and control are also at the core of domestic violence, which thrives in the privacy of monogamy (McCullough & Hall, 2003). Much of the information on domestic violence against men is anecdotal, largely because of the lack of funding to study the problem. Although several organizations explore domestic violence, the biggest single source is the Department of Justice, which administers grants through its Office on Violence Against Women (Watson, 2010).

There is a list of examples of domestic violence against men that is posted on the Healthy Place website, and many of them differ from just physical abuse, which is what most people probably assume. These include:

- Kicks, punches, slaps, or bites you (often, but not always, women target a man's groin)
- Threatens you with weapons like knives, guns, baseball bats, irons
- Purposely scalds or burns you

- Throws objects at you
- Commits violence against your children or pets
- Violates court visitation orders by willfully stopping you from seeing your children
- Verbally humiliates you in public or private
- Constantly ridicules and makes fun of you
- Calls you names and berates your self-worth
- Blames you for her own failures
- Destroys your personal items
  Turns your children against you (parental alienation)
- Threatens to ruin you financially if you leave her
- Isolates you from family members or family functions if your family is nearby
- Destroys fixtures in the home (i.e., cabinetry, walls, appliances)

The problem is that American society views men who are battered by women as being weak. Gluck (2012) writes that, "Many people view male victims of domestic violence as sissies or as weak. This typical attitude makes them reluctant to admit that their partners physically abuse them for fear as being labeled as weak or unmanly" (pp. 1-2).

Such foolish assholes. The black man is not afraid of the white man and we sure aren't weak. But back in the day when that white boy was beating the shit out of us, our fear as that behind him stood more white boys, mobs, the army, the marines, the navy and the National Guard. We would take that ass whipping because we didn't want to get lynched or gunned down. That is how they act; you rarely see a white man take on a black man one-on-one. If we don't fight back it's because we understand the long-term implications of beating the shit out of this white boy. Short term pleasure will surely yield long-term pain.

It's the same way with bitches when they dare to take us on. We don't fight back because we know what the long-term stakes will be. For the most part, the law is on their side and so is society. A man who blazes on some broad, even after she hits him, is going to be viewed as an "abuser." It has nothing to do with being viewed as "weak." Let me give you an example.

"Jerry Springer" is a popular, low-rent show that features relationships, usually guys who mess around behind their wives' and girlfriends' backs. Now this show is nationally syndicated and yet these people appear on stage to spill their guts, air their dirty laundry and then engage in fist fights, brawls and name calling. Most of this is done by women, white and black. Before I continue, read the information that was provided earlier regarding the list of examples of domestic violence against men that was posted on the Healthy Place website.

When on stage, these women – white and black – will haul off and clock these guys; not just slaps, but open fist. They will push them, charge them and it appears as if they are going to try to truly do harm. They will push them in their chests so hard that these men almost fall off stage. None of the bodyguards appears to want to do anything when it is the woman charging and swinging at the man (when the women fight each other, a bell rings and they are allowed to go at it). Now why would a woman do this, in front of a live audience and on national television, unless she knew that she was "protected"?

After all, these guys are far bigger than these women, but one thing comes across: these bitches have done this before, but they most likely knew what would happen. But when they're on "Springer," they are protected by these professional bouncers. These are men who appear to be separating or breaking up the onslaught, but they always manage to let women get in punches. It is clear that the men are held in check by a pre-show lecture because they guys don't even try to punch back or defend themselves.

What does this have to do with domestic violence against men? Clearly, most women can see that they can be overpowered by the men in their lives. But they also know that, like the bouncers on the "Jerry Springer Show," they will be protected. They will take their lumps so that they can have some long-term damage inflicted on the guy (an arrest, perhaps a violation placed on his record, temporary or long-term eviction from the home, perhaps grounds for divorce, etc.). These women are dangerous – all of them. I'm not talking about the ones who are taking Zumba classes and martial arts training: I'm talking about the ones who have emotional issues and when they snap, the man is going to pay. This then, is domestic violence against the male.

Overall, there is evidence that women use IPV against their male partners. The evidence suggests that criminal justice and social service agencies are unsure of how to respond to or provide services to female perpetrators or male victims (Hines & Douglas, 2009: p. 582).

At the group level, a final study investigated gender differences among 45 male and 45 female IPV primary perpetrators in North Carolina who were mandated to attend treatment as part of their probation … This study showed that although men had a longer history of domestic violence offenses and other nonviolent criminal offenses than women, the majority of women did have criminal histories (Hines & Douglas, 2009: p. 577).

At the Macrolevel and domestic violence against men as equally as powerless when it comes to equal protection under the law. This would involve the criminal justice system and within that context, the problem continues to be convoluted. The predominant criminal justice policy that has affected female perpetrators of IPV has been mandatory arrest policies which mandate (or in some states, strongly encourage) police officers to make an arrest in any call involving IPV. These policies have led to an increase in women being arrested for intimate physical violence, particularly in "dual-arrest" situations – those that are seemingly mutually volatile and in which the police cannot determine whether one party is the perpetrator of the assault, and therefore arrest both parties (Hines & Douglas, 2009: p. 576).

Right now the laws appear one sided. One testimony from a report called Domestic Violence Statistics offers an interesting concern by a male victim:

> Men are victims. I am currently serving a 2 year probation period for a simple assault with DV. I am a man. I was also hit, scratched, kicked and more by my ex 3 years after leaving her she stopped by my home. I couldn't get her to leave. I made a huge mistake by grabbing her and removing her from my home then locking the door. I should not have grabbed her. It doesn't (nor did it matter) that she was hitting me and threatening me. I lost my firearms rights, my home, job, damaged credit, dog and 90% of my personal belongings. Fines, mandatory jail time, embarrassment and more is a cross that I bare (Michael, August 15,2012 at 2:49am) (Domestic Violence Statistics, 2013 : p. 3).

There is no doubt that domestic violence against men can be reduced; the domestic violence initiatives of the past 40 years have brought a hidden crime to light and provided protection for millions of women. The next step is to admit that domestic violence is not a male or female problem, but rather a human problem, and that a lasting solution must address the cruelty – and suffering – of both sexes (Watson, 2010).

Here are the facts: men, for the most part, are stronger than women. Women, for the most part, are going to do whatever it takes to fuck up as many men as they can, especially those who have wronged them. Fact: the law is going to protect women as much as possible in these cases. Never hit a woman? Again, there should be no blanket protection of anyone. Back in the day a black man couldn't even look a white man in the eyes. When Emmett Till allegedly whistled at a white woman, he was tortured and lynched. Today, the person getting lynched with an almost blanket refusal of protection is the male and, more specifically, the least powerful of the males, the black male.

MARRIAGE: A FINANCIAL FARCE

Never hit a woman. 'Til death do we part. Through sickness and health, richness or poorer. If I should die before I wake I pray the Lord my soul to take. And other bare-faced lies that we tell without realizing what the hell we are really saying and committing ourselves to. All this shit ties in together to pit the sexes against one another, to create a hierarchy where one will rule and the other will be ruled. You decide which one you think is which.

Violence begats violence. The person who creates the conditions for violence – men hitting women and women hitting men – should be considered just as guilty as the individuals directly involved. Marriage, in my view, provides an arena for violence, and it always has. You can call it domestic abuse, spousal abuse, intimate partner violence, family disagreements or whatever: forcing someone to be obligated to another person is, in my view, the beginning of creating an arena for violence to take place. From adultery, premature ejaculation, post-menopausal sex problems, bad ass kids and so on, violence lingers over the institution of marriage. Let me provide some preliminary notes, ideas that provide a nugget of where I'm coming from.

A 2004 *Newsweek* article tried to explain and report on adultery in America. But it was not the first time that this misogynistic culture attempted confuse the issue regarding so-called "adultery." In fact, a topical news story from 1997 provided fodder for discussions of who was being "faithful" and who was not; in this case First Lieutenant Kelly Flinn, a young single woman (26 years old) was court-martialed for military charges of adultery. Check this out: the guy she had he affair with, Marc Zigo, a soccer coach at Minot Air Force Base, was married to an enlisted woman, but told Flinn he was separated. Then, based on this lie, he had an affair with Flinn, who was also charged with "fraternization," lying to Air Force investigators, disobeying an order (to stay away from Zigo) as well as "conduct unbecoming an officer."

Flinn was later discharged and the country was angered because of the way she was treated. From that incident, involving yet another white woman, the article by Hoffman appeared in the May 18, 1997 issue of the New York Times under the headline, "Casting Pebbles in the War Against Adultery." Following are the main points of that article, and my analysis of it.

> To the Air Force, a 26-year-old bomber pilot who fell hard for a
> four-star bad boyfriend deserves to be court-martialed for a
> handful of military crimes including adultery, the quintessentially
> biblical sin. To most Americans, she does not. They have been
> reacting with amazement, not least because for decades, civilian
> courts have responded to adultery with a big yawn. It's not that
> adultery laws don't exist. It's that they're not enforced. Although
> 75 percent of Americans believe adultery is always wrong, the lack

of enforcement reflects a certain ambivalence over whether the government should be peeping into bedrooms (Hoffman, 1997: 6E).

America primes its public for adultery and a form of acceptance of it as "alright." Oh sure, the claims are the opposite and there may be laws against it, and the Christian religion "forbids" it, but the popular culture media is a worthy enough opponent to override all of these. In fact, just the fact that there are laws and the Bible speaks of it and popular culture thrives on it proves how awesome a temptation "adultery" really is.

The previous excerpt claims that 75% of Americans believe that adultery is wrong. But just because they believe it's wrong doesn't mean that they don't admire those who practice it, worship those who promote it or are not engaged in it themselves. The temptation is just too great: too many sluts out there and too many man-whores who get "married" and then find out, too late, that marriage is a crock of shit. And when they find out that sleeping with the same person night in and night out for decades is about as boring as life can get (unless those people truly care for each other), then they strike out on their own and seek sexual gratification with other people.

The debate over it, despite its dubious, unlawful and immoral nature simply reinforces its relevance all that much more. Check out the following:

> In half the states, adultery is still a crime. In some, including Oklahoma, Idaho, Michigan, Wisconsin and Massachusetts, it's even a felony. Professor Katharine B. Silbaugh of Boston University law school, a co-author with Richard A. Posner, a Federal judge of "A Guide to America's Sex Laws" (1996), said state laws vary according to which lover should be prosecuted: "The married one will always be guilty," she said, "but the question is whether the unmarried one is also guilty" (Hoffman, 1997: 6E).

This places the onus on a belief that marriage is somehow "sacred." Judge Judy (Judith Scheinlin) in all of her Jewish arrogance, often deals with cases of people living together. She usually prefaces her decisions with a statement like, "You two decided to live together without the benefit of marriage …" Benefit?

Such bullshit, elevated by social beliefs and religious mythology to the level of sacred observance. Marriage is a white man who claims to be a representative of God uttering some words from a book that is supposed to be the word of God, and getting two people to agree with some "vows" that are made in the name of God. Marriage is a way for the state to generate money and keep track of its citizens;

you get two "slaves" for the price of one, and then further link people to the system. Now they've got to buy a house, get cars, file taxes jointly, plan vacations, have kids, clothe those kids and so on – paying more to be a part of, get accepted by and become more dependent upon, the system.

It's all a giant scam aimed at generating profits for the system. If you love somebody, you should not have to be forced to marry that person. And look at the 70% divorce rate – all the people who got married who found out that when all was said and done, their "love" as sheer and shallow as a pair of Casper the Friendly Ghost's draws.

So from here, the issue of who is "guilty of adultery" is as somewhat twisted. If a "married" person goes to bed with someone else, there has to be a reason. If that person is not happy, is being abused, is not being sexually satisfied, or is just an outright slut, then that person – male or female – has the right to fuck someone else if they choose to. That person is guilty of nothing more than "seeking an alternative." And that is what marriage keeps you from doing: you are supposed to be happy with the person you're with "for better or worse," which is ridiculous.

If the person who is unmarried is involved with a person that is married, what's wrong with that? Both people have to consent and agree that they want to screw one another. If that agreement is made between two sane people, then who is the government to intervene in the arrangement. Look at all those unhappy housewives coming to the black community to pick up young black boys and fuck them – they're married. Look at the white coaches who molest and abuse young kids in locker rooms and elsewhere – they're married. Look at all the white men who come to the barrio and the ghetto looking for some ass – they're married. Think about it.

Enforcing the law on adultery is like passing a law against somebody because they don't know how to fuck. Even if you don't know how, that's not the system's call to make – it's up to the person that's getting the raw deal and in most cases, that's the woman. But my logic is based on sound reality, not bullshit game playing like the kind found in the following passage:

> … in Arizona, for example, both parties are guilty of a misdemeanor, as long as one is married. By contrast, the District of Columbia holds that when the act is between a married woman and an unmarried man, both parties are guilty, but that when lovers include a married man and unmarried woman, only the man is guilty (Hoffman, 1997: 6E)

Again, it seems that the issue is "marriage" and the "fidelity" that supposedly accompanies it. The rules change because people have different views of what adultery is and when people have ideas that come together, those ideas become policy – laws. This is why the issue of adultery is so flimsy and hypocritical: monogamous marriage does not make sense and was only created so that the fathers of the child could be identified. But leaving kids out for a minute, what fuckin' sense does it make to pledge yourself to a person "for the rest of your life" or "until death do us part"?

The rule makers just can't come to an agreement or consensus, it seems:

> Maryland has declared adultery a misdemeanor, but the punishment is just a $10 fine. (Some people have quipped that the state income tax could be jettisoned altogether if the fine were raised to $1,000 and platoons of officers unleashed to enforce the law.) And in Minnesota, the misdemeanor of adultery, said legislators in 1963, is an act between a married woman and a man other than her husband. Sex between a married man and an unmarried woman is not prohibited (Hoffman, 1997: 6E).

And then there is the gender bias, such as is the case in Minnesota. When men make laws, women are going to be disrespected. When men write books – like the Bible, for instance – women are going to receive short shrift. That's the name of the game, and adultery and the "laws" that govern it, are no exception. It's about money and about making the woman look like a slut while the man, if charged at all, becomes some kind of "super stud", "playa," or "mack daddy."

Moving on:

> Prosecutions, though rare, are not unheard of. Professor Silbaugh said they usually accompany another crime, or are used to go after troublemakers. And so in 1970 a Pennsylvania jury found a man guilty of adultery and bastardy, and the case, which resurfaced in the courts 13 years later, was used to compel the defendant to keep up his child support payments (Hoffman, 1997: 6E).

Child support payments. That's what it's about in some cases: paying the state, once again. First you get a blood test and then pay for a marriage license. Then you pay some lousy minister to perform the ceremony. Then you pay for all the shit for the wedding, which costs thousands and then you wear these buffoonish costume in front of all your friends. This is what marriage is all about, and cannot really be justified logically. If you love somebody, you love them. But that's not enough: the state wants evidence that the love is strong enough to keep those payments coming. Adultery threatens this system's money making apparatus and the bullshit myth of "love" that is at the root of getting married.

> In 1983, a Worcester, Mass., woman challenged the
> constitutionality of the state adultery law, for which she was
> arrested after police officers watched her get into a van with a man
> and have sex with him. But the Supreme Judicial Court of
> Massachusetts said that although her concerns about a right to
> piracy had merit, the state had an interesting prohibiting conduct
> that would threaten the institution of marriage (Hoffman, 1997:
> 6E)

And there you have it: "threatening the institution of marriage." And the reason why these are threats is because they threaten the economics that surround marriage and family. This is not a social issue: it is an economic and financial one. It may become social after the economics are threatened, but believe me when I say that marriage in the U.S. is a financial arrangement and the more people who marry the more money (taxes and otherwise) this country can generate for itself in both the short- and long-term.

More evidence follows:

> And in 1990, a 28-year-old Wisconsin woman was arrested for the
> felony of adultery after her husband swore out a criminal
> complaint. Charges were dismissed after she agreed to go for
> counseling, but the case created an uproar. A state legislator
> wanted to decriminalize adultery, but beat a hasty retreat when
> voters warned him they considered his proposal an affront to
> family values (Hoffman, 1997: 6E).

When adultery is "investigated," why don't the officers delve into the marriage relationship? If the husband was not screwing his wife or if he was cruel to her, don't these facts represent the kind of extenuating circumstances that would justify adultery? In such a case wouldn't adultery be viewed as an alternative to divorce?

The fact is, the Bible says that adultery is one of the main reasons, the only reason, for divorce. But the Bible, being the sexist document that it is, was quick to blame the female (just like she got the blame for what took place in the so-called Garden of Eden).

The fact is, adultery is so common that the attitudes about it started to change and what did I say about attitudes? I said that they tend to shape policy and policy becomes law. Want proof? Take note of the following:

> Adultery is considered even less odious in divorce court than in
> criminal court. Following the divorce reform of the 1970s, all
> states have no-fault divorce, which means that a party no longer

> has to allege a specific fault, like adultery, as grounds. A minority
> of states also allow adultery as grounds, but that usually only
> serves to speed the process. In fact many heartsick spouses who
> fantasize that a judge will wreak vengeance on the philanderer are
> shocked to learn that when it comes to divorce court, the only
> cheating a judge cares about is on income reporting. And just a
> handful of states say that if adultery is at issue, a judge may, but
> not must, consider it a factor in the division of marital property
> (Hoffman, 1997: 6E).

"Income reporting." "Marital property." These capitalists don't give a shit about sperm, hotel rooms, dick sucking or intimacy. They don't care that lives can be ruined because of an inane belief in "'til death do we part." No. They care about money, plain and simple. The change in the rules to "no fault" saved time and saved the courts money. Trials were too expensive and saving money is a key component of the system's smooth operation. So there you have it. White men change the system whenever their money is threatened. It's not an issue of morality or love.

In truth,

> … the Sixth Amendment just doesn't pack the same oomph
> anymore, The term "adultery" – as distinguished from the practice
> – has grown dusty from lack of use. Instead, today's descriptive
> language dilutes condemnation with a drop of wistfulness.
> Philanderer, rather than adulterer. A faithless spouse has wanderin'
> eyes, a cheatin' heart. Even more watered down – has an
> extramarital affair. Sex opinion surveys ask: "Have you ever had
> sex with someone other than your spouse while you were
> married?" A tenet of the anti-divorce movement is that couples
> should repair the breach of marital trust exposed by the affair,
> because divorce is a far greater family crime than adultery
> (Hoffman, 1997: 6E).

And not just that, but the whole idea of a "separation" is granted so that the people involved can have time to work out the issues without going into immediate divorce mode.

But a so-called "cheatin' heart" and a "wandering eye" are perfectly normal and human! These are normal situations being relegated to a categorical of immorality simply because of a farce called marriage! People are supposed to see and appreciate each other. What's worse: to look and admire or, when you're with your wife, to pretend as if you don't see? Cheatin' heart? Heart don't do nothin' but pump blood! You can't cheat if you refuse to be a part of a game that's rigged in the first place! And if the game is rigged, and you choose to participate in it, then cheating is a part of the established rules of the game!

So what is all this about changing the terminology and the rules so that it sounds more palatable? It's about the concept of "temptation," and all humans suffer from being able to be tempted, do they not? The dictionary defines "tempt" as, "To entice (someone) to commit an unwise or IMMORAL act. To be inviting or attracted to. To provoke or risk provoking. To incline or dispose strongly (Berube, et al., p. 1252).

Wow! The dictionary says as its first definition that to tempt has to do with committing an unwise or immoral (sinful) act. Now these Americans who claim to be Christians want to use the Bible and use Scripture in order to buttress the points – that is until they come up against somebody like me who knows the Bible better than they do. So according to our language, *even Jesus sinned because the Bible says that he, too, was "tempted."* Do I need to prove my point any further? Okay, I will.

When a person is "tempted," he or she first has to think on it before they act on it. Many times we will ponder in our mind whether we should do something that we really want to do but first we will do the best we can to weigh the consequences of our actions. If our "will" is strong enough, we can resist the temptation of doing it. The point here is that we think, ponder and roll it over in our mind, first. Now, check out what Jesus said in Matthew 5:28-29: "But I say unto you, that whosoever looketh upon a woman to lust after her hath committed adultery with her already in his heart. "

So it begins with the heart (the mind), just like it did back in 1980 when Jimmy Carter admitted that he had lusted in his heart "many times," remember that? So it's a mental thing, and that stuff about the "heart" is just a metaphor because the heart don't do nothin' but pump blood. So when the Bible talks about the heart, it is referring to the MIND. Got it? Good.

Adultery. What a joke. Secret lives? Secret to those who don't want to know the truth. Marriage: a financial farce that provides an arena for difference types of violence: social, economic, cultural and physical. Remember: you heard it here first.

THE PRINCIPLE OF "DAWA NA MOTO NI MOTO"

On the December 5, 2012 segment of "First Take," Stephen A. Williams continued to drive home the fact that a man should never put his hand on a woman. But then he turned around and made some impactful statements about men having to "fall on their swords" and sometimes have to "admit to things they didn't do" in order to comply with society's standards so that they (the athletes) could continue to do their jobs and not fall out of public favor.

I say, "dawa na moto ni moto" -- fight fire with fire.

These women are armed, as I've made clear in this book, with weapons that are legal, social, cultural, political – and gender-biased, although the latter is usually shrouded and covered up by the white man's blatant and longtime sexism and glass ceiling-related antics. And all of these components fall under an ideological umbrella, basically a Euro-American one that states that if you hit a woman there is going to be hell to pay. And the subtle and degrading message that women are willing to sell their souls for so that they can retain this power, is that they are "inferior and childlike" and therefore in need of this kind of "protection."

Notice that when this society talks about "vulnerable groups," or when a ship, a burning building of a disaster area is being destroyed, the claim is always, "women and children first." On almost every single level women, no matter how dyke-like or hard core, are viewed as "things to be protected." The emphasis is on "things" because that is just what they are being treated like: objects.

For instance, merely look at the popular culture movies. Go back as far as 1939's "Five Came Back" (Lucille Ball, Chester Morris, Wendy Barrie) about a plane that is wrecked but of the 12 people who were on board, they have to decide which five can re-board because of the condition of the plane. "We have to consider women and children first," is the universal agreement. How about the movie, "Titanic"? The same thing was shouted after it hit the fateful iceberg: "women and children to the life boats first!"
And in this society, what kind of women do men prefer when it comes to seeking a date or a mate? The ones that are the most weak minded, child-like, defenseless and dependent. The whites have a slogan in regard to their age: "I'm 50 years YOUNG" or whatever their age might happen to be. Everybody wants to be a child and that is why being treated like one comes too easy for so many. This is then followed up with another sexist mantra: the man's job is to "take care" of his family, and what does that consist of? Women and children.
Don't take my word for it. Just watch any show where women confront men. Check out those low-rent, trailer trash, ghetto ass talk shows like "Jerry Springer." These women get in these men's faces because they've been told that the men won't hit them, and they tee off on these bruthas. Pushing them in the chest, slapping the shit out of them – and the bruthas can't do anything but hang their heads because of the "rules." Even the shows where violence isn't as pronounced – "Steve Wilkos," "Maury Povich," "Bill Cunningham" – the screaming by these women is every bit as bad, and worse, as it is for the man. She is every bit "the power" that he is. These women think that no matter how big a man is, or how small they are, they can vent their anger with impunity. I say no.

Therefore, "fight fire with fire" is my contribution to making the situation far more equitable. It gives the female back her humanity. It lets her know that if she swings on me, I'm gonna swing on her. If she hits me, I'm going to hit her back. That makes it fair. The argument about "well, you're a man and you're stronger," and that is precisely my point: she knew that! She sees me and knows what I can do! So knowing that, why would she take a swing at me or hit me in violence? Because she lost her temper? Because I made her mad? Because I didn't do what she told me to do? Fuck that!

If she knows that I can kick her ass, then she should take that into consideration before she has the nerve to try to kick mine! She knows she has the courts on her side and if things get bad, a divorce will get her half my shit. She has no business trying to put her hands on an ex-street fighter and think that just because she has tits and a vagina that she won't get hit back.

That shit might work on the ignorant. But not on me.

REPERCUSSIONS, RESPONSE, RETALIATION:
THE STELLY PARADIGM

On a January 13, 2013 segment of the PBS News Hour, it was reported that there had been 350 suicides among military personnel in 2012, and that was up fifty from a year before. Why do you think this is? I believe it's because while men and women are around the world enforcing the imperialist intentions and goals of this country, their spouses and mates are back on the mainland fucking around behind their backs!

Nothing is worse than having someone who has been trained to kill and can shoot a gun come home and find somebody else's cum stains on their sheets! The Stelly Paradigm is about gender equity. I watch these TV shows and read these newspaper articles and there are men out there angry because their wives are earning more money than they are. Say what?
Man, if my woman is earning more money, why in the hell would I hate her for that? It's going in the same pot, isn't it? In fact, I prefer her working and I sit at home and write, do the things that women have been getting away with for centuries. I don't mind being a "house husband" or being "Mr. Mom." It is this role that women use to train the kids to hate our guts and the time that they use to talk to their slut girlfriends and pick up tips on how to make the man's life miserable.
Following then, are some basic principles, principles that I laid out before writing this book.

1. If she hits you, hit her back

2. **If you don't hit her back, she will assume you never will**
3. **Hit her back with the equal force that she used when hitting you**
4. **If she thinks you won't hit her, she will kill you one day**
5. **If she thinks you won't hit her, she will assume you are afraid of her**
6. **If she thinks you won't hit her, she will assume that she is the strong one in the relationship.**
7. **If she thinks you won't hit her, she has no fear in regard to doing anything she wants to your shit**
8. **If she thinks you won't hit her, she'll attribute it to how good her pussy is**
9. **If you tell her you don't hit women, ask her to tell you that she doesn't hit men; if she doesn't tell you that, then take back what you said.**
10. **If she thinks you won't hit her, she'll assume you're a fag**
11. **If she thinks you won't hit her, there's nothing to stop her from emptying your checking account**
12. **If she thinks you won't hit her, there's nothing to keep her from contacting your ex-bitches and saying whatever she wants to say**
13. **If she thinks you won't hit her, there's nothing to stop her from stalking and harassing you**
14. **If she thinks you won't hit her, she'll tell her friends and now you've got a bunch of men cowering from their women**
15. **If she thinks you won't hit her, she'll think you're "soft"**
16. **If she thinks you won't hit her, she'll be more prone toward violence**
17. **If she thinks you won't hit her, she'll say you're violating Biblical scripture because you're supposed to "keep her in line"**
18. **If she thinks you won't hit her, eventually she'll begin thinking you "don't care"**

The previous statements are rooted in common sense, human nature and universal law. Don't put your hands on me and I won't put my hands on you. To borrow from the Christian Bible, "Do unto others as you would have others do unto you."

A BASIS FOR "UNJUST ENRICHMENT"?

In this society if you hit a woman, you are penalized. With relationships being what they are, a penalty for a man is tantamount to a reward for the woman. She gets rewarded when she can "teach a man a lesson."

I want to raise issues and answer questions. I don't like the idea of relying on rules of law because I know the basis of many laws is racial and gender bias.

But at present, there are general and common sense principles we can use to show how one-sided this concept of "you should never hit a female" truly is. Piggy-back on what I wrote earlier: "fair exchange ain't no robbery." So that means if that if an exchange is not fair, then someone has been robbed. In robbery situations, the person who does the robbing is "enriched" – his status has been improved because he stole your shit.

For this reason I want to explore the concept of "unjust enrichment" as it relates to the "advantage" that any female can have if she charges that a man "hit her." This is regardless of the situation, what she did beforehand, what she said about him or the harm inflicted upon his person or property. In sum, because of her gender, far too many of them are getting a free pass.

According to Wikipedia, a scholastically frowned up and yet somewhat reliable (in my view) source of information, "unjust enrichment" is defined as, "a particular type of causative event in which one party is unjustly enriched at the expense of another, and an obligation to make restitution arises, regardless of liability for wrongdoing."

Restitution. An interesting point. A man hits a woman because she hit him first. He pays for it with jail time, desertion, ridicule, an ass whipping from the cops, a divorce, liquidation of his assets, and on-going feelings of guilt. Furthermore, unjust enrichment need not be the product of some conspiracy no the part of the female. The definition informs us that it can be a benefit by mistake or chance, and furthermore,

> Morally and ethically the one who gains a benefit that he or she has not paid or worked for should not keep it to the rightful owner's detriment. The party that received money, services or property that should have been delivered to or belonged to another must make restitution to the rightful owner. A court may order such restitution in a lawsuit brought by the party who should rightly have the money or property.(Wikipedia, 2013).

If a woman benefits from starting a fight and then getting her ass kicked as a result, why should be then benefit? That is where restitution comes in; it need not be monetary, but it can be an apology. Nothing extravagant or extensive just an apology to the tune of, "I'm sorry I made an ass out of myself by assuming that I could hit you and then not expect that you would hit me back." If this was done, more situations could be cleared up much more expeditiously.

With an apology, we solve the restitution problem and no one has to admit any wrong doing. As the definition of "unjust enrichment" further instructs,

> Liability under the principle of unjust enrichment is wholly independent of liability for wrongdoing. Claims in unjust enrichment do not depend upon proof of any wrong. However, it is possible that on a single set of facts a claim based on unjust enrichment and a claim based on a wrong may both be available. A claim based on unjust enrichment always results in an obligation to make restitution. A claim based on a wrong always results in an obligation to make compensation but may additionally result in an obligation to make restitution (Wikipedia, 2017).

There need not be proof of any wrong, but in the case of hitting and violence, the wrong is committed when the person violates your personal space. A woman who hits a man has assaulted that man, and has battered him as well. These are both crimes in any jurisdiction in this country. Retaliation against an assault and battery should therefore be understood and respected regardless of gender. It is the obligation to make restitution that can bring "closure" to the conflict and as a result the woman learns to keep her hands off of anyone, especially someone who she knows she cannot defeat. In fact, hitting a child, someone smaller than you, even if it is about "discipline," should be viewed in the same way. Maybe if we can do that and teach this lesson, this war-torn nation will learn that violence is not the way to settle all scores.

If a person has an unfair advantage in terms of the way they are supposed to be "treated," that is also a form of unjust enrichment. For instance, there was a time when if a black person saw a white person coming down the street or walkway, that black person had to move over and allow that white man or woman through. There was a time when a black person could not look a white person directly in the eye. There was a time when a black child could call a black man a "nigger," hit him or whatever, and that black man could not strike back. All of these are examples of unjust enrichment because they gave that white man an unfair advantage and made him feel superior; his self-esteem was therefore, enriched.

Today, as has always been the case it seems, a man is supposed to take his hat off in the presence of a woman. A man is supposed to stand up if a woman has to leave the table. A man is supposed to open a door for a woman no matter where they're at. If in line while getting on the bus, let's say, a group of men are supposed to stand to the side and let the girls and women board first (I've seen this done for months while living in Dallas, Texas). A man is supposed to pay for lunch or dinner when he takes a woman out and, in fact, he is supposed to pay for the date, period.

Can you now see how the esteem and ego of the woman would be elevated because of this treatment? In these scenarios, and others, she can "expect" a certain kind of behavior by the male, just because of her gender. This, in my view, is unjust enrichment: she gets something by doing nothing more than benefitting from the fact that she is of the female gender.

And then, we top if off by not being able to defend ourselves if she decides, because of that perceived "gender superiority," to knock the shit out of us. We are supposed to stand there and take it. The old movies would show these white women slapping the shit out of these men and the man just took it. Today on these shows like "Jerry Springer", these women do more than that: they tee off on these guys and the men, because of the "rules" have to take it.

If you want to be treated right by somebody, no matter who that person is or what their gender is, you've got to let that be known. I'm not going to give you anything that you don't deserve or haven't earned (unless you're physically challenged or too young to care for yourself). No woman gets a free pass with me because when she's talking with her friends, she's not talking about a free pass. She's talking all that shit about "independence" and "we don't need men to do anything for us." I agree with them wholeheartedly. And with me, that includes a "no free pass" treatment unless I feel like doing it – not because of some unspoken rule of gender-biased etiquette.

CONCLUSION

During an episode of the old "Alfred Hitchcock presents" show, at one point he made the statement that he wanted his audience to "avoid disappointment and future regret." These words were perfect to sum up the gist of what this book is about. If you keep maintaining a double standard in your relationship based on gender, you will grow not to respect yourself and the person you are supposedly "respecting" will, in the long run, grow not only to disrespect you in the future, but will seize every opportunity to make that disrespect known by subtle and not-so-subtle forms of violence against your person.

As I made clear in the introduction to this boo, America has come a long way from when women were afraid of men, would never talk back and would shrink at even the thought of a man getting angry, let alone striking them. Gone are the days when women were afraid that if they spoke out of turn, said something against the existing system, or did something "unbecoming," they'd get publicly humiliated, lynched, sent to the guillotine, burned at the stake, locked up or banished.

Hitting is not acceptable, and should not be tolerated. The only time to make this known is when hit, you hit back. Before you enter a relationship, let it be known that you believe in the golden rule: "Do unto others as you would have them do unto you." That should appease the majority of people who claim to be Christians, even when they're not. Again, *prior to that you owe it to the other*

person to let it be known that you don't believe in any form of hitting, even in jest.
With that warning out of the way, that person owes it to you to respect your position. If that warning is violated, then he/she deserves the inevitable ass kicking that befalls them.

REFERENCES

Adriaanse, M.A., et. al. (2011). Planning what not to eat: Ironic effects of implementation intentions negating unhealthy habits. Personality and Social Psychology, 37, (69).

Ajzen, I. et. al. (2009). From intentions to behavior: Implementation intention, commitment, and conscientiousness. Journal of Applied Social Psychology, 39, (6).   1356-1372.

Becky, A. (2012, November 22). 5 ways to spot passive-aggressive behavior and do something about it. The Stir. Retrieved from http://thestir.cafemom.com/love_sex/146686/5_ways_to_spot_passiveaggressi

Curran, J. (2006). Media and cultural theory in the age of market liberalism. In J. Curran & D. Morley (Eds.), *Media and cultural theory* (pp. 129–148). London: Routledge.

Dalton, A.N. & Spiller, S.A. (2012, October). Too much of a good thing: The benefits of implementation intentions depend on the number of goals. *Journal of Consumer Research* , 39, (3). 600-614

Day, E. (2008, August 3). Depressed, repressed, objectified: Are men the new women? *The Observer.*
http://www.guardian.co.uk/lifeandstyle/2008/aug/03/gender.healthandwellbeing

Domestic Violence Statistics (2013). Men: The overlooked victims of domestic violence. Retrieved from http://domesticviolencestatistics.org/men-the-overlooked-victims-of-domestic-violence/

Floyd, J. (2013, January 14). Floyd: Dallas mayor Mike Rawlings' domestic violence remarks a surprise. Dallasnews.com.

Gluck, S. (2012, July 27). Domestic violence against men: Male victims of domestic abuse. HealthPlace: Trusted Mental Health Information. Retrieved from http://www.healthyplacec.com/abuse/domestic-violence/domestic-violence-against-men

Hines, D.A. & Douglas, E.M. ((2009). Women's use of intimate partner violence against men: Prevalence, implications, and consequences. Journal of Aggression, Maltreatment & Trauma, 18. 572-586.

Hoffman, A. (1997, May 18). , Casting Pebbles in the War Against Adultery. New York Times.

Liveauthetically's blog (2010, May 20). What does being transparent mean? Retrieved from http://liveauthentically.wordpress.com/2010/05/20/what-does-being-transparent-mean/

Luciano, M. (2012, November 28). John Davis, Florida teen shot: Michael Dunn behind bars in Trayvon Martin style incident. *Policymic.* Retrieved from www.policymic.com/articles/19766/jordan-davis-florida-teen-shot-michael-dunn-behind-bars-ni-trayvon-martin-style-incident

McCullough, D. & Hall, D.S. (2003, February 27). Polyamory – What it is and what it isn't. *Electronic Journal of Human Sexuality*, 6.

McDaniel, M.A. et. al. (2008, June). Implementation intentions facilitate prospective memory under high attention demands. Memory & Cognition, 36, (4). 716-724.

Nairaland Forum (2009, November 10). Why should a man not hit a woman. Internet blog.

Oswald, J. (2008, January 28). Why black women are doing the white thing. *The Voice*. Issue 1305. http://www.voice-online.co.uk/content.php?show=12808

Owens, S. G. et. al. (2008). Overcoming procrastination: The effect of implementation intentions. Journal of Applied Social Psychology, 38, (2). 366-384.

Shaw, Jazz (2016, December 21). Joe Mixon and when it's "okay to punch a woman." Hotair.com. Retrieved from http://hotair.com/archives/2016/12/21/joe-mixon-and-when-its-okay-to-punch-a-woman/

Watson, B. (2010, January 30). A hidden crime: Domestic violence against men is a growing problem. Daily Finance.

Whitson, S. (2009, September 30). Backhanded compliments and angry smiles: Passive aggression defined. Psychology Today. Retrieved from http://www.psychologytoday.com/blog/passive-aggressive-diaries/200909/backhanded-compliments-and-angry-smiles-passive-aggression-d

Witkin, G. (1991). The female stress syndrome: How to become stress-wise in the '90s. New York, New York: Newmarket Press.

How Women Get Laid and Paid:
A Socio-Historical and Political Analysis

PREFACE

On July 27, 2016 Democratic Presidential nominee Hillary Clinton became the first woman to ever get the nomination of a major political party. After it was announced, she said, by satellite, "I can't believe we just put the biggest crack in that glass ceiling yet!" That glass ceiling should have never been there in the first place because women have been running shit all the time, but were just forced to keep it under wraps because men are so bitch-like and thin-skinned. And the "crack" that these women used to gain power was the one between their legs. Historically, women have been able to "get laid and paid." This book provides evidence and examples.

Just as a footnote, that "glass ceiling" that Hillary thought was cracked fell in on her ass. The blatant and overwhelming sexism and gender bias that permeates America caught up with her. Cowardly white men, even the Russian leader Vladimir Putin, showed their dicklessness and teamed up against her. Trump was caught making statements about grabbing women by their pussies and America STILL forgave him. He stalked her on stage during the third debate and these Americans still overlooked his actions. The white woman may be in power, but she is not in control: the white man, the new demi-god, is going to make sure of that.

In the 1960 movie "The Facts of Life," two married people are having an affair. They have not yet agreed to tell the people they are married to, but the woman (Kitty, played by Lucille Ball) has brought it upon herself to leave her husband by good-bye note. Later, as she and her lover Larry Gilbert are headed for their hideaway cabin for a three-day weekend, she tells Larry about it. In the 1996 movie, "A Strange Affair," Judith Light says at one point to her daughter: "Every wife has to invent her own life."

These two examples of two ways that white people have created a "new normal" and in doing so, despite the male façade, have handed the power, the money and the family over to the female. Although he is all for it, that is not really the issue.

The issue is for you to see how many women have always and continue, to make major decisions based on what they want and how they figure things and then impose it on the male. Kitty did it twice: once to her husband with the letter and then to Larry. Now he's in a "no choice" situation; she imposed her will on him and did what she felt was "best for them both." Recall the earlier statement: "The hand that rocks the cradle rules the throne."

This new-found confidence is long overdue and is perhaps best summed up in the lyrics from Alicia Keys' 2008 hit, "Superwoman." In part, it goes something like this:

Everywhere I'm turning
Nothing seems complete
I stand up and I'm searching
For the better part of me
I hang my head from sorrow
State of humanity
I wear it on my shoulders
Gotta find the strength in me

I am a Superwoman
Yes I am
Yes she is
Even when I'm a mess
I still put on a vest
With an S on my chest
Oh yes
I'm a Superwoman

For all the mothers fighting
For better days to come
And all my women, all my women sitting here trying
To come home before the sun

And all my sisters
Coming together
Say yes I will
Yes I can
I am a Superwoman
Yes I am
Yes she is

… When I'm breaking down
And I can't be found
And I start to get weak
Cause no one knows
Me underneath these clothes
But I can fly
We can fly, ooh
I am a Superwoman …

But there's another side. In the same movie mentioned earlier, the goodbye note that she left for her husband. She flies back home to take it back but he's already there. He comes in and he's having a drink. The child is crying in the other room but before she goes to see about it, she asks her husband, who has the envelope with the note in it still sealed, to toss it in the fireplace. She goes into the other room to check on the child and this trick does just that: he doesn't open it to see what it says, he just blindly tosses it on the fire.

Superwoman. Gettin' laid and getting' paid. And with all that power and influence can still whine, cry and lie with the best of them.

So just as women manipulate situations and dominate without being "dominative," men are childlike thralls and, for the sake of pussy, do just about anything to get themselves a "girlfriend," "a woman," "a fiancée" and then of course the final scam, "a wife.

This philosophic scenario fits women and their roles in setting up, maintaining and controlling relationships, by way of getting "laid and paid," like a glove.
Not a few people have heard the maxim, "When life gives you lemons, make lemonade." This is supposed to encourage people to be optimistic and have a "go get 'em attitude" about whatever it is they are pursuing. This saying is the perfect way to describe the philosophies of most women when it comes to "getting laid and getting paid." And I'm going to explain to you how I arrived at this conclusion.

Take the concept of lemons and use the word "sperm" instead. In this book I will discuss the sexual tango that goes on between men and women but for the most part the aim and intention of "dating" and this kind of thing is to have sex.

Women view sex differently than men do. In my view they view a potential mate as being more than just a sex partner; they are looking for some kind of financial assistance. That's why they ask you where you work, who you work for, and other questions related to your financial situation. Most, not all of them do this by the time you've gone on your second "date."

A woman who is young and just out for orgasms is one thing. But when they get older they begin to understand how serious relationships are supposed to be as it relates to how their friends and family will view them and also in regard to their future. So now we go back to the adage: when life provides you with a man (or men) who want to screw you, and you find one that has economic potential, then "make lemonade." Translate that sperm into a pregnancy. In many cases she makes the right decision – for her. And once that decision is made, she will figure out a way to impose it on YOU.

By the time most men realize the historical tendency of women getting laid and paid and how, even though held back with gender bias, glass ceilings and sex role socialization, women have seized control of the relationship. They do it with their vaginas, with the mythology and social pressure that surrounds family and sexual relationships, and with the uncanny ability to take over and control family budgets. They have even so mastered the system that they have pussy whipped their white male partners into passing legislation that gives them half of your shit during a divorce and in some cases, entitles them to it even if you are not married to them.

Getting laid and getting paid.

How do little girls learn how to suck dick, trick men into giving them money, take it up the ass when necessary and of course, master the straight fuck? From their mothers, where else? Many learn in the streets of course. But the curiosity is raised by what they see at home. In the day and age of the single mother, young girls grow up seeing their mothers looking and smelling good and then going out on dates. They see men come into the house for long and not-so-long periods of time as the 'boyfriend.'

These are the only logical ways to figure how it is, from one generation to the next, women continue to get over on men one way or another. There is however, yet one more constant variable in this formula regarding how women get laid and paid. And that is the "social psychology" of the dating process, the game playing that goes on, and how easy it is to trap men, get them to pay for almost anything and then use that power to determine what role you want him (or them) to play in your life.

Generally speaking women learn about male desperation, gullibility and peer pressure. Here's how it works. And what they learn they pass on to their children, both boys and girls. But the fact is, there are two different sets of lessons that are imparted. And these divergent lessons come together as the child gets older and grows into adulthood, and at the end of those crossroads is one beneficiary: the female. It might not seem that way because of all the sexist articles in her way, but in the final analysis, no woman in her right mind would ever want to be a man (outside of the workplace, that is).

To begin with, boys learn from their mothers about what a "good woman" is. As part of this programming they are told that you never "hit" a woman, but very little is taught about what to do if a woman hits you. You're just supposed to take it. And you aren't supposed to let her pay for the dinner or the date and so on. The mother hands these tips down to her sons while she is teaching her daughters how to fight, exploit and take full advantage of any "sucker" that comes along. The more soft-spoken, dainty and submissive the boy is, the more the mother likes it.

Using their spoil-happy mothers as a model, the boys seek to find that type of treatment from and that type of person in person in a girl. Grown-ass men are often heard telling women, "that ain't how my mama would do it" and similarly infantile statements. That is one reason why the wife and the mother oftentimes bump heads: each sees the other as competition for this man who is being treated like a little boy by both of them.

Desperation begins to increase as increasing number of their male "buddies" have girlfriends, go on dates and start getting "hooked up." Then they learn how to compare stories and experiences, including the truth, some small lies and of course, the infamous "cock claiming" where they claim they fucked girls that they haven't. That reality is what leads to a number of conflicts, guy on guy and girl on guy. And it is as old as cockhounding itself.

In simpler terms, the peer pressure increases after the first piece of pussy and comparisons are made. Women know about it because they talk amongst themselves and their sisters, classmates and others talk about men and what it took to land one. Women share notes on men and as they get older, begin to see something universal among us: men are crude assholes who can be easily seduced by something that women carry around all the time: pussy.

Women grow not to respect us, although many of them will pretend as if they do, claiming for instance that they want "somebody like my daddy." Realizing that their father wasn't shit either (which is why they never saw him), they nevertheless have to have something to fall back on, lest their mother be deemed or perceived as a slut. So each generation protects the other one. And both have one thing in common: the low regard for the male species that, for some reason, seem to crave and obsess over this thing called "pussy."
After all, what's all this fuss about something that smells, something surrounded by hair, and something that serves no real use other than to get the man off, a factor that is negated by the fact that this same human hole is responsible for

impregnation which tends to tie a man down for no less than eighteen years? That's right: because of desperation and peer pressure, the man seeks out the very thing that is going to trap him and change his entire life. And then there's the issue of gullibility.

It is clear that men are gullible because we fall for the same old shit. We screw a girl and she tells us we are the greatest lover she ever had, that our dick is huge and that she can't resist us. After that she begins luring us into these public displays of affection which is the modern day version of the "brand." By brand I refer to the ways that farmers mark their cattle and other animals. They took a hot poker with initials or a design and tattooed it onto the animal's flesh. That then, was your "brand."

Today and in this case, there are several other types of "brands." The first of these is what I call "The first love tat." This is a tattoo that girls of today get on their arms, breasts, backsides and inner thighs in most cases, with the name of the boy who they "love" emblazoned across their skin. These dumb bitches think and act as if this is the "real deal" just because this guy might have claimed that he "loved" them. Now having had sex with him, they think he'll be around forever, but little do they know: he might not even remember her name the next day. The second form of brand is where women literally "mark their territory" the way gang members (and dogs) tend to do. One way women do it is through public displays of affection: walking up to you when you're with your pals and kissing you, walking down the hall holding hands, flashing the engagement ring you so foolishly purchased so you could get the pussy and so on. Despite their sister-like behavior toward one another, women do not trust each other when it comes to "their man."

By the time we realize that maybe she's not the one, it's too late. She's spread the necessary news and rumors to trap you. And it's about that time that you spot two, maybe three other girls who you would love to screw. But they already know about you and your "girlfriend." Many won't give a shit and will fuck you anyway. But remember this: when the dyad (a group of two) becomes a triad (a group of three) power relationships shift and there is always a tendency for danger on some level. You see it all the time, but on no more show displayed most vividly than the TV program "Snapped." And if you haven't seen it, I strongly suggest you watch it. You might learn something.

Let me close by saying this: I wrote this book to serve as a basis for discussion between men and women and whomever else. You cannot arrive at sane conclusions without someone being able to offer up some sane variables. *This emotion-laden screaming match type bullshit will no longer suffice.* This is a capitalist society, and what is capitalism? It is the ceaseless pursuit of profit. Not just money, not just a paycheck or a stipend, but PROFIT. And in my view women have been paying a huge price for the "profits" they've acquired over the years. We have hurt them emotionally, socially, culturally, physically and intellectually. All the while they were getting paid.

The bleeding has therefore been reciprocal.

Introduction

You took my kisses and you took my love
You taught me how to care
Am I to be just the remnant of a one-sided love affair?
All you took, I gladly gave
There's nothing left for me to save
All of me why not take all of me
Can't you see I'm no good without you
Take my lips I want to lose them
Take my arms I'll never use them
Your good bye left me with eyes that cry
How can I go on dear without you
You took the part that once was my heart
So why not take all of me.

"All of Me"
Ruth Etting, 1931

All of me. Although it was performed by a woman, two Jews – Seymour Simons and Gerald Marks – wrote the words and the music. This song should be re-named something like "The Trick's National Anthem" or "Confessions of a Turned Out John." All of me? For pussy? Come on, y'all. You know that for decades men have been begging for pussy as if it was lined with gold and women, seeing how desperate we were and how low we were willing to stoop just to get some "stank," decided to comply. But that is, after we pay for it with dates, flowers, candy, hotel rooms, trips and cruises, rent payments, car payments, a house and in many cases, a diamond ring that commits us to marrying her. Then and only then, are we promised to get all the pussy we want. But ask any married man: once you're married, you're lucky if you even SEE it once a month, let alone actually get it (that is, unless she's setting you up with a kid).

The fact is, men have been paying for sex and women have been selling it throughout recorded history. For the most part, these activities have been viewed and written about negatively, but it is fair to say that these negative views were put out there by men who were talking out of both sides of their mouths. On the one hand the talk is about morals and about not coveting other people's wives, while in real life, pussy was being purchased using everything from the bartering system and the offer of status to outright monetary exchanges.

How have women been able to get "laid and paid" all these years while appearing to be the victims of male chauvinism? First off, make no bones about it: they were victims. But much like a wolf that swallows a cobra, the results are going to be disastrous even though the wolf's belly is full. He's going to end up fuuuuuuuucked up! And so it has come to pass with the male-dominated, chauvinistic, misogynistic society that we all call the United States of America. The "state" of the female America is "united" when it comes to refusing to continue taking shit off of men. And men are just now beginning to pay for it.

But pay we will. And we will pay big time. Let me show you how by outlining what women "want in a man" based on a survey. The survey results and my analyses, follow.

THE MYTH OF THE "PRETTY GIRL'S CURSE"

The myth on the streets is that pretty girls lose out because they are so pretty that guys don't approach them because the assumption is that they are going to be vain or that they already have a man. This sounds logical but it's bullshit. This society is based on women and their overall physicality and as I point out later in this book on ugly women, any woman in America can get laid any time she wants to, no matter how she looks. But it is the image of "the pretty girl," popularized by television, film and magazines, that has so many young females feeling depressed and fucked up.

One of the biggest musical hits of all time was Roy Orbison's, "Pretty Woman." This 1964 hit described a man who was longing for this bitch, from beginning of the song to the end. His whole worldview was about trying to get this good looking woman to give him a chance. Following are the lyrics:

Pretty woman walkin' down the street
Pretty woman, the kind I like to meet
Pretty woman, I don't believe you
You're not the truth
No one could look as good as you
Mercy
Pretty woman, won't you pardon me
Pretty woman, I couldn't help but see
Pretty woman, and you look lovely as can be
Are you lonely just like me
Pretty woman, stop a while
Pretty woman, talk a while
Pretty woman, give your smile to me

Pretty woman, yeah, yeah, yeah
Pretty woman, look my way
Pretty woman, say you'll stay with me
Cause I need you
I'll treat you right
Come with me baby
Be mine tonight
Pretty woman, don't walk on by
Pretty woman, don't make me cry
Pretty woman, don't walk away
OK
If that's the way it must be, OK
I guess I'll go on home, it's late
There'll be tomorrow night
But wait, what do I see?
Is she walking back to me?
Yeah, she's walking back to me
O-Oh
Pretty woman

Pretty girl's "curse"? This hunk of bullshit is defined as a good looking woman not being able to get a lot of suitors because she is so fine that most men will assume that she has someone already and will bypass her for a woman who looks closer to "ordinary" or "attainable."

This myth says more about the people doing the pursuing than it does about the actual woman. To begin with, women know if they're fine or not. In fact, even ugly bitches think that if they slather on enough makeup, put on some false eyelashes, perhaps some contact lenses that make their eyes green, a wig or extensions. Some underalls and a pantyliner, a pushup bra, a super short micro skirt, and some "fuck me" pumps, they can land a man. And because men are so fucked up, in most cases they can do just that. It has nothing to do with "pretty" or "beauty" because beauty is in the eye of the beholder.j

But remember: so is "booty."

And that is what men pay for: pussy, not looks. Sure, looks help and the call girls that cater to a wealthy clientele look good as far as their faces are concerned. But white men are closet homoerotic assholes and they want their women's features to be tiny: small nose, no lips, flat asses, small breasts and so on. In that way they can pretend that they're having sex with a young girl. So it's the sexual desires of the men that enables women to get "laid and paid," not much else. Perhaps blonde hair doesn't hurt, but there are so many bitches dying their hair today there is no doubt in my mind that Clairol, Vidal Sassoon, L'Oreal, and Revlon – to name but a few – are making a virtual killing.

Where did the concept of a "pretty girl's curse" originate, one wonders? Who knows. More likely than not some loser – or a group of them – were having a hard time getting some pussy. So they came up with an excuse akin to that of the fox and the grapes. Remember that Aesop's fable? In case you don't, let me briefly recap:

> ONE hot summer's day a Fox was strolling through an orchard till he came to a bunch of Grapes just ripening on a vine which had been trained over a lofty branch. "Just the things to quench my thirst," quoth he. Drawing back a few paces, he took a run and a jump, and just missed the bunch. Turning round again with a One, Two, Three, he jumped up, but with no greater success. Again and again he tried after the tempting morsel, but at last had to give it up, and walked away with his nose in the air, saying: "I am sure they are sour." (Aesop, 2001).

In other words, since he couldn't reach them he had to convince himself that something must have been wrong with the grapes – instead of something being wrong with his abilities to reach them. So I believe this kind of failure created the "pretty girl's curse." And I only mention this because in this book on women "getting laid and paid," one might be led to believe that only the fine ones are benefiting. Let me tell you something.

Over the millennia, pussy is the only thing that never loses value. Women learned that a long time ago, even before capitalism was created. They also knew that men weren't about shit and were only good for physical labor, getting them pregnant, and menial chores. In the meantime, they (women) sat at home on their pussies and prepared food, cleaned the house and thought about just how stupid men, who seemed happiest when engaged in wars, bar room fights and other macho struggles, really were. And they waited and planned and have been getting "laid and paid" even before recorded history.

And this is taking place whether the woman is "pretty" or not.

THE TOP 20 TRAITS WOMEN WANT IN A MAN:
A SURVEY ANALYSIS

A March 11, 2016 article on MSN.com carried an article titled, "The Top 20 Traits Women Want in a Man." These "traits" as they called them (what they really meant was "characteristics" – only animals have "traits") are just the kinds of tendencies that enable women to control and further enhance their abilities to get "laid and paid."

These "traits" are rated by percentages based on how important they are as stated by the women themselves. I will address each of these, include the statements that were provided in the original article and then analyze those statements with my own evidence of the control mechanisms that truly show how women control men and in doing so, control their bank accounts of overall financial wherewithal.

These traits are broken down into four areas: character traits, personality traits, practical skills and physical characteristics. There are twenty (20) traits altogether and we are to gather that these traits, based on a survey, are what women want. Now I will break each down and show you the link between money, sex and female security. They all overlap but in American society we refer to this as "love" or "family life." Read and learn.

Top Character Traits: 1. Faithfulness 84%

More than 8 out of 10 women rated "faithful to me" in the top 10 attributes they find sexy in a man. A woman's tendency toward attachment is a biological imperative, a matter of raising offspring right. Reassure her (often) that you're not going anywhere.

This is been the way to ensure a long-term trick with money to take care of "the family," which translates to mean HER. The white man's system is so fucked up that he created sex role socialization where the man "goes out and does the work" and the woman "takes care of the home and the children." Little did this asshole know that while she was at home she was thinking and planning. And as technology became more sophisticated and accessible, she could learn new ways to stockpile money in the name of the children, have a bank account on the side, and lay guilt trips on his sorry ass when he loses his job or starts coming up short with her "allowance."

In order for any of this to have any impact on her wallet, the concept of being "faithful" must be widely circulated and accepted. But not because she gives a shit: it's because if he's out there fucking around, that means that HER money is going into some other woman's purse or pocketbook. She can never allow that. Women are close in a lot of things, but they don't trust other women around "their" men. A man who is unfaithful is a man who is unpredictable and in being un predictable, he is more difficult to control.

Top Character Traits: 2. Dependability 75%

Three out of four women say they look for a man who makes commitments and follows through. Being responsible—even if it's just remembering to pick up salad dressing on your way over to her place—sends a positive signal that someday you might commit.

Dependability is really tied with "faithfulness" in my book. In order for her to keep getting paid she has to be able to count on the man to come up with the money. That is why pussy whipping him is so important. She makes it look like he's talking her out of the pussy or that there's something about him that just turns her on, but these bitches know what they're doing: they know that as men, we are some simple muthafuckas. All she has to do is give us some pussy or some head and we lose our minds. The more and better she does it, the more spoiled we become. The more spoiled we become the easier it is for her to control us. And that control mandates that "dependability" means falling in line with the "men's responsibilities" which means "taking care of and supporting your family" which means taking care of HER.

Top Character Traits: 3. Kindness 67%

Young women may still fall for the bad-boy type, but more-mature women are turned on by kindness, because kindness inspires confidence. In other words, if you treat the waitress well, your date figures you'll treat her well, too.

Kindness? That's a very general term that could mean anything. If the woman wants to get knocked around during sex and the man wants her, he will comply. Is this therefore an act of kindness? Of course not – by most standards. But when these women in this survey were talking about kindness, pay close attention to the defining statement: if you treat your waitress well, your date figures you'll treat her well too. Notice that in the example money is exchanging hands, which means that what I am alleging is valid: marriage and dating are about prostitution. By tipping the waitress you are showing that you are willing to "pay for good service." Not only that, but she's checking out HOW you tip: do you have an attitude, do you complain, do you count every penny? Or do you flash a wad of green or an American Express card. These bitches are checking out every little gesture, movement and nuance and that's why and how they get "laid and paid."

Top Character Traits: 4. Moral Integrity 66%

Having the guts to tell the truth means to a woman that you have the guts to be a good, caring, decent partner over the long haul. White lies are okay; just avoid any that are tinged with gray.

Moral integrity? How can a bitch who wants to find a guy to take care of her have the gall to be concerned about moral integrity? The fact is that she is lacking in it, so she makes sure he has it. Why? Because that means he'll have bought into that whole "man take care of woman" bullshit that she is fishing for. If he's moral he'll buy into a number of other bullshit myths: "a man should never hit a woman," "a man pays for the dinner," "a man opens the woman's door," "a man lets the woman go first" and so on. The higher the moral integrity of the man, the better a trick he makes. Women know this. That's why preachers and ministers get over on so many bitches: women think these guys believe in the religion, but in reality they're pimps using the pulpit as their foundation.

According to the caption above you have to have the guts to tell the truth. That is bullshit. Women hate the truth. They want to be lied to if that lie jibes with what they are looking for. Tell them they look good when they look like shit; tell them that you'll take care of them no matter what – and so on.

And the racism implied about the "white lie" is just the white man's way of making it appear as if it's alright: a white lie is better than a black lie in Euroamerican culture. But a fabrication of the truth hurts no matter what it is. As the old saying teaches, "Dress a liar as you will, a liar is a liar, still."

Top Character Traits: 5. Fatherliness 51%

Being a good dad (or having the potential to become one) is about being a good role model—and about being patient and caring, qualities women like in a partner. If you're not a father, then tell her about your favorite niece or nephew, or the employee you're mentoring at work.

This is one of those "after the fact" traits where she's already set you up – you know – "accidentally" getting pregnant. This can happen before or during marriage but when she decides it's going to happen, trust me – she'll make it happen. And she sizes up the guys that she wants to be the fathers and "fatherliness" is only a minor consideration. You have to have a good job, not have any other children and be a sucka for that "one big happy family" bullshit.

Being a good role model for your child? She only uses that when she's pissed or she thinks you're going to leave her. Then if and when you leave, she will spend years dogging you out behind your back, making sure that the kids hate your fuckin' guts. The kids never ask "what in the fuck did you do to make him want to leave us"? You don't believe it? Turn on a pro game and listen to LeBron James, Dwyane Wade, and all those professional athlete whine about how their mother made them the men that they are.

And where did this woman learn about the importance of fatherliness? From her mother. And what did her mother tell her? She told her that men ain't shit and to be careful of them. When she brings you home to meet her family, watch how her mother looks at you as you shake her hand. First, she's measuring dick length, then your eyes to see if you might be a playa. After that she's making sure that she helps get you on board the "we are family" bandwagon, which makes you a trick for the whole family to game on and enjoy.

Top 5 Personality Traits: 6. Sense of Humor 77%

Being able to laugh at the stresses of this world is a must, according to the women on our panel. You get bonus points if you can make them laugh. Humor tells a woman that you can laugh at—read, handle easily—the many difficulties that life throws at you.

Yeah – being able to laugh will help you offset the reaction you get as you watch the bank account decrease little by little; or watch her continue to buy dresses and shoes that she saves for church or some other bullshit event; or as she continues to complain that you don't "touch her the way you used to" despite the fact that the bitch has gained 60 pounds and has TB – two bellies.

Sense of humor? Laughing at difficulties doesn't provide solutions to them. Cracking up at problems doesn't diminish their impact. Smiling, skinning and grinning don't stop her from doing what she wants to do if she has made up her mind to do it. And when she files for divorce and gets half your shit, all the jokes and wise cracks in the world ain't gonna get your snaps back.

Top 5 Personality Traits: 7. Intelligence 55%

A worldly, interesting man is a man she likes to show off. Men who are take-charge problem solvers make women feel secure, and men who are always improving are never boring.

This is bullshit. She wants an intelligent man to show off so that she can look good for her friends. Her friends will think that since he's so smart and he's with her, she must be a good catch. Other than that, the smarter you are the bigger the threat you are to her goal of getting laid and paid, more the latter than the former.

No matter how intelligent a man is the woman always has the advantage. And do you know why? She knows that no matter how many degrees you have, how high your IQ is or how accomplished you are, you must not be worth a shit or else you wouldn't be with her! She knows that with all that intelligence, for some reason she has something you need – or think you need. And it is that advantage that enables her to maintain the power in the relationship.

Top 5 Personality Traits: 8. Passion 46%

Why have women always melted for musicians? Because rock stars are passionate in public. Women like displays of passion because they're not accustomed to seeing them from men. Get passionate about something: kayaking, impressionistic art, barbecuing, or Habitat for Humanity. It's proof that you care for and about something beyond yourself.

Passion is the key to maintaining control – for HER. Your passion is going to be taken, twisted and shoved right up your ass. Oh sure you used to be a great musician. Oh sure, you used to be able to dunk backwards. Yeah, you used to be able to sit down and write an essay with the best of them. But her very presence and her goals of getting laid and paid are going to take that passion and twist it so that it works in HER image and interests.

The previous description says that being passionate about something is "proof that you care for and about something beyond yourself." And that is the target for her: reversing that trend so that the passion is not about the things you have interest in: it's about taking your interests and re-directing them at HER.

Top 5 Personality Traits: 9. Confidence 41%

A man who feels secure in his own skin makes the woman he's with feel secure. By showing you can handle unfamiliar people or situations, you tell the woman in your life that she need not fear, either.

This one is debatable. Women will answer any kind of way to make it appear as if they see men as human beings and respect them as such. Nothing could be further from the truth. Women see men the same way men see women: as commodities. This is a commodity society, one rooted in the market and in capitalism. You are one of two things: a tangible asset or a crippling liability. Women view men as both, and seek to turn them more into the former than the latter.

When it comes to a man with confidence, this works against the "laid and paid" ethic. A man with confidence won't fall for the bullshit lies, the fake orgasms and the "you sure have a big dick" falsehoods that we have been programmed to fall prey to. A man with confidence will first of all understand a key point that most men miss: anything worth having is worth studying first and foremost. You can understand what you want and what you are after once you understand the nature and essence of that "thing."

Women are not "things" but remember that we live in a commodity society which has men treating women as such in the same way that women treat men that way. Therefore you have to study and know yourself and work to enhance your skill set in the bedroom and socially. Once you do that, and you know what you can do, no one can come along and "flatter you" out of your bank account, money and life. A man who is truly confident is first of all confident in the fact that he knows things. If you know about women, this society, and the tendencies I am outlining in this book, then you can afford to be confident in the correct way.

What was described above in terms of confidence can be misconstrued. For instance, it states that, "By showing you can handle unfamiliar people or situations, you tell the woman in your life that she need not fear, either." Confidence is much more than what was just hinted at. It starts within and emanates outward, not the reverse. Women want to see if you can handle unfamiliar people and situations so that you can protect HER. It's a selfish definition for a woman to view men in this manner. We are more than bodyguards and off-duty cops; and any woman worth her salt is going to know how to protect herself in various situations. If not she's only setting herself up for dependency and abuse.

Top 5 Personality Traits: 10. Generosity 38%

This is more important to women over 35 than it is to those under that age. Generosity, however, doesn't just mean springing for dinner at a four-star. Your willingness to give your time and lend your ear is what women crave.

If this survey was real, this one would be ranked first. The old street saying teaches, "Catch a fool, bump his head." And men have been getting their heads "bumped" for centuries. A smile here, a batted over there, an "oops-I-didn't-mean-to-show-you-my-panties" curtsy and voila! We become their willing thralls.

An age-old maxim teaches, ""Generosity consists not the sum given, but the manner in which it is bestowed." But when it comes to women getting laid and paid the sum is more important than the manner. You've heard it time and time again: women, married or not, taking ass whippings and psychological abuse because the man buys them nice things, is paying the rent or the car note. The sum is very important in a capitalist society because it's when the elites are excluded and it comes down to male-female relationships, what you have left is a "zero-sum game." There simply are no real winners other than those at the top who are defining the game.

Generosity, in fact, is defined as, "the quality of being kind, understanding, and not selfish," and the "willingness to give money and other valuable things to others." If you do not view self as the basis of nation, then you are going to always be someone's stooge. The greatest number is number one and number one should be you. That's what makes you want to help people because as the Bible teaches, ""To those whom much is given, much is expected." So you believe in yourself and you use your skills and gifts to help other people – not allow them to help themselves TO you.

And here's the key to the definition provided above when it comes to male generosity: "Your willingness to give your time and lend your ear is what women crave." Giving your time and lending your ear are the keys to the female assessing or evaluating just how gullible you are and how many resources you have. The more time you give the more money you spend – on HER. The more you listen, the more lies she is set to tell, usually a sob story or some myth about how she "hasn't been with anyone for years." All setting you up to let down your guard and to place your common sense on the back burner. Before you know it you're having sex with her and she's paving the way for finding out how generous you are in bed. But even if you're not, if you are willing to spend and invest money and time, she's got you hooked.

Top 5 Practical Skills: 11. Listening 53%

Pay attention. A woman feels safe and secure when she knows her man will put down his BlackBerry and listen to her. Magic words: "I'm here. Tell me everything."

This one is an extension of the "generosity" principle that I just described. This is the key to the game plan: the more you listen the more you learn. But the fact is, what you may be learning could be bullshit. But the bullshit is based on the stereotypical views that you may already have and hold about women.

Listening is an art. There is regular listening – which is what far too many of us males do and that's how we end up getting bamboozled. But then there is "mindful listening," like the kind that I do. Some people say that I am "too analytical," but in my view, there can be no such thing. This is my life and if I'm going to let anyone else in, I'll decide who it will be. This goes back to what I said earlier about the importance of study. I try to teach my children the same thing. As an adult who went through what most kids go through, what I've learned is that you look at what people produce, not what they say. People will say anything, and that is why mindful listening is so important. But if they produce something, it is an indicator of what they are about, what they believe and what they have the ability to do.

This seems to be the way women think. They want a man who is industrious, and that means willing to bring home a paycheck. That's why women accept a man who is an idiot, works a menial job or degrades himself at work. In the case of black people, that's why so many intelligent and conscious sistahs marry some of the biggest sellouts and Uncle Toms there are: the money is more important than the consciousness or character of the man they married. They don't care what he is producing on the outside – even if he produces nothing – as long as he brings home a paycheck and takes care of her needs and wants. It's called marriage – deal with it.

If you're smart, you'll do some serious listening. Women run their mouths all the time, and the more secure they feel about the amount of control they think they have over you, the more they are bound and prone to talk. This is not to say that they don't have secrets: every single one of them does. And on earth, there's at least one other bitch who knows that secret. Therefore if you listen closely enough not only will she run her mouth, but when she gets angry, that's when the REAL truth comes forward. Some of them have discipline and can control their mouth because they learned, from their mothers, that "loose lips sink ships." But for the most part when a woman wants someone to "listen," it's a key to the control mechanism: she wants you to know something for a financial reason. And even if the reason is a personal or intimate one, in the final analysis it comes down to money. Because if it didn't, she wouldn't be trusting you and telling you in the first place!

Top 5 Practical Skills: 12. Romancing 48%

Romance appeals to a woman's right-brained, less-logical side. Every woman fantasizes about being swept off her feet. Romance is bold because you're displaying your desire for a woman and revealing a softer, more vulnerable side that women find irresistible.

We live in America so I'm going to deal with this "romantic" bullshit that has been promoted throughout American popular culture. Even now the white man and his negro lackeys are having what are called "play dates" for their young sons and daughters, having them play together and go out on fun time dates. This paves the way for the "romance scam" that translates into major income for American businesses.

"Romance" is defined by the Merriam-Webster dictionary as, "Ardent emotional attachment or involvement between people; love." In my dictionary of life I define it as, "the process of spending a lot of money on the person you hope to fuck." That's what it boils down to and it's done through another concept known as "the date."

What is a date? It's turning a trick. If you're a guy, you're spending money on a woman hoping to get in her panties. If you're a woman, you're looking for a guy to take you to concerts, dinner, or to otherwise spend money to expand your social horizons. In 2016 America when you say "I used to date him/her," what that means is that you used to FUCK them. You went out and when the time was deemed right, you got the pussy or the dick (in America, it could be both). Therefore as I view it, "Romancing" the woman is paying for her attention and then based upon her assessments and evaluations, taking her to bed. She will determine how much "romancing" it will take to move beyond the initial sex act.

The previous explanation about "romance" makes the claim that, "Romance is bold because you're displaying your desire for a woman and revealing a softer, more vulnerable side that women find irresistible." Bold? Romance, if anything, is the prelude to what I call "the sucker assessment." You show attention and she decides if you can move on from there. On the streets it's called "choosing." Any man who thinks he "chose" the woman he's with is a damn idiot. They choose the time, the place and the person. They decide when you'll fuck them, how you'll do it, how much money you'll spend before you fuck them and if and when you get to fuck them again. Welcome to America.

When the definition says that romancing reveals a "softer, more vulnerable side that women find irresistible," what they should be saying is that romance shows the degree of how weak-minded you are and how big of a sucka you will be. Romancing in America is linked to spending money, plain and simple. If you're a cheapskate or don't flash that cash, most women won't give you the time of day no matter how "cute" you might be or how big your dick is. Back in the day there may not have been such business-oriented tendencies. But that was during a time when there were a lot more black men around. Today, when you subtract the ones who are locked up, dead, dying from some disease, taking it up the ass (homosexuality) or who are on the downlow, that translates to mean "slim pickin's" for the sistahs. So they have to roll the dice and put family and personal security over good looks and a dick. "Romance," in such a context, is nothing more than icing on the cake of "financial security" that most women seek and crave.

Top 5 Practical Skills: 13. Being Good in Bed 35%

A woman knows that a man who takes care of her in bed will take care of her out of bed. Your enthusiasm for her body is more important than your sexual prowess.

This is one of the keys to the colors of how women get "laid and paid." The bedroom is the arena that you step into once you've passed some of the "tests" that I've outlined in this short book. Let me explain.

Being "good in bed" is something that men are going to have to master even before they get pussy. You are going to have to study the female body, study social customers and learn how to apply them to your concrete needs. You are going to have to find out something about that woman, even if it means studying her astrology sign. I don't subscribe to spookism but astrology does have some accuracy and gives you a basic foundation on learning the characteristics of a person born during a certain time of the year. I'm going to tell you: it's worked for me in as much as it let me know what kind of woman I was dealing with. Sometimes I was wrong; many times, I was right.

If you've learned what I just suggested, it doesn't matter who the woman is. They're all built the same. The only difference is the previous experiences they may have had. And let me tell you something: most of the ones out there are damaged goods because of US. That's right: show me a cute woman who is available and I'll show you somebody who had a boyfriend early in life, got dogged and dismissed and it bitter as hell. And you are going to inherit that bitterness because to her, all men are the same. This is where being good in bed comes in.

Most women know that men crave pussy. Therefore they spend a lot of time dolling themselves up and showing you just enough to let you want to see more. That's why the hems are going up, that's why the thong bikini draws are the rage, and that's why many of them have their breasts hanging out. They want to get dicked because most of their friends are. But first come the wine-and-dine rituals that I outlined earlier. But once you get her to give up the pussy, you have to be prepared to do to her what her previous man may not have done: you have to give her an orgasm.

Back in the old days women didn't seem to give a shit. They wanted dick and that was about it. But in today's America, these bitches will take it up the ass, give up head and lick your balls just to "turn you out" and make you the kind of man that they can use. If they don't cum, they'll either fake it or act as if it doesn't matter. If you've gotten to the point where you've shown them a good time on a date or where they see you as a marketable commodity (read: someone who has or will get a good job) then they'll tolerate you fucking up in the bed.

Two points about the previous definition. The first is where it makes the claim that, "A woman knows that a man who takes care of her in bed will take care of her out of bed." It is up to the woman to determine if she's been "take care of in the bed" or not. Some of them are cum freaks and want to have as many orgasms as they can because they don't plan on seeing you again or they don't plan on you getting the pussy any time soon. Some of them just open their legs, act as sperm spittoons, and then let you get off so that they (the woman) can get on about the business of figuring out what role you'll play in the days ahead.

The fact of the matter is a woman who thinks a man that takes care of her in bed will take care of her out of bed is falling prey to the scam run by most playas and pimps. Those of us who have learned the art and science of mastering a woman's body know how to deal with it in the bed just like we can talk a woman into the bed by saying the right words. We have been doing it for centuries, and while they may fall for it when they're young, once we've gotten what we want, the next guy who comes along is going to pay a huge price. At any rate, compliments in bed should never be confused with achievements in life.

The second point lies in the claim that, "Your enthusiasm for her body is more important than your sexual prowess." Wrong, again. All enthusiasm leads to is premature ejaculation, let's face it. And as for "sexual prowess," unless you're an athlete, by the time you turn 55 that shit has diminished (as has your interest in her for the most part). Enthusiasm that leads to sex is like buying a new car: once you drive it off the lot the value decreases by fifty percent! In like manner, once you get the pussy, the thrill is gone in many cases. Don't get me wrong: you might want to get it again. *But after that first time, all the time, energy and money that was spent on getting it weighs in on how you view having gotten it and whether or not you think it's worth hanging around for after that first time.*

Top 5 Practical Skills: 14. Cooking, Cleaning, etc. 23%

Self-sufficiency means you're not going to expect her to be like your mother. Learn how to make one or two killer breakfasts or dinners, and you'll win her heart.

This is a good practical skill, one that I tried to inculcate into the minds of my sons. But be careful: one woman's "practical man" is another woman's reason to be a lazy bitch. The fact is women have been programmed by their mothers (especially black woman whose mothers actually worked) to keep a clean house, know how to cook and know how to be "a good housewife." In many circles this thinking still exists today, especially in the South. And many of today's men, as gluttonous as ever, continue to look for a woman who is "like my mamma."

Unfortunately for single black mothers, too many of them have raised these effeminate ass boys, known today as "mitches." These muthafuckas act just like bitches, from wearing two earrings and having their "hair did" to skinny jeans. These kids of dudes aren't looking for someone who is going to motivate them to be independent men; these "guys" are a new breed and as such, if they do any cooking and cleaning it's going to be in their bachelor pads as they play the field with women as well as men. The art and science men knowing how to sew, cook, and clean is a thing of the past. Many of them know how to braid but that's only because a lot of them have been locked up and learned how to do that to earn money and keep Bubba's dick out of their ass.

Top 5 Practical Skills: 15. Earning Potential 21%

One in five women surveyed said a man's successfulness in his career contributes to his sexiness. If you've demonstrated talent, goal achievement, and follow-through, you give women confidence that you will be a good provider.

Whoomp! There it is! Earning potential is an essential key to how these women get laid and paid. Their concerns? "Where you work at?" "How much you make?" "Who you work for"? "You gon' buy me a drink or what?" "What kinda car you got?" "You married?" Of course I'm talking about the sistahs because that's what I know. But white bitches, though the vernacular may be different, put their white men through the same "paces."

Now let's get to the "commodification" of human beings that I talked about earlier.

The previous quote claims that, "One in five women surveyed said a man's successfulness in his career contributes to his sexiness." This statements speaks volumes. How can a career contribute to a man's "sexiness" unless that career is generating enough money to take this woman wherever it is she wants to guy, feed her and otherwise give her a lifestyle that she feels like she deserves? If he does all that, then he can prematurely ejaculate all he wants to! The fact is, it is the "career" and that hard work the contributes to men's sexual dysfunction as they get older, and she knows that. But as the jewelry and status increases, so do the lies about how "great" he is in the bed, whether it's true or not. And in fact, a growing number of these "happy women" sleep in separate beds and in many cases separate bedrooms.

As Simmel wrote in his book *The Philosophy of Money*, "money is the ultimate confounding of things." What he means is that money can make the puny look large, the weak look strong, the ugly look attractive and so on. Now add that to the definition that was supplied above: "If you've demonstrated talent, goal achievement, and follow-through, you give women confidence that you will be a good provider." The key word is "provider" – one who provides what? Not dick. Not pussy licking. These are just the ersatz manifestations. She wants a house, a car that will make her neighbors jealous, and kids that she can use to set you up at a later date and a nice bank account that she has access to.

This then, is what "earning potential" has come to mean when it comes to men and women in America.

Top 5 Physical Attributes: 16. Sense of Style 30%

The way you dress reflects on the woman you're with, and she knows it. The man who knows how to match a patterned shirt and tie will notice when she's dressed well, too. (And maybe he'll pay for the Blahniks.) Keep your tailor and your dry cleaner busy, and spring for posh, touchable fabrics like cashmere, suede, pima cotton, and brushed corduroy.

This is some of that "clothes make the man" bullshit that white boys, mainly Jews (who control the garment industry) helped to promote back in the day and it still holds as a constant belief in 2016. The only problem with the belief is that it is only partially true.

As I see it, the way the man is perceived is what makes him and as a result, it doesn't matter if he has on a Hart Schaffner and Marx double-breasted suit or a pair of jeans and a t-shirt. Black men in America are the sharpest dressers on the planet and what has it gotten them? Very little other than token jobs, prison and a few white bitches. One of the richest men in the world is Warren Buffett and he is also one of the slouchiest. Do you think that when he walks in a room with that undeserved "Oracle of Omaha" moniker that people give a shit what brand of suit he's wearing?

And one more thing: numerous millions of women have been duped by sharp-dressing men who weren't worth a shit. Look at these black ministers – they wear nice suits and they are nothing more than pimps in the pulpit. Look at drug dealers: brand name clothes up and down, jewelry and the like – and most of them are no-talent wannabes who may also be borderline faggots. Clothing is one way that men have been able to dupe women, just like an average woman with a mini-skirt, some pumps and some fishnets can land just about any man. Clothing is external and subjective.

If style were power, black men in America would be running the world. But it is not – it is a pacification tool that benefits those who make the clothes (and we know who that is). Being clean is one thing, but donning an expensive suit so that you can impress some woman is not a good idea: she grows to expect this all the time which means you have to keep on doing it. Now you're spending money to impress her and that's in addition to the money you're spending on trying to get her.

I've learned that real style is mental. If you have personality and charm, people will remember you no matter what you have on. Keep that in mind.

Top 5 Physical Attributes: 17. Handsome Face 26%

The science of attraction, which has been studied ad infinitum, says it's all about symmetry. Imagine you have a dotted red line (Nip/Tuck style) vertically through the center of your face, down your nose. Are your features similar in form and arrangement on both sides of the line? Do your eyes and ears match up? The closer one side mirrors the other, the more attractive you are. Women in cross-cultural studies have also ranked men with broad chins, high cheekbones, and large eyes as the most attractive. Best way to improve your looks: Smile more, and make certain your sideburns are even.

Handsome face? This makes some sense. I've read a number of studies that show that physically attractive people fare better in life and at the workplace than those who just look average or who are downright physically unattractive. But my concern here are the descriptors that were just provided, so let's break them down, interject the variable of race, and then see how the shoe fits.

According to the previous paragraph, "Women in cross-cultural studies have also ranked men with broad chins, high cheekbones, and large eyes as the most attractive." According to my research, although the sources are dubious at best, I found that South Asians, Indians (from India), Pakitsanis, Arabs and Armenians, south Europeans (meaning Italians and Greeks) and Sub-Saharan Africans) (Yahoo Answers, 2016). None of these groups are the "typical" white folks in America which, as we know, are mixed up with some of everything.

Here's some evidence based on what I've heard: white women have a saying that they want their men to be tall, DARK and handsome. Why is "dark" in there and what do they mean? Do they mean olive skinned like a lot of Italians of Middle Eastern guys? Or do they mean black men? Judging from the way they clamor for black men, from the rich black guys to the young black men who many of them cruise the ghetto for (while their husbands are at work), one has to wonder.

And here's one more thing: take note that while a quarter of the women sampled rated "handsome face" as a top priority, this doesn't mean anything in capitalist America. Look at all the ugly muthafuckas that have fine women: look at all the beat up old white boys who have fine younger women. Case in point: Donald Trump, Michael Douglas, Phil Jackson, George Bush and so on. They make it a point to attract women who look fairly good to take attention off of their own ugliness. But one thing they all have in common: money and power, and that's all the average bitch cares about. After all, she can always "rent" a cabana boy on the side if she needs to, right?

Top 5 Physical Attributes: 18. Height 15%

Tall, dark, and handsome isn't the be-all and end-all. Women say they like feeling smaller than their men, but height doesn't necessarily mean might. They will feel comfortable as long as they aren't towering over you.

The average male height in the United States is 5'9". Some women have a height requirement because many of them link height to dick length. I don't know if this is accurate enough. Some say it's the size of a man's hands or the length of his fingers. But one thing is for sure: if you're tall and broke, you can hang it up.

Based on the previous definition there is a point that I want to fine-tune; that is where it is written that, ". Women say they like feeling smaller than their men, but height doesn't necessarily mean might." Women aren't dumb – despite the century long attempts by a male dominated society to make them think that they are. They know that if a man is tall he is going to let his guards down once he sees that the woman is shorter. I believe that a lot of these guys that you see on television on shows like "Snapped", the ones lying in caskets, were white boys who were taller than their woman but who let their guard down, started acting real macho and got a cap busted in their ass.

And one last point: no matter how much a man "towers" over a woman vertically, he should remember that a pussy can stretch enough to produce a small human being larger than a good sized watermelon. So all this "I got a big dick" shit falls deaf on the ears of the woman who knows better. Towering over her when you're standing up is immediately nullified when you lie down with her and see how easy it is for your dick to slip in. Feel me?

Top 5 Physical Attributes: 19. Muscular Build 13%

Spend more time with the bathroom mirror and less time with the gym mirror. Nearly three times as many women value a clean-shaven face over the clean and jerk. Muscles help ward off rivals and assure a woman that you won't drop her during a dip, but your overall appearance is more important than the size of your biceps.

As is the case with height, all those muscles don't mean shit to the woman who knows what she's doing.

Take for example, those assholes that take steroids and get testosterone injections. Their balls swell up the size of peas. They might have huge thighs, large chests and great abs, but when it comes to fuckin' they just don't measure up. Women know this shit. When men are young they have fairly muscular builds, but the thing that gets them over on women is the woman's naiveté. But once she starts getting dicked and begins to incorporate the strategies and tactics that she learned from her mama and her girlfriends, those male muscles are only good for two things: lifting groceries and toting them to the kitchen and showing off to her girlfriends to make them jealous.

Top 5 Physical Attributes: 20. Fitness 12%

Women recognize a good body as indicative of a man of discipline and self-control. It tells a woman you can keep up with her, in bed and out.

Being physically fit may or may not have anything to do with muscular build when it comes to men and women. Being in shape translates to mean that you can fuck for a long time. It means that your blood vessels are in good shape and the blood can get directly to your dick or your pussy. I know: the commercials try to make it look like it's more than that but I'm telling you the facts. All those white boys and negroes on the movies doing all this hour long fuckin' is bullshit, and they know it.

Look at what the definition says: "Women recognize a good body as indicative of a man of discipline and self-control. It tells a woman you can keep up with her, in bed and out." But that works two ways. If they see someone who has an average body, many women know he can be controlled. A growing number of women don't even like getting fucked for a long time or, for that matter, don't want big dicks stuck in them. Maybe this is the way it always was, but in our youth culture, we measured sexual pleasure by what we were able to do and what we wanted when we were in our teens and our twenties. I'm not really sure.

But what I *am* sure of is that recognizing a body as a sign of discipline or self-control may not be what you think. If a woman sees a man with what she sees as a good body, she may be targeting him for a pregnancy set up. All women want healthy children and if you're in shape, then you attract someone of the same type. Fat bitches know they can't get muscular dudes, although large numbers of them move on skinny guys. In that way the child will average out to be normal in size. I'm just sharing with you what I've observed among the men and women I've seen in the cities I've lived in.

Keeping up with her in bed is important. According to one website, the recent spate of white men working out, jogging, going to the gym and so on may be at attempt to compensate for lack of dick length. Chancellorfiles (2006) makes the following claim:

> Blacks have larger penises than whites, and whites have larger penises than oriental Asians. All of the other racial groups' and ethnic groups' penis sizes fall on the same level as whites. On one extreme blacks of African descent and black Africans have the largest penises in the world, and on the other extreme oriental Asians have the smallest penises. Whites and all other non-white racial groups have medium size penises thus putting them in the middle between Blacks and Asians (Chancellorfiles, 2006).

There are one billion Asians on the planet meaning that dick length ain't got shit to do with potency. It's about diet and effort, and apparently they have plenty of that. The bruthas with the big dicks are sticking them in each other's ass or so it appears and they learn that from prison and from their mother's spoiling them and turning them into "mitches" when they're young. Their fathers aren't around because too many of them are on the downlow or out chasing some white bitch.

There you have it. How bitches get "laid and paid" based on the words that come out of their mouths. But there's more. Let us now look at *motive and psychological intent*, which I believe lies in the concept of "misandry" – the hatred of men, which is a response to the fucked up way that male dominated societies have mistreated women over the centuries.

SIGNS THAT A MAN IS BAD IN BED

Women have always known the difference between what they want, what they need and what they can tolerate. If they have to fake orgasms or tell an idiot that he has a big dick, they'll do it. Why? Because they have a goal in mind, and that goal involves long-term stability on some level. Even if they don't plan on keeping this particular guy around, he'll make do for now until a better one (read: more money) comes along.

In a 2014 article titled, "The Male Bad in Bed List," Coeli Carr offered up some signs that a man is bad in bed. I am going to share those with you and then analyze them based on how they relate to women "getting laid and getting paid.

Large Waist

In other words, fat. Medically speaking, a man who is fat usually has health problems. According to the article,

> Large waist
> Bigger is not always better. "By consensus, men with a 40-inch or larger waist size are generally defined as having metabolic syndrome," says Irwin Goldstein, MD, director of sexual medicine at Alvarado Hospital in San Diego, and clinical professor of surgery at University of California, San Diego. "Metabolic syndrome increases the risk for morbidity, diabetes, high cholesterol, hypertension, vascular disease -- and also erectile dysfunction … (Carr, 2014)

You who I blame: *black men.* Sure, these women we marry believe that if they feed us well, they'll keep us. Their mothers told them that, "The way to a man's heart is through his stomach." That was bullshit. The way to HER heart is through HER stomach, which is why these bitches are always "sampling" what they cook: take a little bite of this, and a bite of that. What was once an hour glass figure transforms into a hefty bag in no time flat. And the same thing goes for us.

For the hard working man, even we have been fat at times. We might work in a foundry where the heat is mover 100 degrees, construction or the railroad, but when we get home, there's those muthafuckin' chitlins staring at us: beans and rice, gumbo over rice, big chunks of steak and pork chops. So we get fat and we sleep a lot. She's already landed what she wanted: a husband with a job. So she's satisfied.

How could so many men have diabetes unless we got it from these bitches? They're the ones preparing the genetically altered shit being farmed and grown by these god damn red neck farmers! These women care more about coupons and sales than they do about calories and health. Of course, as I say, you can't force someone to do something if they don't want to do it. But these women can get us to do anything with the threat of pussy hanging in the air. If they said, "eat healthy or no more pussy," black men would look the way we looked back in the 1960s when we got together and played pickup basketball and flag football, rain or shine. The white man saw that, imitated it, poisoned us with drugs and then opened up "health spas" that he makes sure we can't afford to get into.

Also in regard to the waist, the author writes that,

> "The connection between a man's large girth and erectile dysfunction is low testosterone, says Goldstein. "If a man has enough testosterone, then stem cells, which are present in all the organs, can be converted into muscle," he says. "If his testosterone level is low, stem cells will convert into fat."The most synergistic remedy is typically lifestyle change, along with testosterone administration, if indicated, says Goldstein. (Carr, 2014)
>
> '

Unless that "lifestyle change" also includes dietary changes, you can forget it. As for that testosterone, that's what fucked us up in the first place. The craving for pussy is what made us susceptible to the lies that these women tells us. Feeding our ego about how "good" we look or perform in bed. And we start spending that money and to make it look good, she might spend a few bucks as well. But with her, any expenditures are a long term investment in HER future. After that comes the, "guess what honey? I'm pregnant." Now you're hooked for 18 years. And as she gets bigger, she makes sure you do, too. In Biblical terms, "fatback begats fat, jack."

Next is something called a "claw hand." Check it out:

Claw Hand

What does a claw hand have to do with being able to fuck? Well, according to this article by Carr, the following is the explanation:

> Claw hand
> Can't high five? "Men who can't flatten their fingers and spread them may also have problems with excessive scarring in the wall

of the erection chambers of their penis, which results in curvature
of the erection," says Goldstein. "These men are often incapable of
shaking hands or grasping objects." (Carr, 2014).

This is why I have issues with these white people and their "sexual analyses." Take note that the author writes that people who can't flatten their fingers and spread them "MAY also have problems with excessive scarring in the wall of the erection chambers of their penis." How? Prove it. If it is a fact, then instead of saying that it "may" be the case, it should be WILL be the case.

At any rate, an attempt at an explanation by the author follows:

Goldstein says that the conditions, called Dupytren's contracture,
are often seen in men with Peyronie's disease. "Both are metabolic
disorders of connective tissue -- there's difficulty in stretching the
thick tendons in the hands or penis" … Because claw hand is a
systemic condition, both hands are typically affected, says
Goldstein. "Fortunately, pending FDA approval, there's a remedy
in the wings: Collagenase, an enzyme which can digest excess
collagen and can be injected into the erection chamber's thickened
walls to decrease penile curvature." (Carr, 2014).

I have issues with Jews when it comes to anything medical. It seems to me, having researched what they do as a group, there is a tendency to promote anything that directs people toward purchasing medications or getting operations of some kind. It is already a fact that the Israelis have worked out a way to manipulate the genetic codes so that DNA can be distorted or "altered," and now we have this. The claim is that "connective tissue" is the key and the question I have is this: does this apply to ALL humans or just the white folks that these people tend to use in their theoretical constructs? I have already proven over the years that medicine is "racialized" and that indeed, we are NOT all the same under the skin.

So if that is the case, then who is Goldstein talking about? Other Jews? White folks? How could it pertain to everybody when diet and surroundings impact one's physicality? Are Asians impacted the same way? And then he has a "remedy" already in mind even though most of his concepts are theoretical: "hey, just by some of this and you'll get a boner." I say don't trust any doctors any further than you can throw them. They get paid to promote certain medications to their patients, and we all know the history of Jews and their orientation toward "profit at any expense." Their "clawed hand" seems to always be draped around the cash register button or a wad of bills.

Short Arms

Short arms? Again, this Jewish doctor seems to be engaging in what real social researchers refer to as an "ecological fallacy." If you think the "clawed hand" was weird sounding, check out his explanation of being good in bed and having short arms:

> Men whose long-sleeved shirts fall way past their fingers may be in for a shock. "Longer measurements from men's underarms to the tips of their middle fingers are statistically associated with long-sized penile erections," says Goldstein, editor-in-chief of The Journal of Sexual Medicine and co-author of When Sex Hurts, Generally, he says, an erect penis is about five-and-a-quarter inches long. When it is longer than that, the arms will be longer, too. Unfortunately, the opposite is also true, he says, noting, however, that for many partners, size is not the most important issue. (Carr, 2014).

His measurements of the length of an erect penis is collected by taking averages of the dick lengths of the majority of men in this country who are, after all, white. Just the fact that you've got people measuring other men's dicks is in itself fucked up; but now they want everybody to think that they have shrunken dicks just because the white man's is. By the white man's own mythology and social statements, black men's penises are larger. So if we can establish that the statistics on dick length are skewed toward white men, then why shouldn't we further conclude that the findings in the "Journal of Sexual Medicine" and the findings in Goldstein's book, When Sex Hurts, are equally as biased? In fact, the reason why sex probably hurts is because the white man realizes that he has a shrunken dick! Ever think about that?

Low-Hanging Gut

Low hanging gut? What about these bitches? The new "thing" appears to be for women with pot guts to wear tight blouses, expose their tits, wiggle their way into a pair of skinny jeans, put on some pumps and waddle their fat asses down the street. What's that about?

According to Carr (2014), "Most men would love to make their guts vanish. But when it comes to sex, men should ask what part of the anatomy their low-hanging guts make disappear. Turns out, it's the penis. "Statistically, a small penis is associated with a pear-shaped gut, also known as the pannus." says Goldstein. "Because the pannus extends out several inches -- and the shaft of the penis is also several inches -- the pannus can obscure the penis. The medical profession often refers to this condition as 'buried penis ….'" (Carr, 2014).

The fact of the matter is that if you look around, most of the men who have power have these guts. That is because they have sedentary lifestyles because they are rich – they call the shots. These hard bodies that you see on TV and in movies may appear virile, but they work FOR these fat assholes. In your view, the hard bodies – who you call "celebrities" are rich. But the fat boys are wealthy. The rich men and women receive the checks – the guys with the low-hanging guts SIGN those checks.

In a capitalist society, it doesn't matter what you look like because money, as George Simmel points out in his work The Color of Money, is the ultimate confounding of things. It makes the ugly appear beautiful, the small appear large, and the low-hanging gut types – when wealthy – appear most attractive. And guess who finds these fat boys attractive: the women who get laid and paid. Do you think the average bitch gives a fuck if you've got a fat gut if she's on your yacht or riding in your private jet?

So once put in the proper perspective, all this shit about what women like or dislike in bed is bullshit. Even young women will fall for an out of shape guy if he has money. If she has enough game she can always get some dick on the side. But what she wants and is attracted to is power and money.

Finger Ratio

Growing up I had a lot of bitches tell me I had long fingers and nice hands. And that is when I started hearing shit about you can tell the size of a man's dick by his hands. I immediately bought into it and as part of some of my approaches to women, I'd often say, "see these hands?" and they would automatically know what I meant. So I guess the belief in the fingers and the hands is a widely known belief.

Now here's what Carr (2014) has to say:

> A man's fingers can reveal a lot about libido, if you know where to look. "Studies have shown a correlation between the length of the index and ring fingers and behavioral traits based on testosterone," says Goldstein. In what's known as the "2D:4D Digit Ratio," he says, there's less libido when the index finger (2D) is longer than the ring finger (4D), which indicates that the man was exposed to more androgen while in the womb. There's more libido – -- a sign that a man was exposed to high levels of testosterone during gestation – -- when his ring finger is longer than his index finger. Heredity has everything to do with these ratios. "A mother will

pass on her own high or low testosterone levels to the fetus," he says.

This one sounds like bullshit, although a number of women do go by that "big hands big dick" philosophy. So it stands to reason that if you have long fingers, then these same female types would view it as a reflection of dick length. Valid? I don't know and to tell you the truth, I don't give a fuck. Why? Because women are liars and will shout and scream about how big your dick is when you haven't even put it in yet! So how can you rely on finger length when most of them have pussies so deep you could stick your leg in it and barely touch the sides!

Tubercle Prominence

More weird sounding shit is to follow, this one having to do with the lips – no, not the pussy lips – the ones surrounding her mouth! Check it out:

> The tubercle -- the slightly plump protrusion found at the bottom-center area of the upper lip -- has a surprising connection with pleasurable sex. In 2011, a study published in The Journal of Sexual Medicine cited that the greater the prominence of a female's tubercle, the more likely she is to experience a vaginal orgasm. (Carr, 2014).

What? Now let's try to figure this out logically. This information was gleaned from The Journal of Sexual Medicine. Sexually speaking, who are the most fucked up folks on the planet? White people. Now, since they only care about themselves, who would this "journal" be aimed at? Their fellow white folks. So, when we start talking about lips, who most closely lacks lip texture and has lips closest to those of chimps? White people. Knowing all this, how could a plump spot on the lips of women who are lacking in lips determine their likelihood of having an orgasm? Let's delve a little deeper:

> "This relationship between tubercle and orgasm has been studied primarily in women, but it may also exist in men, pending further research," says Goldstein. "In the sexual medicine field, what happens in women usually happens in men, and vice versa." (Carr, 2014).

But the question is, who created this journal and for what purpose? Do you actually expect me to believe that they are concerned about the sexual health of blacks? The fact is, they have been working to destroy our sexual vitality for centuries! That is what castration and pseudo-science were all about! No, it's about the white woman who is lacking in lips (hence the rise of botox) and her man, who is equally lipless. That may be why they lust to kiss one of us, the full-lipped black man and woman and once they do, they apparently can't get enough. Now study THAT, peckerwoods!

Man Boobs

This is nothing but an extension of the fact that if you get fat it's going to impact on your sexuality. If you've got a fat gut then there's an effect. Now we find that if you have fat around your tits – as many men do – then it's going to have an effect. What if you have "man boobs" but a big dick? What then, white boys? At any rate, check out their theory:

> Man boobs, which occur when excess fat is deposited in the chest area, are no laughing matter. "The condition is caused by excess estradiol -- an estrogen hormone -- and insufficient testosterone," says Darius A. Paduch, MD and Ph.D., director of sexual medicine in the department of urology at New York Presbyterian Hospital/Weill Cornell Medical College. Not surprisingly, man boobs appear in overweight men whose bodies convert testosterone to estradiol. "In addition to having feminine-appearing breasts, a man will also lose his libido and have difficulty sustaining an erection because of the decrease in testosterone and his high levels of estradiol." (Carr, 2014)

This makes sense until you interject the variable of race. A black man who is overweight can still be physically fit because our people usually work blue collar jobs. Those fat bruthas you see in the bar who are dressed to the nines used to be janitors, bricklayers, foundry workers and the like. They just got fat because they ate a lot of red meat, and eating greedily is an after effect of being born poor and not having a lot of food. So when you grow up and get a job, you tend to over-do it. This behavior can lead to the formation of man boobs in later years.

But again I have to ask, is the previous conclusion based on a study of a white male sample? That is what they tend to do and then they try to "generalize" their bullshit findings and apply them to other races of men. Now I don't think a Sumo wrestler has enough dick to compensate for his fat tits and gut. But we're black men and there's plenty of white bitches who will testify to the fact that they black man's "man boobs" don't stop him from shoving boocoo dick up her pussy (and ass, if she swings that way). Look at these black and white linemen in the National Football League: many of them have manboobs, but they are still in shape.

I think that this area might need to expand and so a cross-racial study. But wait: there's more!

> Paduch advises men with this condition to lose weight, which will help reduce testosterone conversion, and to cut down on the consumption of soy products, which contain phytoestrogens. (Carr, 2014)

How about this: grow a dick! In that way, no matter how fat you get, you can still get enough of a boner to have sex with your woman. How about that? Testosterone is important and white boys are injecting it every day. And it's not just them: black men have found out about testosterone and human growth hormone and are over dosing on the shit (just like we did when we found out about the effects of cocaine, marijuana and crystal meth!). So man boobs may be a hazard, but up to this point in our history, these bruthas have produced a lot of kids and even though they might die early, they die with a smile on their faces.

Snoring

Snoring means you're overweight and therefore may have a problem breathing. But Carr is only discussing physicality: if I'm bored with this woman lying next to me, I'm doing to take my ass to sleep. So boring is a symptom of being bored shitless in this case – it's not the origin of it! Here is what Carr claims:

> Snoring, which in men is associated with obesity and low testosterone, often indicates the sleep disorder called sleep apnea, says Paduch, associate professor of urology and reproductive medicine at Weill Cornell Medical College. "Sleep apnea causes grogginess on awakening," he says. "When you combine an already low testosterone level with the chronic fatigue that results from sleep deprivation over time -- which further lowers testosterone -- there's little or no energy for sex." (Carr, 2014).

And what would make a man allow himself to get this fucked up? First of all, if he's married or in a relationship, his woman is loading him down with carbs in the name of "good cooking." I believe this to be especially true of black women and Latinas. People of color have been programmed to "feed their man" and that "the way to a man's heart is through his stomach." But since most of these bitches are the ones with TB (two bellies), it appears that the way to HER heart is also through her stomach.

Not only that, but low testosterone levels are inevitable. If your relationship is totally reliant on sex, then you don't have one and she has all the advantages. Even after menopause, all she has to do is gap her legs and she can have sex. Not so for the male. So sleep apnea is the result because you allowed yourself to get fat. And you got fat because you got comfortable. If bad sex is the result, then all you have to do is condemn your physical state with the introduction and establishment of its opposite: in other words, stop eatin' so much, muthafucka! But seriously, even if you do eat a lot, if you exercise regularly you can steal keep from getting a pot gut, belly overhang and snoring. I know one sistah who is 66 years old and has the body of a 36 year old. How? She works out. She eats like a dog and is still svelte. Why? Because she cares about how she looks. Now don't get me wrong: she's batty as a bed bug, but her body is in great shape.

Moving on, the writer adds that, "Paduch advises men with this condition to lose weight and get treatment for sleep apnea to restore healthy sleep patterns." (Carr, 2014). There is another alternative: stop fuckin'! When you eat you will get fatigued unless you're in shape. Don't each after 8pm and maybe you can force a boner so you can stick it in this bitch so she'll stop running her fuckin' mouth about how you don't "love her" any more. You can buy that bitch all the flowers, candy and presents you want to, but if you ain't sticking it to her, the automatic conclusion is going to be you don't want to love her – or that you're "giving it" to someone else.

This is the perfect lead-in for the next issue addressed by Carr:

Depression

According to an article that appeared in the May 25, 2011 edition of the Huffington Post, **Nineteen percent** of Americans will suffer from depression at some time during their lives. Sadly, depression hits the young and old alike. Fifty percent of children and adolescents and 20 percent of adults report some symptoms of depression." As you can see this information is over five years old so the numbers have increased without a doubt. If we are to buy into Carr's claim of depression and its impact on sex, is there any wonder why the birth rate among white people (no doubt the primary people who were tested) is on the decline.

This is not to equate sexuality with pregnancy, but it can be an indicator. Carr's article makes the following observation:

> To have good sex, you need to focus. "Unfortunately, men who are depressed, despite their best efforts at sex, have too many other things on their mind," says Paduch. In some cases, he says, their depression is associated with anhedonia, a condition that makes it

> difficult or impossible to experience pleasure, even when having
> sex. (Carr, 2014)

This is but the tip of the iceberg. Good sex is partially linked to mystery. As a major player in the sex game, I know that the quest is as important as the conquest. If a woman has a dress on so short you can smell her pussy and tits pushed up under her chin, where is the mystery? That plays a role I am sure. As for depression, who wouldn't be depressed as one's consciousness and awareness grows when it comes to male-female relationships? You begin to realize that it amounts to the male being a "trick" and the female selling pussy to the highest bidder. This is known as prostitution folks, despite the fact that it is referred to as "dating" in the American lexicon.

Continuing:

> Paduch notes that men who've gotten into a "not-in-the-mood" groove need to distinguish between what might be their temporary moratorium on sex -- because of illness or after certain disruptive events -- and long-term avoidance. Trusting your sexual partner is critical, he says. And, adds Paduch, antidepressants should not be a permanent solution. "Many anti-depression drugs, especially SSRIs, have significant sexual side effects." (Carr, 2014)

And that includes Viagra, Cialis and Levitra, despite their claims. The white man doesn't give a shit about side effects. He wouldn't even be printing or broadcasting warnings about side effects if he hadn't been forced to by law. For decades these quacks have "prescribing" this and "recommending" that and people have been dying. If you take a pill to deal with this ailment you might end up paralyzed; if you take medication it doesn't cure anything – it just brings about temporary relief.

Stiff Walk

White men know it. Their scholars watch black men and have named what we do and have tried to emulate it, with no success. Elliott Liebow wrote about Tally's Corner and how black men carried themselves and then there was Cool Pose, written by Richard Majors about the young brothers and how they act on the streets. Everybody sees the walking style of black men (except the trained Uncle Toms, who still do it but not around their white bosses). They admire the hell out of it as do women, black and white alike.

Carr writes that, "An easy rhythmic walk is a good indicator of how well you'll perform in bed. When the pelvis lacks total mobility, there's less chance of having a good orgasm, says Paduch, and an inflexible spine may be associated with nerve impingement." I believe that the same can be said of activity on the dance floor. White women are watching as black men gyrate and other try to imitate those moves. White women move madly on the dance floor in an attempt to display some sense of eroticism, but it's like a young baby who keeps beat with the music and adults consider it "dancing." As Karenga (1967) once wrote, "Whites can imitate or copy soul, but they cannot create out of that context."

Carr continues:

> When it comes to sexual response, the nerve signal goes from the brain to the spinal cord, where nerves travel through the vertebrae to tell arteries in the penis to open," says Paduch. "This results in increased blood flow and an erection." But, he says, if the vertebral openings are squeezed because the spinal column lacks flexibility, those signals won't get through to the penis. To improve flexibility, Paduch suggests a combination of exercise, yoga, muscle-relaxing practices, and acupuncture. (Carr, 2014)

There you have it. Back in the day, black youth played basketball religiously on the courts. White men drove by and saw it. Black people, until recently, were always in good physical shape. The best way to offset that is by impacting on the diet, so here comes inferior quality food stuffs at markets that serve a black clientele. Here comes an overload of malt liquor, usually not even sold in suburban siores. Here comes crack cocaine and on-going sabotage of the black family's life chances. Here comes mass incarceration of black males and prisons just recently snatching weights and other exercise equipment out of the prisons for fear that black males, who can already kick their ass, will just get stronger and stronger, and increasingly "buff."

Want proof? A book I reviewed and analyzed, *What Cops Know: Today's Police Tell the Inside Story of Their Work on America's Streets*, was a lengthy interview with Chicago police officers, and they spilled their guts to the author, Connie Fletcher. One part of it deals with this issue of black men and their walking style and physique, and here is an excerpt from those statements and my analysis:

> You can tell if somebody's just out of prison just by looking at them. They've got what we call a "joint body." They do the prison strut when they walk down the street. Say you're a young fellow, you're five-ten, weigh only 160 pounds. You go into prison. You're fresh meat, baby. You're gonna be breakfast for these cons. The first thing you do – you start pumping iron to have strength to survive in the joint. You get a big chest, huge arm muscles. It's an attitude you want to give off to people; it says, get outta my way,

don't mess with me. These guys get out of the joint, they come at you down the street, they look like gorillas. They swing their torsos when they walk; they look menacing. You see somebody like that walking toward you, you get out of his way, right? He's got the joint body, the prison strut. You can spot an ex-con in a second that way (Fletcher, 1990, p. 25).

See? White men – including cops -- have always envied the bodies of black men. Black men have different muscle structure, much of it coming from hard, menial work. Since slavery, this white man has admired the black physique. These cops suffer from that same thing; even young black males who haven't done time have a "cut" physique, and white boys know it.

Calling that look a "joint" body is the white man's way of dealing with his sour grapes. There are white boys who go to prison and come out fat, overweight and sloppy looking. Even when they lift iron, they seldom have the cut of the black physique. Ask any body builder what the standard is.

As for that "prison strut," black men have always had a certain stride, a certain gait, if you will. The old school brothers used to call it "percolating." The white man is well aware of the walking patterns of blacks because he all too often admires us from a distance. It's part of the black cultural style. We call it "the pimp walk." The white man calls it the "prison strut" because, once again, he wants to take that which he craves and can never obtain, and consign it to a category of negativity. By calling it the prison strut, he can explain why he lacks the rhythm to do it: "I've never been to prison."

And there you have it. Reasons why men may be "bad in bed." And that is why the prostitution industry is multi-billion dollar industry. Men who ain't shit can still get pussy: they can prematurely ejaculate or not even be able to get a boner, but if they can pay, they can find a woman who takes the money and will say what he wants to hear, pose the way he wants her to pose and do what he wants her to do. And being a housewife is a more socially acceptable form of the same prostitution that you see on the streets and in the suites. And as a result, women continue to "get laid and paid."

THE FOUNDATION: MISGUIDED "MISANDRY"

Many people have heard the term "misogyny" in reference to a lot of what's going on and being said today by white men, including Donald Trump. It translates to mean "the hatred of women," but it's far older than trump. In fact, one of the first movie shorts ever made by the Three Stooges was a 21-minute piece consisting of a long rhyme. The movie was called "The Woman Haters Club" and that was back in 1934. Here we are today some 83 years later and the issue is still a reality.

The Woman Hater's Club

This was in 1934 when television was still in its embryonic beginnings. And even back then white men – specifically Jewish white men – were pawning off sexist mistreatment and commentary off as "laughs." They even had women in audiences laughing at themselves.

In "Woman Haters," the Three Stooges – Moe and Curly Joe – join the "Woman Haters Club" and take a pledge to never have anything to do with women. In the meantime, Larry gets married anyway and tries to hide it from his buddies. But they take a train trip and Moe and Curly end up finding out. I actually saw this one several times, and in my view it is one of the most misogynistic movies ever made. These guys HATE women and trade stories about how they got messed over and about how insane it is to be married. It was billed at the time as a "musical novelty." But what was novel about the system-wide maltreatment of women, forcing them into the "Ozzie and Harriet" mode of living? At the woman haters club meeting, you hear comments like, "they need quiet, not a riot." They meet for the 7th time to convince member of the club that romance is a crime. Check it out:

> Speak up like a hero
> Your speech not be rehearsed,
> It's Mr. Zero.
> "Alright I'll speak up first."

This may have been done for laughs, but men had no reason to hate women during that time or any other. The fact is, men of that era (and today) seem to hate the responsibilities that come with women. We want to be boys all of our lives, "kicking it" and having a good, or so it would seem, while she stays home with those bad ass kids that we helped to make, and that is why the battle of the sexes lingers on to this day.

Larry comes in and says, "Fellas I have to quit the club I joined last week," and explains that the reason he has to quit is that he fell in love. The response, led by Moe, is overwhelming:

> "What are you thinking of?
> If you violate the rules of the club
> you'll be just as good as dead.
> If you do, you'll b e carried out with a lump on your head.

Laughs? Of course. But sometimes that which is "said in jest is meant in earnest." Violence against a man because he falls for a woman? No more farfetched than the black fraternities who brand themselves, label themselves as "dogs" and abuse women, even though they have wives at home (the wives passively allow such behavior in far too many cases).

Larry is convinced by the words and the threat, and says he'll cut off the relationship, and to show that he's serious, he'll put up his bankroll and sign an agreement for life. The response?

> Now that you've signed
> Please bear in mind
> No women around of any kind.

In one particularly racist scene, a black porter asks Larry, "Is that all?" referring to Larrys' luggage. Larry replies, "that's all that I want with you." Then he tips him. At the same time, Moe and Curly are looking for Larry and ask the porter if they've seen a curly haired fella. "Sure did, she's hot stuff," says the black man. Say what?!

In my view, this was the worst "Three Stooges" short of all time. They tried a music and combined poetry, and it fell flat. When you add these two mistakes to the subject matter – hating on women – then it becomes clear that the Stooges improved as they found themselves – their comic niche, so to speak – and began to do movies that were less political and more physically abusive and slapstick-oriented.

You have to remember something about television that was true in 1934 just as it is true today in 2016. Somebody had to write that poem and then somebody read it and a committee of people approved it. Then somebody put it in television dialogue format, ran it past the "Three Stooges" and got them to memorize the script. This was a group effort, and it is doubtful if a single woman was involved in the production. And here we are some 83 years later still able to watch it during re-runs on various television stations. Sexism, like racism, won't end until the white man admits that not only does it exist, but that it is perpetual and will continue. Now that we understand how deeply misogyny runs, we can gain a better understanding of why misandry exists and how it manifests itself in the form of what could be called "socioeconomic payback."

On-Going Misandry

Sexism, as one writer might put it, is nothing short of "fragmentation of the human whole" (no pun intended). But there is another term that is rarely used, but is more prominent than one might believe. The term is "misandry," and it basically means "the hatred of men." Some background is in order before moving on and showing the link between the hatred of women and how women continue to get "laid and paid."

According to one source,

> Misandry, a word which appeared in the nineteenth century, is parallel in form to 'misogyny'. The form "misandrist" was first used in *The Spectator* magazine in April 1871. It appeared in *Merriam-Webster's Collegiate Dictionary* (11th ed.) in 1952. Translation of the French "Misandrie" to the German "Männerhaß" (Hatred of Men) is recorded in 1803. *Misandry* is formed from the Greek *misos* (μῖσος, "hatred") and *anēr, andros* (ἀνήρ, gen. ἀνδρός; "man") (Wikipedia, 2016).

These white people knew that such hatred could exist, despite the stranglehold that men thought they had on women's minds, beliefs, values, pocketbooks and goals. And that's pretty much the way it is today: men thinking that they have all this control when, in reality, *they don't control anything more than what women dupe them into believing and thinking they control.*

The misandry has been disguised, camouflaged with sex and other forms of social control. Women pretend to submit, feign being "talked out of their panties" and fake orgasms. They have been doing this for centuries. And in return to this feeling of "machismo" that the white man (and others) feel he's "earned," they are given increasing amounts of leverage and leeway, access to bank accounts and token access to power. The white woman has learned her lessons well: "The hand that rocks the cradle rules the throne."

Farrell (1993) has written a book that gives scholarly verification to a fact that most men in the streets have long known: that being the fact that men are "disposable." He cites as evidence of this the fact that men are in the most dangerous occupations, of which he claims the military is one. He claims that life expectancy is lower in men and suicides are higher. These points are relevant in only one way: as a point for discussion. Other than this, this white man sounds more like an apologist for men than anything else. The reasons for short life spans is the preoccupation with trying to justify and live up to the bullshit that men have created about themselves – things that they knew weren't true from the get-go.

More on this later.

Misandry is very real. I, for one, tend to believe that the claims that man-hating is a myth is in itself, bullshit. Women DO hate men and they have every reason to do so. You can hate someone and still be passionate about them; in fact, hate involves passion as does love. The opposite of love is not hate – it's "ambivalence." If you can say you don't care one way or the other about a person, that is the opposite of loving them. If you say you "hate" someone, you are nevertheless passionately connected. That's why so many people end up killing people they love as well as hate. Don't believe it? Watch an episode of "Snapped" and you'll see what I'm talking about.

How are you not going to "hate" someone who sends your daughters and sons off to war and claiming it's being done to protect YOU? He didn't ask you shit! He just started some shit and then sent the woman's kids off to fight for him. These old white men who talk all that shit and start wars can't fight! So they send kids off to do it. You don't think women see this shit?

You don't think women know that they get paid less for doing the same job a man gets paid? You don't think that these women use their spare time to study what is going on around them? You don't think women are smart enough to PRETEND to be "the weaker sex" while all the time puss whipping the hell out of men to get whatever they want or need? If you know this, then you have the basis for passion and that makes it hate. Because there is no way that an oppressed person can be "ambivalent" about the person who is oppressing him/her!

So misandry has to be the basis; this doesn't mean it has to be expressed behaviorally or verbally. In fact, these white feminists and their dyke counterparts are playing right into the white man's hands when they use the word "hate." As a black nationalist I have never written or said that I 'hated' the white man. I deplore his ways and I despise his traditions and history. But spending time hating him is like an obsessed bitch who claims that it's over but continues to stalk the guy that she claims to hate. It's like the punk ass guy who claims that he "quit" that woman but nevertheless talks about her every chance he gets, hoping to convince other guys not to go after her. All that "hate" does is waste energy, time that can be spend planning the next setback of the person you are ambivalent about but still as yet someone who you know is harming your people.

Women get laid and paid because they know that these are the male's two weakest areas: his wallet and his dick. They know that if they can control these two areas, they can gain a stranglehold. The fact of the matter is that if they can effectively control one of the two, they can automatically gain access to the second one, no matter which one is first or second. They have it like that and the male weaknesses are just that universal and easy to gain access to.

In the introduction to *The Great Comic Book Heroes*, though only h80 pages long, Jules Feiffer makes some great points about the super heroes of the 1930 and 1940s comic books. One point in particular is relevant to the issue of how men are viewed. In this case, Feiffer makes the comment that this is Superman's joke on the rest of us. Clark is Superman's vision of what other men are really like. We are scared, incompetent, and powerless, particularly around women (Feiffer, 1965). And this is exactly how women see us as well.

Super man could have assumed any identity: a construction worker, a pro athlete or even a radio announcer. He chose being a reporter so that he could keep up with what was going on, but to also fly under the radar. In Clark Kent, he wanted to be, as the promotion for the television version told us, "a mild-mannered reporter for the Daily Planet." Why "mild-mannered"? Because Superman saw earth men as pussies, that's why. And just as he saw us is how women see men for the most part: as violence-prone pussies who are desperate for pussy and will do whatever it takes to get it.

Misandry is payback for centuries of the stronger sex being projected as being "the weaker sex." Even William Shakespeare, in several of his plays, makes the point that men ain't worth a shit and that women have to "settle" just to be able to marry one. You don't have to hate men to see them for what they are. But women are trying to eke out an existence in a sexist society and on some level they are going to have to "deal with" the male of the species. So they pretend like they respect and love us, admire us and then dupe us into believing that they've bought into this misogynistic system called a "democracy."

But misandry is at the root and we deserve to have it inflicted upon us. But as I say in the case of racists, stop pretending you care about black people. Call a press conference, tell the world, "we hate niggers" and be done with it. In the case of the misogynist, the point is somewhat different: they need pussy in order to survive (although even now they are working on test tube alternatives to the vagina) and as a result, they pretend like they respect women by putting more on television, more on the movies, showing them kicking male ass, allowing them into the military to right wars that men started and so on. Far too many of them are duped into believing that such actions are signs of progress when *nothing* could be further from the truth.

THE BLACK WOMAN AND THE RISE OF THE 'SISTER DYKE"

Women, no matter what their sexual preference, are going to get paid and gain power in some capacity. This section of the book is dedicated to the black woman who may not be a full lesbian, but who – because of the lack of men – may opt to adopt the role of the muff diver, lounge lizards, or the Saturday Night lesbian – just to have company and sex.

Back in the 1960s, this white senator named Daniel Patrick Moynihan labeled the black family a "matriarchy." He said that it was run and dominated by the woman, and Black scholars, including myself, dogged the shit out of him and basically pawned it off as racism. But the system worked to make this statement come to pass: Since the 1960s it is the black man who has been shot down by cops and arrested in huge numbers and placed in prisons. A large number of them have come out of the closet and of course, want nothing to do with a female. This has left the black family in the hands of the black woman who, for the most part, already thought she was in charge. Now it has REALLY gone to her head.

Hence my name for this hybrid female: the "sister-dyke." This is the sister-dyke: not necessarily fucking other women, but assuming the role traditionally held by and attributed to that of an aggressive male when things get tough.

How else to explain these women walking up on football sized men and taking swings at them? How else to explain women slapping men so hard that it sounds like a shot was fired? How else to explain some of the insults and curses hurled by these women at men, women and children when they become angered? This comes from the transformation that I am alleging exists: the black woman is the new super-dyke stereotype. And I'm going to prove it.

I believe that when it comes to the Black family, what appears to be a patriarchy is really a lesbian-oriented matriarchy (either overtly or covertly). An article titled, "Patriarchy," by Allan Johnson (printed in In Paula S. Rothberg (Ed.) Race, Class and Gender in the United States. New York: Worth Publishers. 2001.) provides information that I will now flip to show that what I say about these "transformed sister-dykes and their "power" rings true.

I believe that Johnson's article, written in 1997, had two major points . The first appears on page 133 where he writes,

> Because patriarchy is male-identified and male-centered, women and the work they do tends to be devalued, if not made invisible. In their industrial capitalist form, for example, patriarchal cultures do not define the unpaid domestic work that women do as real work, and if women do something, it tends to be valued less than when men do it."

Using the concepts of "male-identified" and "male-centered" as the nexus for the reminder of the article, Johnson then begins to touch upon issues that are obvious, and yet eye opening. For instance, he writes that, "If you want a story about heroism, moral courage, spiritual transformation, endurance, or any of the struggles that give human life its deepest meaning and significance, men and masculinity are usually the terms in which you must see it ... Male experience is what patriarchal culture offers to represent HUMAN experience and the enduring themes of life, even when these are most often about women in the actual living of them ... " (p. 132.)

But when it comes to today's black community, especially the majority which is locked into the urban core, and when what was just written is flipped and applied to the new single head of household, the new Black female -- the sister-dyke. She wants to be viewed as a white woman by whites, wanted to assume the role of "boss" when it comes to Black men, and wants to be viewed as the shot-caller for the black community when it comes to responses by white decision makers. She wants to be both loved and feared – much like a Mafioso boss.

This is so true. Even in the study of African-American and African history, the women are usually mentioned either only in passing, or they are women who assumed courageous roles, in other words, roles that most people would assign to males. But they assumed masculine approaches to fighting the system. We have Harriet Tubman and Sojourner Truth, for example: two women who dealt with the system in different ways, but who are cited because of their appeal to men: Harriet Tubman because she showed extraordinary courage in leading the enslaved out of bondage, and Sojourner Truth because she appealed to the patriarchal system and was therefore invite to meet the president of the United States. You can add Ida B. Wells to that list.

Now lets' take the previous paragraph and better understand how the "sister-dyke" is now the norm when it comes to the black community.

The new black community, riddled and torn up by racist cops, illegal arrests, drug abuse, teen pregnancy, gang domination, mass incarceration and black on black homicide, is now run by women. In addition, Black men because of our actions, are viewed as docile derelicts. So to re-write the first sentence of the previous paragraph, we have this: "Because the sister-dyke is female-identified but male-centered, men and the activities they engage in tend to be devalued, if not made invisible. The sister-dyke has largely learned to ignore the Black man, except on an "as need" basis (e.g., rent money, an escort for a social gathering of some kind, child support, occasional sexual trysts, getting their "hair done," pocket money, etc.).

There is also a racial twist when we flip the previous words by Johnson. Today's reality would go something like this: "In their industrial capitalist form, for example, sister-dyke communities do not define the unpaid relationship work that men do as real work, and if men do something, it tends to be valued less than when women do it." See? The society we live in has deformed male-female relationships for everybody, but it is more evident and pervasive among us than it is among others. After all, as the saying goes, "when America has a cold, black folks have pneumonia."

Black female courage is nothing new. Kwame Nkrumah once wrote, "The degree of a country's revolutionary awareness may be measured by the political maturity of its women." And in black history, as I alluded to earlier, it was black women who were out there dealing daily. From sisters like Ida B. Wells and Mary McCleod-Bethune to Fannie Lou Hamer, Rosa Parks and Angela Davis, black women have been right there on the front lines of the struggle. The same is true in every single African struggle. But in the U.S. these women have become so frustrated, bitter and angry, they have re-defined themselves and their relationships. And the sister-dyke is what you get.

A second key point made in the article appears on page 135. Johnson writes,

> For women, gender oppression is linked to a cultural devaluing of femaleness itself. Women are subordinated and treated as inferior because they are culturally defined as inferior AS WOMEN, just as many racial and ethnic minorities are devalued simply because they aren't considered to be white. Men, however, do not suffer more because maleness is devalued as an oppressed status in relation to some higher, more powerful one (emphasis original).

Here's how the previous paragraph about "patriarchy" should read as it describes the status, style and substance of the "sister-dyke: "For the sister-dyke, gender oppression is linked to a cultural devaluing of both femaleness and blackness. Women, in general, are subordinated and treated as inferior because they are culturally defined as inferior. So they adopted a defensive formulation of toughness and self-defense. She is also angry because wearing her long extensions, makeup and using skin lightener still as yet doesn't enable her to be considered "acceptable" (white). Black Men, the new faggots, do not suffer more because their maleness is devalued as an oppressed status in relation to some higher, more powerful one. In fact, these Black men have abandoned and are now apparently re-defining their maleness.

Dykes want other women as mates, but such a choice is socially unacceptable so some hide it. Even in this day and age, lesbians are frowned upon for the most part. These "girlfriend clubs" and "girls night out" bullshit you see going on: this is the hunting ground for the dyke. They are systematically adopting male roles and even male dress. They want to shake hands like the brothers, use the terminology of the brothers and so on because they both hate and admire us. They want that black male swagger because most of them feel they'll never find " a good man" because, as most of them think, "all men are dogs." So if you can't find a good man – then just BECOME one! As the character Hud said in the movie by the same name, "no use shooting the whole pack of dogs when only one has fleas." But you cannot convince these bitter and oftentimes abused black women of this.

We have always had sister-dykes in our midst. One source documents it:

> Although a number of lesbian and bisexual blues singers--
> including Bessie Smith, Ma Rainey, Josephine Baker, and Ethel
> Waters--attained a level of sexual openness in their music, these
> women generally hid their same-sex relationships behind a public
> guise of heterosexuality. Only rarely did their lyrics even allude to
> their sexual desire for other women, and generally all such
> allusions were tinged with an ambivalence suggesting an elusive
> sexuality ... (GLBTQ, 2009).

Does knowing that Josephine Baker, Bessie Smith, Ethel Waters, or Ma Rainey were lesbians make you appreciate them any less? Of course not. I'm just saying admit what you are, act it out so that I can tell, and then I know where that relationship is going to go. The social stigma was great, so they hid their desires from the public. But the fact still remains that too many sister-dykes are living a lie the way the sisters just mentioned had to do. In a patriarchal society, the sister-dyke is living a life of self-deception which, in turn, forces her to deceive others.

I have always believed that even the dirt poor white hillbilly could identify with someone like George Bush because both were white. But the male aspect is also a factor and Johnson explains that nicely on page 132:

> Since patriarchy identifies power with men, the vast majority of
> men who aren't powerful but are instead dominated by other men
> can still feel some connection with the IDEA of male dominance
> and with men who ARE powerful. It is far easier, for example, for
> an unemployed working-class man to identify with male leaders
> and their displays of patriarchal masculine toughness than it is for
> women of any class ... In this way male identification gives even
> the most lowly-placed man a cultural basis for feeling some sense
> of superiority over the otherwise most highly placed woman
> (which is why a construction worker can feel within his rights as a
> man when he sexually harasses a well-dressed professional woman
> who happens to walk by?)

But it is also this way for sister-dykes.

For instance, the previous paragraph about patriarchy would read like this when discussing the sister-dyke:

Since patriarchy identifies power with men, the vast majority of Black women who can't locate men and/or hate the men they can still feel some connection with the IDEA of male dominance by becoming "sister-dykes" and adopting the role of father and mother, protector, provider because they are tired of being used and dumped by men who they allowed into their lives. It is far easier, for example, for an employed working-class sister-dyke to identify with white male leaders (demi-gods or "meta-humans") and their displays of patriarchal masculine toughness than it is for women of any class to accept a black male who is gradually turning into a faggot In this way male identification by the sister-dyke gives even the most lowly-placed Black woman a cultural basis for feeling some sense of superiority over the black man and other men of color.

The ranks of the sister-dyke are growing. Some call them lesbians, but there are a lot who are pretending to be in that life just so that they can have companionship and as a result, like most adult human beings, get a nut whenever they can. Just like many Black men are on the down low, black women have been sexing each other up for decades. And they not only get laid, but they can keep on getting paid: *from him and from her.*

The sister-dyke can assume dual roles: that of slut that is male oriented or that which is dyke, where she can go after what she really wants: *pussy*. She's tired of sperm running down her leg as the man snores next to her, tired of the lack of pillow talk, tired of not getting head, tired of sucking foot long dick and ending up with a facial, tired of him thinking that cuddling is for sissies (a cover for the fact that he is really on the down low) and tired of him getting a quick nut and then disappearing out the door. She's tired of having to beg for massages or being touched "in that place" when, if she switches sides and gets a girlfriend, she won't have to worry about these things. And she can STILL get paid.

Put another way, following the white woman's historical example, the sister-dyke has learned how to use "pussy politics" to control her life in a number of ways and further, to use the white man's system to secure a lifestyle albeit an impoverished one. And it is this version of "pussy politics" that, to this day, dominates the "sister dyke's role as "family backbone" and aids and abets in the black man's assumptive role as effeminate. Let me explain.

To begin with there's the "I don't need no man" shit that the white woman started with her "Women's Liberation" movement. Other versions of the new liberated woman, which created the philosophy for the sister-dyke, can be found in statements regarding how silly a man is, how easy a man is to seduce, and how expendable they are include, "all a man is good for is a fuck," "if you're going fishing, you gotta use the right bait," and of course," If you get over one man get under another one," and "men are like buses: there's one coming down the street every hour."

All of these are versions of "social and sexual independence" that white women feel and strive for, and now the black woman is following suit. The white woman adopts lesbianism out of choice; the black woman does it after a forced choice or necessity. For the sister-dyke, her dual role is one of survival.

The heyday for the black woman now turned quasi-dyke was the advent of the Blaxploitation movement, where movies and characters like, "Foxy Brown,' "Sheba, Baby," "Cleopatra Jones" and "Friday Foster" paved the way for the

super fine, super independent woman who only associated with men when they could join her "team" and serve as her willing thralls. In those movies the sisters were large (sometimes literally) and in charge, and all men were asked to do was serve as sidekicks, flunkies and occasionally, a love interest. And one more thing: all of these sisters had their own cars, houses – and they got PAID.
From there women started dressing for each other, going on in groups, dancing together and as you can see, it is considered "sexy" by some males (not me) to see two women making out with each other. The acceptance of the sister-dyke had arrived!

Today is much the same as black male numbers dwindle at an alarming rate and the belief that "all the good men are taken" or "there ain't no good black men" seems to dominate most of their thinking. Even when they hang out in clubs or lounges, they're basically in there looking for some money attached to a penis – when back in the day, it was the other way around. They're on the prowl at the club, at the supermarket, in the library, or even in church -- perhaps to set some brother up with a pregnancy, but only after they check his credit rating, driver's license and other identification like the white woman trained her to do.
They now have their own money, their own cars and in some cases, their own homes (sometimes left behind by a deceased husband or other family member). All they aspire for now is a serious relationship so that their girlfriends won't think they are dykes. They might even go so far as to get pregnant to stabilize their cover. But they know that they tread dangerous ground with their deception, so they need legal protection. That's where the spike in "domestic violence' comes in.

These women in general and the sister-dyke, in particular, are armed with weapons that are legal, social, cultural, political – and gender-biased, although the latter is usually shrouded and covered up by the white man's blatant and long-time sexism and glass ceiling-related antics. And all of these components fall under an ideological umbrella, basically a Euro-American one that states that if you hit a woman there is going to be hell to pay. And the subtle and degrading message that women are willing to sell their souls for so that they can retain this power, is that they are "inferior and childlike" and therefore in need of this kind of "protection." And in this society, what kind of women do men prefer when it comes to seeking a date or a mate? The ones that are the most weak minded, child-like, defenseless and dependent. But it's just a front: the sister-dyke might play possum during a date, but once the relationship is "safe" (e.g., with a pregnancy set up, a marriage proposal, etc.) she goes into that nurturing mode which increasingly becomes more and more dominant. And since the black man is slowly becoming more effeminate and bitch-like, the relationship flips: she wears the pants and makes the decisions, he wears the earrings, gets his hair done and when possible, takes it up the ass from the neighbors or his pals. This is taking place while she treats the male in the relationship like a child who can't even hold his own dick when he takes a piss. The whites have a slogan in regard to their age: "I'm 50 years YOUNG" or whatever their age might happen to be. Everybody wants to be a child and that is why being treated like one comes too easy for so many. This is then followed up with another sexist mantra: the man's job is to "take care" of his family, and who does that consist of? Women and children. The sister-dyke goes so far as to use HIS paycheck to horde away a little money on the side (for "night clubbing purposes") and make sure the home is cared for. After the first few years he tires of her, stops fucking her, hides in his "man cave" which in turn, paves the way for three things: (1) a whole lot of jacking off and pornography viewing with the door locked, (2) the "downlow" with some of his equally effeminate pals, and (3) opportunities, for her, to date women (commonly known as "girl's night out")

Popular Culture

The sister-dyke is not just a status but also a role – Black women with the equivalent powers of a black man, doing the bidding of the white system. Although the white man still gives the orders this new wave black woman has a masculine image and usually a high position – a position that no Black man would ever be entrusted with or assigned to. And – she gets PAID.

For instance, there's "Scandal," which stars fine-ass Kerry Washington, and the plot is so unbelievable you have to ask yourself: whose dick did she suck to get this part? America is really going all out putting these black women in these prime time roles - anyone is better than a Black male (who white female viewers might find "attractive"). Witness, for instance, Taraji P. Henson in "Person of Interest" (killed off but then lands a lead role in Fox's "Empire"), Meagan Good in NBC's "Deception ," And "Sleepy Hollow" is filled with black women: the sister Abbie Mills appears to have a thing for the white boy Ichabod Crane, and then the woman who plays her sister, Jennie. Both shot guns, stab and slice demon s, fight monsters and so on.

The lone black man on the show, Captain Frank Irving, is played by Orlando Jones. And even though he's the police captain, nobody really respects and in many ways he comes off as the effeminate side piece. To add to his impotence is his ex-wife, who appears now and then to show him the pussy he'll never get again and brings his young daughter along to flash, just to egg him on more. In other words his role, like the roles of most black men in the lives of the sister-dyke (and society in general), is weak, second-rate, and limp. He's also another in a long line of police chiefs that no one listens to.

Why "women firsts" when it comes to bad situations? They want to be a male's equal, but they still expect their doors to be opened. You call it chivalry; I call it acting a damn fool.

For instance, merely look at the popular culture movies. Go back as far as 1939's "Five Came Back" (Lucille Ball, Chester Morris, Wendy Barrie) about a plane that is wrecked but of the 12 people who were on board, they have to decide which five can re-board because of the condition of the plane. "We have to consider women and children first," is the universal agreement. How about the movie, "Titanic"? The same thing was shouted after it hit the fateful iceberg: "women and children to the life boats first!"

Strong black women taking the place of black men. And as the new black men, look at how they are presented: no shuffling, no skinning and grinning, but in positions of power. They are the new black men only when working with and taking orders from, the white man. These women have juice, carry guns, seduce powerful white men and do battle with bad guys. Sister-dykes, one and all.

In a society where pussy is craved and sought out like the ore of the Gold Rush of the 1800s, craving booty was a male domain. Having seen that, women have flipped the script and upped the ante: since it appears that men want it so bad, they must now **pay for it unlike any other time in history**. Not only with money, which is why prostitution is the world's oldest profession, but with a secure lifestyle and blind obedience that begins with something called "the date."

I'm writing about the American version. Although dating is probably universal in European culture (which this society is based on), Americans have added their own twists and modifications to turn it into a romance-laden, capitalist extravaganza. And whatever the white man does for and toward his mate, the black woman sees it and turns around and manipulates the black man, in his quest for pussy, *to do the same thing to and for her.*

It is popular culture, spurred by magazines, television, and the social network, that is perpetuating this, ""that's okay to be a dyke" bullshit. Young girls in middle school think it's cute to kiss each other and "experiment" with girl-girl dating. Women enrolling in what we called "self-defense" classes, but really they're classes that train them to focus on men's nuts. You can use your knees, you can kick or you can duck and land a jab – as long as you hit him in the nuts, he'll be disabled.

Finally, as long as men keep fucking up – and we will -- the sister-dyke ranks will grow and inevitably become more visible. Black men are abandoning their families, chasing white women, hanging out in bars, getting fucked up on alcohol and drugs, taking it up the ass from their "pals," and a host of other things that the police and media protect white men from being caught doing. So if we know that, all we gotta do is to stop fucking up. The sister-dyke might be a genetic reality, born a lesbian. But whether the tendencies come from nature or from nurture, she's here to stay. Some will try to disguise it; some will be outright including public displays of affection.

Facts are facts: roles have changed because of personal, social and cultural need, and the recent approval of homosexual marriage. The sister-dyke, as quiet as it's kept, is the protector of our community and in some cases, of our secrets. You normally don't see her on TV babbling about her Black family concerns like these bitch-like male assholes are prone to do.

THE PUSSY PRINCIPLE: CONCEPTS AND CHARACTERISTICS

The pussy principle is very simple and has been in effect for centuries, across international boundaries, cultural boundaries and of course, enacted to perfection here in the United States.

Pussy and the craving of it is a part of the male onset for the overwhelming majority of his life. Even after being rendered impotent by disease, natural causes or some kind of accident, men still spend huge amounts of money for "female company." After all, as the women say, "If you can't use the hips, use the lips." And so it has come to pass: the "pussy principle" is not only alive and well, but it is thriving in present day America.

What I am about to share is how the premise of the "mistress" enables a number of women, married or single, to get laid and paid.

Let me provide some examples.

Pro Athletes and "Mistresses"

Getting laid and paid is evident when it comes to the institution of marriage and these so-called "housewives" who control the family budget, but it's all over the place. Let's take a look at the article about and comments of this porn star named Lisa Ann, who was the focus of an article in the Sporting News in March of 2016. The headline was, "Porn Star Lisa Ann Warns 25 Percent of NBA Players Have Faced Blackmail." According to the article,

> NBA Pro athletes engaged in affairs with porn stars and strippers should watch their step, warns adult film star and director Lisa Ann. She estimates 25 percent of NBA players have faced blackmail at some point in their careers. Writing for Complex, the basketball aficionado warned that rich NBA stars, particularly married players, have become targets for hustlers looking to steal their money, wallets, jewels, even their Playstations. If they're not

stealing, they're trying to hustle players into paying their rent or
buying them fancy cars (McCarthy, 2016).

But let's place the blame where it belongs: cockhounding-ass black men
who see a white bitch in the stands and lose their minds. White society knows what
these Kardashian-oriented women are about, and so do the teammates of the men
who spend that money. But who really cares? Do these men give a shit about
having "wives" at home or children who may be affected? Of course not. And this
is one more piece of evidence that backs up my later claim and contention that men
are viewed as children by women: immature "boys" who chase pussy and need a
"mommy-type" to take care of them.

The previous quote by Lisa Ann posits that, "rich NBA stars, particularly
married players, have become targets for hustlers looking to steal their money,
wallets, jewels, even their Playstations." Play stations? Grown ass men? Jewelry?
Are these men or bitches? So all that material acquisition slowly directs these
males toward what they REALLY are and what they really crave: pussy –
preferably white pussy. The article adds that, "If they're not stealing, they're trying
to hustle players into paying their rent or buying them fancy cars." I ask, how is
this any different than what the housewife is doing? Blackmail won't work if the
man knows what's going on in terms of his relationship at home. "Tell her – she
already knows," should be the response. But these cowardly effeminate assholes
are AFRAID of the women they married. And so they pay the blackmail to keep
the ho quiet.

And what a "get laid and paid" scam it is. According to Lisa Ann,
I've heard girls say they make sure he is married or in a relationship before going
back to his hotel with him. Once there they wait for their moment alone with his
wallet and take photos of all of his credit cards and his ID. The final part of the
plan is blackmail. You would be shocked how many NBA players have had been
blackmailed in an effort to keep their privacy. My guess is a minimum of 25
percent of NBA players have dealt with blackmail at some point in their career.
I've heard girls brag about long-term hustles where they have a player paying their
rent and expenses just to keep them quiet and out of their family life.(McCarthy,
2016).

Snitch-ass Kobe Bryant got busted by his woman after he "raped" a white
bitch while he was undergoing therapy in Colorado. I mean he bent the bitch over a
chair and everything. So she blackmailed his ass. He came clean at a press
conference, but that wasn't good enough. He added that, "I should have just paid
her off the way Shaq does with his women." Now Shaq was married at the time,
and his wife has since divorced him. Did Kobe's comments have anything to do
with it? Who knows. But I know this: Shaq had kids and those kids watched

Kobe's press conference. So Kobe is a snitch and a bitch. And his fine-ass Latina wife threatened him and he had to go out and buy her a million dollar ring and hasn't "gotten out of line" since. She definitely got "laid and paid."

Getting laid and getting paid. And for what? Pussy? I understand that men have their needs, but the problem with far too many of us (black men) is that we let our needs dominate and direct our thought processes. White men probably do that as well, but I don't give a shit what happens to them. I am talking about the few brothers who get the chance to make big money and who should be donating that money to community-based organizations (not the church) to defend and develop the black communities that spawned most of them. Instead, they know that these women want their money because even the ugly muthafuckas like Dennis Rodman can get approached by these women.

But it's not just the cockhounds from the NBA who get "punked" right out there in the open for all to see (clad in underwear, standing and listening to a little white man tell them what to do, having child-like temper tantrums when the referee makes a call they don't like, etc.), it's also the men from the National Football League and pro baseball as well. But beyond sports, politicians buy into it as well. I will address women getting "laid and paid" by the politicians and how it has functioned using a few case studies.

Politicians and "Mistresses"

America is a conglomeration of its own contradictions, preaching morals on the one hand and fucking around like there's no tomorrow on the other hand. An article titled, "Twenty Presidents Who Were Rumored to Have Mistresses," by Caitlin Bussman, which appeared on a website called "rantpolitical," provides a basis from which we can clearly establish why America is on the moral decline.

In this section I show that it is not pussy that brought down these men or impugned their reputations; it is the desire to get pussy, to seek it out, to control it that is the problem. See, the thing is, you can never control pussy unless you control the woman who is carrying it. And despite the games and claims to the contrary, no man can EVER control a woman, and this is especially true once kids come into the picture.

Let me provide some examples, borrowed from an incorrectly headlined article titled, "Twenty Presidents Who Were Rumored to Have Mistresses," and analyze, in retrospect, the role that sex plays even when the guys are borderline impotent, ultra-busy or borderline gay. Even when men have unlimited power, the pussy principle kicks in and is always at work. It's about conquest and power, and in some cases, getting a nut. At any rate, this mentality and tendency lends itself to "how women get laid and paid."

George Washington and Venus

Who is the hell is "Venus," you may ask. According to Bussman (2014),

> George was rumored to have an affair with a slave named Venus,
> resulting in the birth of a son named Wes Ford. Descendants to this
> day deny it ever happened, and refused any kind of DNA research.
> (Bussman, 2014).

I don't know what black woman in her right mind would name a lovely black girl after a white mythical character. But there she was: enslaved and vulnerable and the white boy who is still considered, "the father of our country" was taking advantage of some under aged pussy. Do you know any white folks named Washington? There are, of course, probably tens of thousands but what is noteworthy here is that there are probably millions of black people with that last name. And in fact, when you hear that surname, you assume that the person was black.

The grade schools, middle schools and high schools offer history and civics classes boasting about their bullshit presidents. They lie and revise history to make them look like they were great men. But when you enslave another human being and then take pussy that shows your true character. The only response the white historians can offer are denials, revisionist lies, and shame.

Abraham Lincoln and Joshua Speed

The man who black people love so much and who is still attributed with "ending slavery" (a damn lie – he ended it in areas where he had no jurisdiction), was married and was probably a fag. According to Bussman (2014), "Yes, you're reading that right. The two lived together for four years, and were rumored to have shared the same bed. A second 'affair' was said to happen with his bodyguard David Derickson."

Now, in today's racist white popular culture, they have the gall to offer us movies like "Abraham Lincoln: Vampire Slayer." What? There is no such thing as a vampire, you stupid muthafuckas. But guess what? How about a movie called "Abraham Lincoln: Fudge Packer"? Or "Abraham Lincoln: The Rump Roaster Who Would Be President"? Again, I don't put anything past a race of people whose men walked around in powdered wigs and called themselves "judges." They were waging war and killing unarmed people by day and taking it up the ass and sucking dick by night. Now – put THAT in the history books!

John F. Kennedy and Mimi Alford

Whether you take pussy or buy pussy, you're lacking in game and character in my book. And when you're president of the United States and you're doing it, risking it all (can you say Bill Clinton?), there is something wrong with you. Check out the following:

> No president liked to wander more than JFK, which will become evident in this list. The biggest cheater to ever reside in the oval office, has a never-ending list of women who claimed to have had an affair with him. And unfortunately for Jack, several of them have been confirmed. One of his first conquests was White House intern Mimi Alford -- who was 19 at the time. The two had an 18-month relationship, until he became tired of her. (Bussman, 2014).

Why aren't there any theories about Kennedy's assassination being the result of a plot designed by Jackie and one of his bitches? Wouldn't it seem logical? She had to know what he was into because the women he was messing with were highly visible and fine.

Like Clinton, he decided to fuck a White House intern. But we can't put it all on him. Women know what they're doing and they know that men, regardless of their power and titles, are as weak-minded as hell. She probably hiked her skirt up, bent over so he could see her panties and he got a boner. He snatched into one of those back rooms and prematurely ejaculated all over her and then gave her the day off. She was only nineteen years old and that's how white men – and a growing number of black men – seem to like their women: young, dumb and ready to be filled with cum.

This was no "fling." I consider a year and a half to be a long time, especially when Kennedy was married and surrounded by body guards (who had to know about it) and Bussman claims "until he got tired of her." No way. That bitch got PAID. If he hadn't paid her it would have been all over the newspapers. He knew that. So he probably gave her a giant wad of cash and threatened her. And, like most white women who get laid and paid, she kept her fuckin' mouth shut.

John F. Kennedy and Marilyn Monroe

Now this was some class pussy right here. The only problem was she was fuckin' almost everybody! This bitch was giving up more pussy than the local pet store! According to Bussman,

> Well, let's knock this one out of the way, shall we? The two had a
> romantic rendezvous at Bing Crosby's house in Palm Springs
> shortly after meeting. It's reported that Monroe got in touch with
> the President's wife, Jackie, and told her about the affair. Jackie
> was well aware of John's wandering eye, and responded by telling
> her to move in and marry him, and then she would have all the
> problems! (Bussman, 2014).

I don't know how valid this statement by Bussman is because I believe that Jackie was a dyke all along and just used men like JFK and Onassis as a "front;" JFK wasn't fucking her and Onassis was too old to fuck. So Jackie, who couldn't divorce JFK because of the scandal that would be involved, probably just bumped pussies with some women behind closed doors. I really don't give a shit but I'm only citing this excerpt and others to prove one thing: bitches know how to get "laid and paid," and Jacqueline Kennedy-Onassis was no exception.

John F. Kenned and Judith Campbell Exner

Revisionist history keeps this pussy hound from being exposed for what he really was. Black people kissed his ass and many older blacks have pictures and paintings of John, his brother Robert, and Martin Luther King standing shoulder to shoulder. And rightfully so: all three fucked around on a regular basis, including the fact that Robert also fucked Marilyn Monroe ("sloppy seconds" behind his brother), and King was fucking white women galore behind Coretta's back.
But in the case of JFK and this woman Exner,

> Introduced by Frank Sinatra, the two began their affair in 1960 in
> Vegas. In interviews since the affair, Exner described him as being
> "so reckless" and even admitted to aborting his child, although
> those allegations have never been proven. (Bussman, 2014).

I believe Exner. I believe that JFK didn't use condoms and didn't give a shit if she was using birth control. When he wanted pussy he wanted it with the quickness and that is what she meant by his being "reckless." What did he care? If push came to shove, he could have that bitch capped. He was fucking her at the same time that the Rat Pack was hanging out, which means that Peter Lawford, Sinatra, Sammy Davis, Joey Bishop and the rest of the "hangers on" knew about it as well. JFK wanted to be a part of the group but couldn't because he had big dreams; but his past is secure because the revisionist historians who dominate the American publishing estate make sure that the truth about these dog-ass white boys never gets out. He'd better be glad that there was no social media back then, or he'd be busted just like that bastard Donald Trump is even now being exposed in 2016.

John F. Kennedy and Ellen Rometsch

Check out the following JFK debacle:
If you're going to cheat non-stop, why not make one a prostitute? Rometsch was from Germany and resembled Elizabeth Taylor on a bad day. She attended secret naked pool parties at the White House and would routinely visit for quickies. Apparently, brother Bobby threatened to have her deported but it's not stated whether or not that followed through. (Bussman, 2014).

Laid and paid. This guy had all the pussy he wanted, was married, and still had to find a bitch that he PAID money to. This is white boys for ya. Since those days the concept of paying for pussy has attempted to become normalized in popular culture, led by that worthless Charlie Sheen and his popular TV show, "Two and a Half Men." Not only did he buy pussy, but he used his money and his beach house as a recruitment tool for hos! Then he would brag about it and even his under-aged nephew knew about it.

As it relates to JFK, how can you have a "secret naked party" at the White House? How did this asshole find out? Where were the secret agents and government men? Where the fuck was Jackie? It was no secret except to the public. These white people show their true nature when they get some power and can afford some semblance of security.

Grover Cleveland and Maria Crofts Halpin

Another child born behind the back of a president's wife. How can this be? This guy was unique in that, according to one source, he was an American politician and lawyer who served as the 22nd and 24th President of the United States.[1] He won the popular vote for three presidential elections – in 1884, 1888, and 1892 – and was one of the three Democrats (with Andrew Johnson and Woodrow Wilson) to serve as president during the era of Republican political domination dating from 1861 to 1933. He was also the first and only President in American history to serve two non-consecutive terms in office. (Wikipedia, 2016).

But that means nothing: these white men with all that power continue to pay for pussy and take huge risks. Those bitches know everything because the white man, like his woman, is a gossip. Check out the case of Grover Cleveland:
The 1884 presidential elections got ugly. Cleveland's opponent James Blane alleged Cleveland had fathered an illegitimate child with Halpin while practicing law in New York. In Blane's defense, Cleveland had been paying child support to

Halpin. In Cleveland's defense, Halpin admitted she was a whore who slept with the whole law office and had no clue who the father was. Cleveland paid because he was the only bachelor there, and just assumed... (Bussman, 2014).

Another president with a "whore." He later got cancer and had it operated on aboard a yacht while on vacation. These white boys not only got "laid and paid," but they got away with it on both counts.

Bill Clinton and Monika Lewinsky

I believe Clinton "paid" as well as got laid. According to recent accounts by his wife's opponent Donald Trump, he was fined $850,000. But we'll get to that later.

The fact is, Clinton seduced that young girl because he was president of the United States, a man who knew full well that this girl was the same age as his own young daughter, Chelsea. One source gives us the embarrassingly unbrotherly facts of the case:

> In 1995, Lewinsky, a graduate of Lewis & Clark College, was hired to work as an intern at the White House during Clinton's first term, and was later an employee of the White House Office of Legislative Affairs. While Lewinsky worked at the White House, Clinton began a personal relationship with her, the details of which she later confided to her friend and Defense Department co-worker Linda Tripp, who secretly recorded their telephone conversations.(Wikipedia, 2016).

Linda Tripp wasn't always overweight and ugly. But obviously her lackluster love life made her depressed and she turned into a hefty bag. So she was jealous when this young girl divulged that she had just sucked Clinton's dick, not just once, but several times. And Tripp couldn't keep her mouth shut and probably wanted some of the limelight. So here's what took place:

> When Tripp discovered in January 1998 that Lewinsky had sworn an affidavit in the Paula Jones case denying a relationship with Clinton, she delivered the tapes to Kenneth Starr, the Independent Counsel who was investigating Clinton on other matters, including the Whitewater scandal, the White House FBI files controversy, and the White House travel office controversy. During the grand jury testimony Clinton's responses were carefully worded, and he argued, "It depends on what the meaning of the word 'is' is,"[6] with regard to the truthfulness of his statement that "there is not a sexual relationship .(Wikipedia, 2016).

Clinton was already in trouble with Paula Jones – who also ended up getting paid. She is the one who got the $850,000. And here is now, in 2016, still trying to do harm to Clinton by appearing at Donald Trump's campaign debates with some other bitches that Clinton allegedly "sexually assaulted." Laid and paid, plain and simple.

Clinton looked like a complete ass in front of millions of people, lying his ass off. Then he had to recant his statement and admit that he lied to the country and to his wife. And don't think Hillary wasn't pissed. I don't think she's said a word to that muthafucka since 2001. Now she's running for President and is using him in her campaign, and will probably use him in her cabinet if elected. But her attention is on Chelsea, their daughter and her grand kids.

Bill Clinton was 49 years old at the time and Monica was 22, and a White House intern. He fucked her life up, although she tried to do some writing and did go away and get a degree. And what about Billy boy?

> President Clinton was held in civil contempt of court by Judge
> Susan Webber Wright for giving misleading testimony in the Paula
> Jones case regarding Lewinsky and was also fined $90,000 by
> Wright. His license to practice law was suspended in Arkansas for
> five years and later by the United States Supreme Court
> .(Wikipedia, 2016).

So getting some head behind your wife's back cost him his law license and a bunch of money. I hope that this shows that it doesn't matter if you're the President of a pauper, if you want to get laid in America you are going to pay one way or the other.

<u>James Buchanan and William Rufus King (probably)</u>

I don't know what Bussman wrote "probably" because if it didn't happen, then he had no business printing it. I date a lot of pretty women and when nosey assholes see us out, they know my reputation and assume that I 'probably' fucked them. See what I mean? At any rate, here is how this particular situation evolved, although it sounds like a homosexual tryst:

> After Buchanan's wife, Anne Coleman, died; he and future VP
> William Rufus King became very... close. King and Buchanan
> attended social functions and lived together, referred to themselves
> as a "communion", and Andrew Jackson called them "Miss Nancy
> and Aunt Fancy." After King died of TB, Buchanan became
> President and once wrote in his journal: "I have gone a wooing to

several gentlemen, but have not succeeded with a one of them."
(Bussman, 2014).

So Buchanan was gay, which means he was gay when he was married. And this is one more example of these powerful white men living double lives while their wives know what's going on but they enjoy the comforts and the status so they keep their mouths shut. Why? Because they may not be getting laid, but they are sure enough getting paid!

Buchanan was the 15th president of the United States and always favored the South in his decisions. He is quoted as having once said that, "slavery is of little practical importance." His woman knew this just like these other white women knew that their husbands were racist. But they kept their mouths shut and nodded their heads in approval. And why? Because they got "laid and paid"!

Warren G. Harding and Nan Britton

This president was known for his cockhounding and apparently didn't give a shit about who knew. The rumors were that he was of "mixed race," but whether he was or not, he was caught in a scandal that almost rivaled Bill Clinton's many years later. Check it out:

> Throwing it back to 20's for this cheating commander-in-chief who strayed more than once. His first conquest was Nan Britton. Britton claims that right before Harding took the presidency, he fathered her illegitimate child. She made the announcement of her daughter and the cheating scandal well after his presidency ended in 1928. She described him as a womanizer and swore til the day she died in 1991 that her child was Harding's. (Bussman, 2014).

Sound familiar? And you don't think this woman got paid? These women aren't giving away booty for free because these old white man can't be that great in bed. They were getting wined and dined and given money to pay this bill or that bill because this was back in the days when prostitutes were more frugal and practical than those "buy me a diamond necklace" type bitches that you see today.

Warren G. Harding and Carrie Fulton Phillips

> The most well-known of Harding's affairs. The two were together for a long period of time when Harding was just a senator. The affair between the two ended around the time he became president when she tried to blackmail him. Not only did she try to blackmail him, she was successful. (Bussman, 2014)

Again, key points that you are not going to find in any history book in the American school system. Why? Because their goal is to make their presidents appear to be as moral and ethical as possible. That is where the myth that "George Washington never told a lie" and "Abraham Lincoln chopped down a cherry tree" came from.

Dwight D. Eisenhower and Kay Summersby

> Kay Summersby was Eisenhower's chauffeur and secretary during World War II. Eisenhower was not President at the time, and the two went their separate ways when he returned to the United States. This affair was never confirmed, but the two spent more time together than anyone else and were rumored to be very close. (Bussman, 2014).

Of course they had an "affair," as it was called. These guys have all this power and oftentimes the only female in the office or in nearby proximity is their "secretary." She knows she's going to give up that booty and so does he – it's just a matter of time. Clinton had his interns, JFK had his intern and Grover Cleveland had his office worker and FDR had his secretary. And the list goes on. And the American people, even when they find out, they don't really care as they showed when they found out that Donald Trump openly admitted grabbing women by their pussies. What kind of country elects these kinds of men? I think it is pretty clear, and that is why women continue to get "laid and paid."

Thomas Jefferson and Sally Hemings

> One of the biggest affairs in Presidential history was between TJ and his slave Sally Hemings. It's been suggested that the couple had six children together, four of which survived and went on to be free. This could be the most scandalous of all on the list, seeing as race relations then are definitely not what they are today. (Bussman, 2014).

To begin with, race relations today are really no different if you look at what is said behind closed doors when an interracial couple is spotted. And second of all, why would this matter? The fact is this is a man who felt black people were inferior, and was on record claiming that the enslaved male was "less amorous" toward his female than the white male. Well this is a lie, but if it were true, maybe it was because the black male had white men like Jefferson whipping his ass every day and when he (the enslaved) got back to the shack, some peckerwood was straddling the black woman!

Franklin D. Roosevelt and Lucy Mercer

The affair between FDR and his secretary Lucy was discovered first by none other than Eleanor Roosevelt herself. She wanted a divorce, but the President would have none of it, fearing that the scandal would become public and put his political career in jeopardy. (Bussman, 2014).

The word was that Eleanor was a lesbian. Who knows and who gives a shit? The main thing is that she stayed put as do most white women. They talk all that shit about sexism and gender bias, but they all seem to have a price. Hillary Clinton sure had one, and evidently she wasn't alone.

James Garfield and Lucia Calhoun

James Garfield went the younger route when cheating with his mistress Lucia who was 18 at the time. She was a NY Times reporter whom the president had much admired. When wife Lucretia found out, he was given the ultimatum of wife or mistress, to which he played smartly and picked his wife. (Bussman, 2014).

No, he "pretended" to pick his wife. That young white girl was having an affair with the President of the United States and she wasn't going to give it up. He was getting head from a young woman who was someone he could talk to, and he wasn't going to give that up so he could go home to Lucretia. He lied and said he'd give it up and then he had his aides and others falsify some "fake business trips" or other junkets that they claimed were related to the job, trips that he would take the young woman on. That's how it's done, folks.

John Tyler and the Majority of His Slaves

John Tyler holds the record for having fathered the most children of any president. In his two marriages Tyler fathered 15 legitimate children. What remains murky is the persistent rumor that he'd fathered children with many of his slaves. Oral history among slaves confirms this -- however it's nearly impossible to prove by DNA, since all the children were reportedly sold off. (Bussman, 2014).

The question is why this information is not discussed in the American history and political science courses around the nation. Why don't white kids learn about all this "illegitimacy" among the "founding fathers" and other famous white men? What is there to hide? I think we know the answer. Black women who were held in bondage had no choice and surely did not get paid. The white man's history is the one that legitimately made rape legal. This is a point that should be studied in the law and civics classes of America. After all, isn't the oath in court "to tell the truth, the whole truth and nothing but the truth"?

George H.W. Bush and Jennifer Fitzgerald

Big daddy Bush's affair was never confirmed, but this rumored couple met within the White House walls. Jennifer was the White House deputy chief of protocol and the affair was reportedly discovered by an aide to Bill Clinton. How convenient? Of course he screwed around, and this doesn't include all the pussy these guys buy straight out, the concubines in various cities that they might have, and so on.

Like father, like son. The White House, as we can see in this analysis, has always been a hotbed of lewd and lascivious behavior. And yet it remains hidden behind those closed doors and those falsely named "hallowed" halls.

Lyndon B. Johnson and Alice Glass

As Bussman (2014) put it, "No stranger to cheating, Lyndon Johnson did this routinely. One of his most infamous scandals was with Alice Glass, whom wife Lady Bird has admitted to attacking. Nothing like a cat fight in the White House!" And it was kept out of the newspapers in the same way that John Kennedy's affairs with Marilyn Monroe, Robert Kennedy's escapades with the same woman, Cisneros paying off his mistress and so on. This is the real America. All that talk about "the first amendment" and the importance of "the fourth estate" is fruitless when the variable of race is interjected. These white people are cutting up behind closed doors, paying for sex, engaging in sexual harassment and assault, and the public is none the wiser.

In this case, another Texas loser gets into the white house (like Big Daddy Bush) and decides to sow his oats while his wife is right in the next wing. And these are the people who help perpetuate stereotypes about black people being sexually out of control, the myth of the black rapist and the myth of the loose black female. Meanwhile, these white men are in the White House and having sex with women who are getting laid and paid.

<u>John F. Kennedy and Angie Dickinson</u>

Dickinson was a slut that probably laid down with Sinatra and other members of the Rat Pack, of which JFK was an unofficial member. She played the role of a slut in the movies and on television and even in the TV flick "Police Woman," she was a loose cannon. As a female lead in the original movie, "Ocean's 11," she was on set with some of the biggest cockhounds in Hollywood. Is there any doubt that she gave up the ass? Of course, JFK had also had affairs with Marilyn Monroe, Mimi Alford and Jill Cowen (both of them secretaries in the White House) and a stripper named Blaze Starr.

<u>Mayor Marion Barry</u>

While he was not directly a trick, he acted like one on enough occasions where, once he got hooked on crack, it appeared that Mayor Barry simply threw caution to the wind. According to Crilly (2014),

> He had had suffered a string of health problems in recent years,
> including diabetes, prostate cancer and a kidney transplant …
> Aside from his very public downfall - captured on video in a hotel
> room smoking a crack pipe in an FBI sting - he was always known
> as gregarious and charismatic, earning the title of Washington's
> "Mayor for life". (Crilly, 2014).

Bad health. A lot of crack heads experience that, and with Barry's track record, it could have been much worse. But as is far too typical of black people, we give assholes like this the benefit of the doubt no matter what they do. The same thing we did for Jesse Jackson and others of his misguided ilk. Crilly offers up the following assessment:

> Mr. Barry managed to earn the title of the most notorious drug
> abuser in North American politics, long before Rob Ford was
> forced to take a leave of absence from his job as mayor of Toronto
> to deal with his drink and drug problems this year. Yet at one time,
> Mr. Barry was a rising star of the Democratic Party, seen as one of
> America's most promising black politicians. He served three terms
> as mayor from 1979 before his personal life overtook his political
> career. (Crilly, 2014).

I don't know about that. Rob Ford smoked crack, talked shit on live TV, and admitted that he "copped" from drug dealers who were in the nearby vicinity. At least Marion Barry tried to keep his shenanigans under cover. But then again, this is a white reporter so what can you expect: when the issue is a negative they are more than willing to give black people "numero uno" status.

Marion had power and when you find a man with power you find someone who is more than willing to spend money on women. Many keep it under wraps but as in the case of Barry, who was like some kind of "godfather," he did his dirt and continued to do it, term after term.

Then came the point where "pussy politics" began to dominate and direct his life:

> In 1990 he met an ex-girlfriend, Rasheeda Moore, at a Washington hotel. Unknown to him, the room was rigged with hidden cameras. The 83-minute video captured him fondling Miss Moore and asking about the possibility of sex before taking two long drags on a crack pipe. At that point, FBI agents and police officers burst into the room. The court - sitting at the time of a crack epidemic and amid rising racial tensions - also heard allegations that the pair had used cocaine as many as 100 times. (Crilly, 2014).

The bitch set him up. She got paid after being laid many years earlier. Just the fact that he was able to fondle her shows that she knew what time it was. And if I remember correctly, she took a hit off the crack pipe as well. The only difference was that he was the political figure and was the one the authorities wanted to get tabs on. And that taped was aired on every major television station in the nation. And the bitch probably got paid after Barry got arrested. .

Continuing:

> Mr. Barry's lawyers accused law enforcement agents of entrapping the mayor and eventually the jury found him guilty of only one lesser charge of cocaine possession. He was sentenced to six months in prison. He later reflected on his troubled third term. In his autobiography, he described the build-up to another drug-fueled encounter at a party: "It was a mix of power, attraction, alcohol, sex and drugs". (Crilly, 2014).

He calls it "a mix of power, attraction, alcohol, sex and drugs." And reader, let me tell you: all five of these areas have something to do with the female persuasion. Men don't use drugs unless there is sex on their minds; men with power don't sit around drinking unless there is a woman somewhere in the vicinity. And in many cases these men are married, so that's one woman who's getting "laid and paid" from the get-go. But for some reason she's just not enough. And so it goes

Corey Booker, Newark Mayor and Senate Candidate

This guy, as of 2017, is being bandied about as a candidate for president in 2020. Really? Why not? He's half white just like Barack Obama is, but he has a lot of baggage. Some of it having to do with the kinds of sexual antics that have been outlined in this section of the book.

Booker was one of the speakers at the 2016 Democratic Convention in July and talked a whole lot of shit about how great America was and why the masses should throw their votes behind Hillary Clinton for president. But what it shows is that most people have short memories and as a result, Booker – like a number of black politicos in city after city – can do dirt and still get away with it. Look at the silly shit this black man, who was at the time running for a senate seat in New Jersey (which he won), got himself into:

Could you call it a scandal? It's not exactly clear *who* is outraged. But Lynsie Lee, a Portland, Ore., stripper who once exchanged private Twitter messages with Senate candidate Cory Booker of New Jersey, is enjoying the attention while it lasts. The story is basically this: On Wednesday a BuzzFeed reporter -- perhaps with sexually challenged New York politico Anthony Weiner on the brain -- posted a story about Lee exchanging private messages with Booker, the bachelor mayor of Newark, N.J. (Pearce, 2013).

As I stated earlier, he won the Senate seat and he continues to be an articulate spokesman for the Democratic party. But I hope you can see why the white man has documentation that the white woman is the black man's "kryptonite." We just can't seem to keep away from those bitches, in person or on line. Why would this black man whose future is bright (in their system, of course) risk it all to engage in a Twitter exchange with a bitch who strips (and probably sells pussy) for a living?

The fact is you can be politically astute and say all the right words at press conferences, staff meetings and during talk shows and still be a complete and total clueless asshole in real life. Want proof?

> The private exchange with Booker, tweeted by Lee, was in February, after the mayor had done some characteristically goofy Twitter bantering with his followers. Booker tweeted to his followers that he wanted to be president of New Jersey's Star Trek club. Lee, who works at a vegan strip club in Portland, publicly tweeted at the ambitious mayor, "if you're ever POTUS I call dibs on First Lady." (Pearce, 2013).

And they wonder how these women end up getting laid and paid. They set these guys up, put on a short skirt and go after them. The guys will pay one way or the other, and it will more likely than not be a long-term "contract" whether the guy knows it or not. Elsewhere in this book, I include an article about the percentage of NBA players who are being blackmailed.

Corey Booker, like Jesse Jackson Jr., Marion Barry and so many other black men who think they are "politicos," can't seem to stop taking steps that will lead to their own undermining and eventual self-destruction. And speaking of these types of bruthas, let's take a look at a man who claimed to be a "reverend" (just like Jesse Jackson) and ended up with his nuts in a vise.
\

Rev. Benjamin Chavis, NAACP

Speaking of getting "laid and paid," Rev. Ben Chavis, a long-time activist whose column I used to run weekly when I was editor of The Milwaukee Courier, got away from addressing issues of "environmental (toxic) racism" and ended up being selected to lead the NAACP.

In July of 1994, the following was reported:

> ATLANTA -- NAACP Executive Director Benjamin F. Chavis Jr. denied yesterday that he sexually harassed a former employee and said he agreed to pay the woman up to $332,400, without telling his board of directors, to "protect the NAACP." (Fletcher, 1994).

How can he protect the NAACP when he is the leader of it? By keeping his indiscretion away from his board of directors he was already violating policy – it's called "malfeasance." And whose money was he using to pay off this woman? More likely than not it was money that he earned as the director of the agency. So he was wrong on yet another count – unapproved expenditures of company funds. Let us continue with his "story":

> In his first public response to Mary E. Stansel's allegations in a lawsuit that she was discriminated against, sexually harassed and fired unjustly, Dr. Chavis told a news conference: "I made an administrative decision to protect the NAACP from exposure to false and slanderous allegations. I believe it would have been irresponsible of me . . . to have allowed this matter to linger." (Fletcher, 1994).

No, what was "irresponsible" was for him to be screwing around with this woman in the first place. These women know what they're doing when they're secretaries to so-called "religious men." Ministers, preachers and the like are the biggest cockhounds there are. That skirt got hiked up a little higher and the compliments starting coming, responded to with a chickenshit smile. Then came the lunches and the late "snacks" in the office. And then he fucked her.

Just like Jesse Jackson, former HUD director Henry Cisneros (who would later be pardoned by President Clinton) and so many others before him, Chavis took the bait. And then when the tables got turned and the woman wanted to get paid, he tried to play the role of the victim.

Now pay close attention to the similar reactions by the wives of these cockhounds. They stand there while the man gives his side of the story, the same way that Vernon Jordan's wife did when she had to stand by his hospital bed after he got shot in the ass by a white man while he (Jordan) was on his way to some white woman's house "for lunch." Remember that? Now, check out the Rev. Ben Chavis situation:

> At times holding hands with his wife, Martha Rivera Chavis, who is pregnant with twins, the 46-year-old NAACP leader said that Ms. Stansel's allegations are "completely false and have no merit. . . . I do not minimize the harm of sexual harassment, when it happens." Ms. Stansel, a former legislative aide to Democratic Sen. Howell Heflin of Alabama, worked briefly as an interim employee at the NAACP in early 1993 but was dismissed. She had been a volunteer in the campaign to make Dr. Chavis the civil rights group's executive director. (Fletcher, 1994).

Pregnant with twins and now holding hands with a man who was getting his dick sucked by a subordinate. She volunteered to help someone she believed in and it got turned into her getting on her knees – just like Bill Clinton did to Monica Lewinsky and Henry Cisneros did with his (paid) mistress. Women get laid and paid and they know how weak men are; it seems to be that the more power these men think they have, the more arrogant they become and the more likely they are to believe that they are above the law. Chavis, like Jesse Jackson, started out being a champion of the people and ended up being nothing more than a cowering cockhound.

And just as these women get laid and paid, the people who have to do the paying stand by and support the criminal perpetrator. The board of the NAACP did just what the wives of these scoundrels tend to do. Check it out:
The 64-member NAACP board was not told of the deal that Dr. Chavis made with Ms. Stansel in November 1993. The out-of-court settlement committed the NAACP to pay her up to $332,400 unless Dr. Chavis helped find her a Washington-area job paying $80,000 a year.

The NAACP should have been disbanded a long time ago. Ever since Thurgood Marshall stopped winning cases, the organization has been under the control of their corporate and Jewish dominated board of directors and have taken control of local chapters by demanding that these local chapters "get permission" in order to pursue certain issues and cases. That slows up and convolutes the entire "civil rights" process – and the N AACP knows this. And meanwhile what is the Board doing: covering the ass of people like Chavis, as in the following example:

> Board Chairman William F. Gibson yesterday defended Dr. Chavis, saying that he had "complete, full executive authority" to make the deal with Ms. Stansel without consulting the board. Dr. Gibson said he knew in late 1993 of Ms. Stansel's threat to sue. "The board had not in the past dealt with such types of complaints and, in this case, there was no reason to deviate from standard operating procedures," he said, flanked by a handful of board members, including vice chairman Ben Andrews Jr. (Fletcher, 1994).

And this is why the NAACP is now moribund – that is, at the point of death. The cycle of Neanderthal activity continues because these negroes are beholden to the white man who is their chief funding source. Their board of directors is chock full of powerful white people and most of them are Jews. But what can you expect when DuBois and others "allowed" these white folks to be a part of the start of the organization? What can you expect when you have a group that talks about advancing "colored" people? And in all those years they have not bothered to alter the name a single time. And therefore it should be expected that behavior like that of Chavis would continue to be covered up.

And when you know your actions, no matter how perfidious, are going to be protected by the President of the Board of Directors, what do you do? Check it out:

> Dr. Chavis refused to discuss in detail why he settled with Ms. Stansel. He also did not talk about the nature of his relationship with her; the news conference was limited to procedural questions surrounding the breach-of-contract suit.(Fletcher, 1994).

Several of the "negro" board members called for Chavis to resign and others wanted to stall time to investigate, but it was clear Chavis would get away for the most part. The point to be made at this juncture is that the woman got both laid and paid, Chavis' wife went for the okey-doke (as did Vernon Jordan's wife, Bill Clinton's wife, Donald Trump's wife and so on) and this is how the cycle is perpetuated.

<u>Henry Cisneros, Dept. of Housing and Urban Development</u>

An article titled, "Cisneros Pleads Guilty to Lying to FBI Agents" offers up evidence of at least another woman "getting laid and paid" by some high ranking politico. Using government money to pay for pussy? Come on. But it's not just the black bruthas doing it; Cisneros proved that Latinos make some of the same mistakes that negro leadership makes.

Check it out:

> Former housing secretary Henry G. Cisneros pleaded guilty yesterday to a single misdemeanor charge of lying to the FBI about money he paid to a former mistress, ending a wide-ranging independent counsel investigation that lasted more than four years and cost more than $9 million. (Miller, 1999).

So he lied and lied, just like Marion Barry was doing until they found him out on tape. Cisneros was accused of lying about the amount of money he had provided to former mistress Linda Jones, a political fund-raiser with whom he had an affair beginning in 1987. But in the case of Cisneros, all those lies were costing more money with the courts. And he still got off relatively easy. While Clinton was getting his dick sucked by an under-aged intern, Henry was battling in the courts to keep from getting butt fucked in a prison:

> Cisneros, 52, is the first Cabinet member of the Clinton administration to plead guilty in a case brought by an independent counsel, though the consequences of the plea proved relatively mild: Cisneros agreed to a $10,000 fine and a $25 court assessment, but he will serve no time either in prison or on probation and he will be free to seek elected office. (Miller, 1999).

He could still seek elected office if he chose to, and only had to pay a small fine. Not only that but,

> As part of the plea agreement, Cisneros was required to admit that he had knowingly given false information to FBI investigators. He told U.S. District Judge Stanley Sporkin that he regretted his "lack of candor" and added, "It is my hope that other people who aspire to and follow in public service will also perhaps learn . . . that truth and candor are important in the process of selecting people for governmental positions." (Miller, 1999)

So Cisneros was able to bullshit his way out of paying for buying pussy. And this woman got laid and paid. Miller writes that as part of his guilty plea, Cisneros, "admitted telling an FBI agent that he had paid Jones roughly $2,500 a month after their relationship ended, when in fact the payments were considerably higher. All told, prosecutors said that Cisneros provided Jones with more than $250,000 from 1990 until 1994." (Miller, 1999). What? Even after things were cut off she STILL got paid? That's bullshit. Why was he paying to keep her quiet and not get any pussy? Trying to adopt the role of the "white knight" check out Cisneros' reasoning:

> When the judge asked why he had lied, Cisneros answered, "For one thing, I wasn't sure about the numbers personally. I had never calculated them up. But beyond that, I was trying to protect [Jones], who didn't want the information out, and my own wife, who didn't know precisely what the number was. And in the final analysis I've attributed it to the pressure and confused sort of fog of the moment where I gave an incorrect number." (Miller, 1999).

But the fact is, Clinton was the standard bearer and a lot of the people in his administration got busted for criminal activity. For instance, Miller (1999) documents that, "Cisneros is one of several Clinton Cabinet officials to be targeted by independent counsel investigations. Former agriculture secretary Mike Espy was acquitted of corruption charges after a trial last year, and investigations of Interior Secretary Bruce Babbitt and Labor Secretary Alexis M. Herman are still ongoing." (Miller, 1999). It should be noted that Herman, who was accused to accepting kickbacks, was cleared of the charges.

Women getting laid and paid. It's as American as apple pie

Eliot Spitzer

This guy had credentials, juice and a good life. He had a law degree from Harvard and another degree from Princeton. He was a prosecutor in the Manhattan District Attorney general's office and had a job as a private attorney with several New York law firms. HE then served as Attorney General for New York from 1999 to 2006. As if that wasn't enough, this power-hungry sonofabitch ran for and then was elected governor of New York where he served for just over a year until the roof caved in: Eliot Spitzer definitely got laid and paid. But he paid a high price for it. As it was reported in March of 2008,

> On March 10, 2008, *The New York Times* reported that Spitzer had previously patronized a high-priced prostitution service called Emperors Club VIP[92] and met for two hours with a $1,000-an-hour call girl. This information originally came to the attention of authorities from a federal wiretap … Spitzer had at least seven or

> eight liaisons with women from the agency over six months, and
> paid more than $15,000 ... (Hakim & Rashbaum, 2008).

You should have seen the picture in the New York Times: poor Mrs. Spitzer standing next to her man and then in another picture, holding his hand while they scurried away from the podium following his resignation announcement. All that money and power, and this peckerwood couldn't keep his dick in his pants. Just like so many of the others: they start thinking they're above the law, but there's a factor that most of the media seem to consistently overlook.

What about these women? They know who they're screwing and they lay out a plan. With them there is a "plan A" and a "plan B." Plan "A" is to screw this guy and get money for it. They know who he is and after the act is done, they want to make sure that its on-going and that he pays well. If he seems to be the "one night stand" type, then they can rig it so that they get him on film or in some way convince him that he is going to keep paying or they will jeopardize his career. This is one of the ways that these women "get laid and paid."

What was with this guy: no pussy is worth a thousand dollars an hour unless you're getting an hours' worth! These guys are prematurely ejaculating and then lying there waiting to get some head. They might load up on Viagra, Cialis or Levitra and keep a long-time boner, that that's still an issue of give and take! These women have convinced these men that having sex is a one-way street and that they (the men) are one-way beneficiaries of some kind of "gift." They (the women) are getting dicked as well! What's up with that?

Continuing:

> According to published reports, investigators believe Spitzer paid
> up to $80,000 for prostitutes over a period of several years while
> he was Attorney General, and later as Governor ... Spitzer first
> drew the attention of federal investigators when his bank reported
> suspicious money transfers under the anti-money laundering
> provisions of the Bank Secrecy Act and the Patriot Act ... The
> resulting investigation, triggered by the belief that Spitzer may
> have been hiding bribe proceeds, led to the discovery of the
> prostitution ring ... (Hakim & Rashbaum, 2008).

He was manipulating bank accounts, deceiving his wife, lying to his family and buying pussy even while he was working in the attorney general's office. How sick can you get? This means that he had sex on his mind around the clock, and his bank account proved that to be the case. What was his wife doing all this time? Was he even sleeping with her. She was no beauty but still they had three daughters and had been married for 26 years (1987-2013) before divorcing. How can you have three little girls at home sitting on your lap, a wife slaving away in the kitchen and taking care of your over-sized home and still have the gall to be staring down on the head of a prostitute while she sucks your dick?: This, in my book, describes a man with absolutely no conscience and waaaaaayyyyy too much time on his hands!

But he threw all caution to the wind, betraying the constituents of the largest state in the union. And it eventually came to a resounding conclusion:

> In the wake of the revelations, Spitzer announced on March 12, 2008, that he would resign his post as governor at noon on March 17, 2008, amid threats of his impeachment by state lawmakers … "I cannot allow for my private failings to disrupt the people's work," Spitzer said at a news conference in New York City. "Over the course of my public life, I have insisted – I believe correctly – that people take responsibility for their conduct. I can and will ask no less of myself. For this reason, I am resigning from the office of governor" … (Hakim & Rashbaum, 2008).

And that's how it ended. And now people have forgotten because such scandals are common place. Donald Trump may be a lousy human being, but he is not the first nor will he be the last. And that is the point I want to make. There is an old saying that, "all men and most rivers are crooked because they choose the path of least resistance." My version of that quote is that, "all rivers and most men walk around wet because they get all kinds of pussy and forget to wash their ass afterwards." I didn't say it made sense.

Anthony Weiner

Three years after the Eliot Spitzer incident and even more bizarre resignation took place in New York, this one involving a man who couldn't stop showing his dick to under aged girls on the internet. His name, quite appropriately, was "Anthony Weiner."

> American politician Anthony Weiner, former member of the United States House of Representatives from New York City, has been involved in two sexual scandals related to sexting, or sending explicit sexual material by cell phone. The first, sometimes dubbed **Weinergate**, led to his resignation as a congressman in 2011. The second, during his attempt to return to politics as candidate for mayor of New York City, involved three women Weiner admitted having sexted after further explicit pictures were published in July 2013. (Wikipedia, 2016).

There had to have been money involved on some level. Why not mention it? This guy is showing his dick to under-aged girls and anyone who wanted to see it and you mean to tell me that these women didn't see that money could be made? It was so bad that he had to resign, so why did he do that? What prompted him to step down? What was the threat? His reputation had already been besmirched. Was there some extortion or bribery involved? You mean to tell me that of the three women involved, none of them practiced the art of "getting laid and paid" and went after this well-heeled politician?

Continuing:

> The first scandal began when Democratic U.S. Congressman Weiner used the social media website Twitter to send a link to a sexually suggestive picture of himself to a 21-year-old woman from Seattle, Washington. After several days of denying media reports that he had posted the image, he admitted to having sent a link to the photo, and also other sexually explicit photos and messages to women both before and during his marriage. (Wikipedia, 2016).

Have you seen Weiner's wife? This woman is beautiful and dark-skinned. She is powerful, a close friend and confidante of Hillary Clinton. He had it made. This hook-nosed honkey had this lovely, talented and accomplished brown-skinned beauty and they even had a child together. But that wasn't enough for this white boy. What does he do? This perverted bastard decides to flash himself on social media. Where is the money? It has to be somewhere because he did it without even going after any booty – or so he claimed:

> He denied ever having met, or having had a physical relationship with any of the women. On June 16, 2011, Weiner announced his intention to resign from Congress with his official resignation occurring on June 23, 2011. (Wikipedia, 2016).

So he was a straight-up pervert. His wife Huma Mahmood Abedin of six years (2010-2016) was busily working in politics just as he was. But he was so sick and disrespectful of this woman of color that he just threw caution to the wind. When they got married Bill Clinton officiated the wedding ceremony which, to me, was the kiss of death right there. Weiner and this beauty – who is a Muslim by faith – had a son, Jordan Zain Weiner. But you are what you associate with; by being close to Bill Clinton some of the perversion was bound to rub off on Weiner.

But Clinton finally got caught and ended up paying off some of his former mistresses; Weiner was a different story:

> A second scandal began on July 23, 2013, after Weiner returned to politics in April 2013 by entering the New York City mayoral election, when more pictures and sexting by Weiner were released by the website *The Dirty*. They were allegedly sent under the alias 'Carlos Danger' to a 22-year-old woman with whom Weiner had contact in late 2012, and as late as April 2013, more than a year after Weiner had left Congress. (Wikipedia, 2016).

The alias of "Carlos Danger"? What kind of "contact" did he have? There had to be a money exchange somewhere because he had plenty of it and any woman that would "meet with" a pervert like this has to have a financial plan of some kind. But what he did was not forgiven: "Weiner admitted sexting at least three women during this period, and although called on by the New York Times editorial board, among others, to leave the mayoral race, he remained in the race until the end, when he took fifth place in the Democratic primary, with 4.9% of the vote" (Wikipedia, 2016).

THE RICHEST WOMEN IN THE WORLD

How could I write a book about women getting "laid and paid" without sharing with you what I view as the key underlying dynamic of both? Men's lust is exploited and pimped by women and the values of the society. Even the Bible is filled with lies and bullshit that place women in a subservient position. What they have been able to do is take their vaginas and place a market value on them; at first it was through marriage and the provision of a house, land and other assets, which of course they had to pay for by bearing children. But if those children were girls, they were able to train them about boys and men and how easy it is to manipulate both.

Wealth is defined as, "abundance of valuable material possessions or resources." Back in the day in Europe and Africa there were "arranged marriages," but the man had to have some kind of wealth: land, money or otherwise. Once married into that family, the woman had to "obey" and do her "womanly duties." This meant giving up a whole lot of booty whenever the man wanted it. If he prematurely ejaculated, so what? If she didn't get a nut, so what? James Browns' rather sexist 1966 song, "It's a Man's World" pretty much lays out the foundation for the global system of gender discrimination. Remember?

This is a man's world, this is a man's world
But it wouldn't be nothing, nothing without a woman or a girl
You see, man made the cars to take us over the road
Man made the train to carry the heavy load
Man made electric light to take us out of the dark
Man made the boat for the water, like Noah made the ark
This is a man's, man's, man's world
But it wouldn't be nothing, nothing without a woman or a girl
Man thinks about our little bitty baby girls and our baby boys
Man made them happy, 'cause man made them toys
And after man make everything, everything he can
You know that man makes money, to buy from other man
This is a man's world
But it wouldn't be nothing, nothing, not one little thing, without a woman or a girl
He's lost in the wilderness
He's lost in bitterness, he's lost lost

While admitting that this "man's world" would be nothing without a woman or a little girl, what the lyrics seem to overlook is that every man is born of a woman and raised by one. So it's actually a woman's world and it is my belief that they knew this all along. But without power what could they do? Men were physically stronger and if women stood up, they'd get their asses kicked or labeled as witches or burned at the stake.

Wealth then came through marriage and even then, the male-run courts made the decision regarding the division of property if the man died or there was a divorce. In fact, women couldn't even own land or property in some cultures. So they waited and over the centuries, increased their impact and influence on powerful men who, in turn, through a pussy whipped stupor, passed laws that began to ease the burden that had been placed on the female of the species.

Now with my rather bizarre interpretation of history out of the way (the truth can oftentimes be viewed as "bizarre"), let's fast forward to today's world and a March 7, 2016 article by Bartie Scott titled, "Forbes' Wealthiest Women in the World." I share this article and the list with you so that you can see that on some level, these rich women "got laid and paid" and came into their wealth. Now, remember the lyrics to James Brown's song. And even with women using "pussy power" to gain more and more control, it remains a "man's world" because he continues to control the wealth.

As importantly the male also controls the policies and the politics of wealth. That means he can lie, distort and control the contractual elements involved in business and the economy, This is what she exploits: the knowledge that she has to have her own money so that she can do things her way. Put another way, "you cannot have political freedom without an economic base" (Karenga, 1967). And in the case of almost every single one of these women, the big money came from some man, either directly or indirectly.

Let's take a look courtesy of Forbes' wealthiest women in the world 2016.

Liliane Bettencourt, whose wealth comes from L'Oreal. Her net worth is $36.1 billion, but get this: she maybe the richest person in the world but she's an "heiress." In other words, she got the company from somebody else. Research tells us that,

> In 1909, Eugène Paul Louis Schueller, a young French chemist of German descent,[7] developed a hair dye formula called *Auréale*. Schueller formulated and manufactured his own products, which he then sold to Parisian hairdressers. On 31 July 1919, Schueller registered his company,[8] the Société Française de Teintures Inoffensives pour Cheveux (Safe Hair Dye Company of France). The guiding principles of the company, which eventually became L'Oréal, were research and innovation in the field of beauty. In 1920, the company employed three chemists. By 1950, the team was 100 strong; that number reached 1,000 by 1984 and is nearly 20,000 today.

So another woman gets "paid" because some male founded a company and she somehow stumbled into it. The specifics are not even important. This French company shows that the white man is paying for pussy just like his American counterpart. Now this rich woman has been paid. And what is their slogan? It's "Because I'm worth it." Name one woman who doesn't believe in this maxim.

Alice Walton is the second richest woman in the world, worth $32.3 billion and is the daughter of Sam Walton, the founder of those Wal-Mart stores.(Scott, 2016). So she is the product of a woman who got laid and now she has gotten paid.

Jacqueline Mars is worth $23.4 billion and is the daughter of the man who inherited the Mars candy empire along with some pet food companies. In other words, another "heiress." She has brothers who share in the inheritance, but remember this: all of them came from the woman who seduced and then married. According to Forbes magazine,

> Jacqueline Mars (born October 10, 1939) is an American heiress, and investor. She is the daughter of Audrey Ruth (Meyer) and Forrest Mars, Sr., and granddaughter of Frank C. Mars, founders of the American candy company Mars, Incorporated. In 2014, *Forbes* described Mars as the 20th richest American. (Forbes, 2014).

Mars has evolved according to the research. According to Yahoo.com, "The Mars bars were sold as such in the US until 2002 when its name was changed to Snickers Almond Bar. It contained then, and still does, plain nougat, almonds, caramel and milk chocolate." Snickers remains a favorite for the most part, and Jacqueline and her brothers keep raking in the dough.

Maria Franca Fissolo of Italy is worth $22.1 billion. She's another candy heiress, this one with Nutella and related chocolates. An obvious case of "getting laid and paid." According to Scott (2016), "She is the widow of Michele Ferrero, who built Ferrero Group and died on Valentine's Day 2015. The private company is owned by Fissolo and her son Giovanni, the CEO; its products include the popular Nutella spread, Kinder chocolates and Tic-Tac mints." So she hooks up with some rich Italian, gives up the booty and has kids by him, qualifying her to inherit all his shit. Now she's the owner (along with her son. See how it works?

Susanne Klatten is the daughter of a woman who got laid and paid, and is the owner of BMW after her mother died. Although Klatten is credited with steering German pharmaceutical and chemical company Altana AG toward $2 billion in annual sales, the fact has to remain that the "roots" of her wealth come from being the daughter of a woman who, again, "got laid and paid." Like Donald Trump, she was born with a silver spoon in her ass … oops! I mean MOUTH. You can afford to be an innovator when money is never an object.

Then there's **Laurene Powell Jobs**. Name sound familiar? It should. While she's an accomplished woman, she is also the widow of the late Steve Jobs, founder of Apple Computers, and it worth $16.7 billion. According to the research,

> Laurene Powell Jobs is an American businesswoman, executive and the founder of Emerson Collective, which advocates for policies concerning education and immigration reform, social justice and environmental conservation. She is also co-founder and president of the Board of College Track, which prepares disadvantaged high school students for college. Powell Jobs resides in Palo Alto, California, with her three children. She is the widow of Steve Jobs, co-founder and former chief executive officer of Apple Inc. She manages the Laurene Powell Jobs Trust.(Scott, 2016; Wikipedia, 2017).

See how it's done. She's blonde and cute and allows him to talk her out of her panties. He becomes a billionaire, dies at an early age (she had to have found out he was ill), the necessary paperwork is in place and then, voila! The one who used to get laid has now been paid. She also owns a chunk of Disney.

Abigail Johnson is worth $13.1 billion and her wealth comes from "money management." Again, we find someone who got her start based on what she got from a man – her grandfather. As one source informs us,

> Abigail Pierrepont "Abby" Johnson (born December 19, 1961) is an American businesswoman. Since 2014, Johnson is President and Chief Executive Officer of US investment firm Fidelity Investments (FMR), and chairwoman of its international sister company Fidelity International (FIL). Fidelity was founded by her grandfather Edward C. Johnson II. Her father Edward C. "Ned" Johnson III remains Chairman Emeritus of FMR. As of March 2013, the Johnson family owned a 49% stake in the company. In November 2016, Johnson was named Chairman and will remain CEO and President giving her full control of Fidelity with 45,000 employees worldwide … Johnson's wealth of approximately $14 billion making her one of the world's wealthiest women. (Healy, 2014).

So her grandmother set everything up by screwing her grandfather, who handed the empire to his son. Then, he handed control over to Abigail. So again, a woman gets a hand me down from a man who impregnated that woman's mother and gave her a lifestyle of wealth. Getting laid and paid.

Charlene de Carvallio Heineken is worth $12.3 billion. I know you recognize the last name. That's right, she's from the Netherlands and she's another heiress. Her parents had money as well. Check it out:

> Charlene de Carvalho-Heineken (born 30 June 1954) is a Dutch-English businesswoman and the owner of a 25% controlling interest in the world's third-largest brewer, Heineken International. Charlene Heineken was born on 30 June 1954, the daughter of Freddy Heineken, the Dutch industrialist, and Lucille Cummins, an American from a Kentucky family of bourbon whiskey distillers. She was educated at Rijnlands Lyceum Wassenaar, followed by a law degree from the University of Leiden.

So her mother got laid, impregnated and paid and this makes Charlene another heiress. See what I mean? This gives an entire new meaning to those James Brown lyrics I shared, especially the part where he croons, "This is a man's world/But it would be nothing/without a woman or a little girl." He was right. The man continues to the species after impregnating one of these women who then gets all of his shit when he dies. So she can then go out and find another guy who is well off and the plutocracy (government by the wealthy) therefore perpetuates itself: getting laid and pad.

Christie Walton is the daughter-in law of Wal-Mart founder Sam Walton. Her net worth is "only" $5.2 billion after dividing her late husband's estate with their 29 year old son, Lukas.

THE GROWN MAN AS CHILD

During the airing of what was originally a January 2, 1962 episode of the western, "Laramie," we find that even back then, during the days of the wild, wild west, the tendency was to treat men like children in order to be an "acceptable" woman.

In this episode, "After saving the life of an Arapaho girl in a fire and helping acquit her in a trial for killing a man, Slim (Sherman, played by John Smith) finds her his possession due to Arapaho law. When she won't leave him, he takes her in but soon finds he has feelings for her." At one point the beauty, whose name is Winona, draws Slim a warm bath without him having to tell her. They walk into his room and he asks her, if she learned this kind of treatment of a man back on the reservation. She tells him, "They taught us how to bathe small children. And what is a man but a small child grown up?"

And there you have it. At first it may seem like a contradiction: the big, bad macho man making sure that the female remains his social, cultural, political, educational and physical inferior. But there is one thing that he overlooked: she has always been his intellectual superior. And because of that, his machismo and political cravings are always manipulated by her and committed in her name. Keep in mind that, "the hand that rocks the cradle rules the throne."

This has always been the case. Don't be fooled into thinking that the rise of white bitches like Hillary Clinton, Elizabeth Warren, Nancy Pelosi is something new: white women have been in control of the men who appear to be in control. And they do it because behind closed doors, they treat him like a child. And he likes it and accepts it. And black people have mocked this pattern of behavior in the way the women treat the men and society has taken notice. Especially the advertising world.

Witness this spate of insurance commercials. What do you see? These mealy-mouthed effeminate "men" (husbands) kissing their wives asses and acting as if they don't know what to do. Companies like Metropolitan Life, Colonial Penn, Liberty Insurance, Mass Mutual, and many others have targeted black elderly married couples, scaring the shit out of them about dying and leaving behind huge funerals bills, and do it by showing the woman large and in charge while the man, admitting that "his health" might be a problem and may impede their qualifying for life insurance, stands back like some scatter-brained bitch while she makes the decision that yes, indeed, they may well need such insurance.

And it's not only the case with health and life insurance. Just look at the family on television: the man is the perennial fuckup, the excuse-maker and the clownish buffoon. On one such commercial, Liberty Mutual insurance commercial this white boy talks about he is leaving for work with his ten gallon jug of coffee and he's backing out of the driveway and then "accidentally bumped into his wife's car while she was watching," and that "she forgave him later on -- eventually" and then goes about attacking the insurance company. Forgave him? He didn't do it purposely so why should he have to apologize to that bitch?

Oasisi Express Cash features this effeminate sounding black man who promotes the product. Another one named "William M." comes on sounding even more bitch-like than the narrator. Mark S. is another one, who calls Oasis Financial "a blessing" is the third "coon" that comes on the air sounding like he was in need of a panty shield. And the list goes on and on. And here is what you have to remember: these "men" were selected over scores of others who auditioned to tell these lies. They were chosen by a committee of white men who weighed their attributes and how they would "come across." This effeminate shit you're *seeing is all by design.*

Or how about the Buick commercial (aired during the summer of 2016) where the young white couple is on vacation. Clad in bathing suits they sit in the shade next to a pool. She asks him if he remembered to handle an issue with their Buick, he assures her he did. Even as the words are uttered she then asks him if he remembered to close the windows in the apartment. He claims he did as she whispers, "You're the greatest." But out of her vision is this chickenshit look in his face as he re-thinks his position on the windows. Cut to the apartment with pigeons flying in and are all over the place.
Again, the woman is the responsible one (although she should have shut the damn windows herself) and the man, who is probably paying for the vacation where she is relaxing, is the asshole. She is large and in charge and of course, getting g laid and paid.

In other commercials, the ones where the man is not totally left out while the single mother who looks like a Victoria Secret model is shown having it all under control, the man is a simpleton. Swiffer wet mops shows this giant of a man mopping up behind his bad-ass half-white kid instead of putting his foot in that kid's ass the first time he fucked up. Another time the little half-white daughter is concerned about her daddy's heart so after talking with her white mommy, the daddy, who is asleep on the couch, wakes up and finds Cheerios all over his fuckin' chest. The little girl was told that Cheerios are good for your heart.

In addition, these effeminate rapper faggots are really a trip. They walk around in skinny jeans acting like children. You've got the likes of Pharrell Williams, Usher, Young Thug, 50 Cent, P-Diddy and so many others either actually gay or what they might refer to as asexual, pansexual, and/or bisexual. What does this have to do with being a "child"? It begins with denial of black manhood. Once you do that, you can be used or manipulated into being anything, including gay and a child. That's the connection. And it's being exploited by white people because they have always had childish tendencies and orientations and it is reflected in the way they act, think and talk once they reach maturity.

RISE OF THE CHICKEN HEADS: EVEN UGLY WOMEN CAN GET "LAID AND PAID"

Under a separate heading I wrote this essay as, "The Rise of the Chicken heads: When Beauty IS a Beast!" In California they define a "chickenhead" as a woman who is a gold digger seeking out a man to pay her bills. In Milwaukee a "chickenhead" is basically a crack whore to gives up head and booty for a hit of dope. In my vernacular, and that of the people I grew up with, a "chickenhead" is just another name for an unattractive female.

At any rate, the point being made here can be found in an anonymous maxim: "Showing cleavage doesn't fix your face."

Ugly women are the new fine hos. Seriously. At least, that's the way it is in their minds and in this culture. Look at television and you can see it: white, black Asian, Latina – whatever. If you can walk in a pair of five inch heels and wear a skirt up to your panty line without actually exposing the panties (thanks to the thong, a thing will keep your panties from showing,), then you qualify.

Aiding these chicken heads in their quest for "pseudo-beauty" is the white man, who is the expert. After all, he's succeeded in making his pale, no breasted, flat-booty woman a standard of beauty for the world. And now the women of color all over this country are trying to look like her, but let me not get ahead of myself. First, we share what makes a woman ugly.

To begin with, it's her shallowness and attitude. And some of these fashions that I've alluded to aid and abet her in this "crime." She's flinging back her fake hair and has her hands on a waist held in place by a girdle and truly thinks that she's 'the bomb.' There are men who find this attractive. But he's encountering someone who has serious esteem issues and who is so obsessed with being accepted by her friends and being with the "in crowd," that she also mimics the attitude that will get her noticed as being "independent," "a down chick," "a strong woman" and so on. What it does is bring attention to what she really is: a modern day emotional troglodyte.

Now after the shallowness and attitude issues we come to the image issues which piles on additional dimensions of shallowness. How do I notice thee? Let me count the ways.

First, the extensions and the wigs. I venture to guess that more than 60% of black women in this country between the ages of 18 and 60 have some fake shit in their head. But the fact is, these women are putting it in the heads of their young daughters as well. Maybe they're too damn lazy to comb it, but the other day I saw a little girl about nine years old with extensions in her head – including blonde ones! What is this telling her about herself and culture? First it was the straightening comb, now it's this shit! (And black men: don't forget those "conks" that you used to put in your head so you could have textured hair like that cracker).

Anyway, these women are spending hundreds of dollars on this shit. Just so they can flip it back in anger or when they turn their heads – the way they've seen the white woman do for decades. And what's so cold about it is that they really seem to think the shit is theirs! And if you ask them (which I will do every time I get the chance) they'll say something flippant like, "yeah it's mine – I paid for it!" Self-image issues, pure and simple.

So it's not just the extensions and wigs, but many of them add color. I've seen more honey-blonde black women in the past five years than I saw during the previous 53 years of my life, combined. Even worse, the young generation has added new colors to their fake-ass repertoire: green, blue, blood red (and maroon), platinum and I've even seen purple. The older ones whose hair is graying refer to it as "silver" and then do whatever it is they do to make it appear as if they have more than they've got. I think they're called "hair pieces."

Now the eyes, which are supposed to be the "gateway to the soul." Based on the length of these eyelashes these women are wearing, I'd have to say that the gateway to the soul needs a pruning! Some of these eyelashes are a full half an inch long! Then they glue them to the ones they've got and they still look like shit. These women's eyelashes are so long that when you kiss them, you know when they open their eyes because the lashes brush your face!

The eyeliners and all that color, including glitter that they use – man, save that shit for the circus! This is the kind of makeup that used to be reserved for the bride of Frankenstein, Clayface and other feature creatures! They don't spare the nose: now it's vogue to have your nose pierced, sometimes on both sides, which prompts a thinking person to ask: what happens to the buggers and snot?

For a long time earrings have been modified in the name of being "hip." These women went from studs to earrings the size of bicycle rims. I mean, they are huge and some of them have the nerve to wear three and four earrings in one ear! When they do that you can hear the jingling and jangling halfway down the hallway!

And then, the breastseses. I am one of the men who can spot the "type" of breast no matter what you try to do to veil them. There are small breasts embellished with a padded bra – oftentimes complete with fake nipples. There are the sagging ones (I call them "droopers") that are pulled up and out with these new-fangled bras that have been developed. The breasts look alright with that bra on, but when they take it off, those things fall to their knees. There's the bra that helps them look larger, more full and can push those puppies right up under their chins, which is the way women seem to be wearing their blouses these days.

Speaking of blouses, there is an increasingly popular style that accommodates these "tittie-fakers." You've seen 'em: these newfangled blouses and shirts that are deep-V cut and allow propped up breasts to be exposed. They're not really "new," because trollops, saloon girls, street hos, women at dance clubs and other night crawler types wore them back in the day. But this "look-at-my-tits" style is even now being accepted in the workplace. And when they hit the club or some social event, you can almost see everything but the nipple.

The waist line can be equally well disguised. They've got these body suits that serve double duty: prop up the boobs and hold in the butt at the same time. They've got the girdles that hold in the gut and firm up the butt. They've got the ones that bring in your waistline only. There's so many looks to choose from, but let us not get it twisted: all this shit is about two types of deception: self-deception and social deception. The former is aimed at convincing yourself that you "still have it" and the second is aimed at convincing others – friends, relatives – that you don't have any psychological issues about "losing it" in the first place. In both cases, they are dead wrong.

Now before moving on, consider this: imagine getting up and having to put all this shit on, manage and arrange it and then live in pain all day along, thinking about avoiding certain things, the lies – both implicit and explicit – that you have to live each and every day. Now can you see why black women are always pissed off? They're not mad at you because you never asked them to do all this shit: they're mad at themselves and their mad at other women, white and black, for looking so "good" that they have to put on these fronts and facades in order to "fit in." Feel me?

So we've got the hair, the ears, the eyes, the nose, the breasts, waist, hips and ass. Let us move on and describe more evidence of the "image issues" that permeate far too many females in this society.

The feet. Most black women have big feet and they apparently don't like the fact. I think many have accepted it, because it's the only way to explain why they bring so much attention to those feet. They paint their toenails and then wear open toed shoes. Fine. But why do that when you're bringing attention to something that is bringing you pain, namely, those damn shoes!

These women are wearing five- and seven-inch heels, man! They're towering over everybody just so they can "look good" (or so they think). They are in pain because the human foot wasn't made to have all that weight (and some of these women are huge) on the falls of the foot. It's almost laughable how they maintain balance and some will even walk on gravel and uneven surfaces rather than taking their shoes off. Some even have the nerve to wear ankle bracelets, which bring even MORE attention to those feet.

The underalls which serve to also hold in the butt cheeks and give shape to sagging, unflattering asses, also serve to shape the legs in many cases.

There we have it: a female version of Frankenstein, Jr.! What could the psychological and emotional implications be for someone who is so manufactured, so fake, so committed to accepting the falsity of their looks? We know this much: it cannot, on any level, be positive. Psychologically, you are creating another person's because the person that you are, the way that you look, are realities that you simply cannot accept or deal with.

Emotionally, it's even deeper. You have to maintain this shit when you enter a relationship or go visit the family during the holidays. You have to keep this front up when you go out with the girls. You have to keep all this stuff up to snuff when you have an important engagement or go to work or to church. In other words, you have to be fake in order to be emotionally secure. But you cannot be emotionally secure unless you accept the fact that everything about you is fake.

The only people who see the "real you" (other than yourself) are your children, and they can't stand you with your "image issues" having self. Why? Because you chastise them and kick that ass for them being "bad" or out of control when it's YOU who's out of control. So much to the point that while they're getting ready for school, you're putting on all that fake shit I just described. When they're home doing their homework, you're stripping out of all that "goon gear" I just talked about. The quality time that you ought be spending with them is spent "relaxing," which is really nothing more than "decompressing" from the freak show that you have become.

Somebody with image issues needs you to affirm her womanhood. Well, they really don't "need" it, but they think they do. And when it comes to women, what they think is their world. That's why they when they enter a relationship they feel it's their goal to "fix," "repair, "mend" or otherwise "improve" the male. And why is that? Because they can't let you go on being your "natural" self while they go through the transformations that I've just described! They want control and the only way they can control you is to make you think you're just as f----ed up as they are!

No matter how much makeup or camera filters you shoot them through, a chickenhead is a chickenhead. Wanna name names? I'll offer a few so you won't think that what I've just provided is nothing more than a cacophony of emotive labeling. Here we go: Margaret Cho (comedienne), Sarah Jessica Parker ("Sex in the City"), Cheryl Underwood ("The Talk"), Jamie Lee Curtis, Tori Spelling, Joan

Rivers, Carla Hall ("The Chew"), Renee Zellweiger, Kristen Stewart, Barbara Walters, Courtney Love, Hunter Tylo, Amy Schumer, Whoopi Goldberg and Sandra Bernhard.

Can I make it any plainer?

THE REALITY OF ALIMONY: KA-CHING!

As someone who has studied sociology at the doctoral level and written extensively on a number of sociological topics ranging from marriage and family, collective behavior and social stratification to culture, urban activity and deviance, I found the on-going defense of "alimony" an interesting one. So I looked into it and found that much of what is written does not really fit into its actual practice and application in the real world. Let me share with you some of my findings, observations and perspectives.

To begin with, what is "alimony." Involves a great deal of judicial and legal "discretion." I have found in my studies that when it comes to discretion in the hands of white people, it means carte blanche when it comes to fines, penalties and meting out punishment, especially when it comes to the application of the law and how to use it as a means of "control." Controlling women and entire families is another area where judicial discretion can be applied with extreme prejudice.

According to the on-line Free/Legal Dictionary, alimony is described thusly:

> The purpose of alimony is to avoid any unfair economic consequences of a Divorce, even after property is divided and Child Support, if any, is awarded. Courts set few specific guidelines to attaining this broad goal: instead of telling judges how and when to award alimony, most courts simply grant them broad discretion to decide what is fair in each case (Burton, 2007).

When the words "fair" and/or "unfair" are used by this American system, what it really means is what constitutes "fairness" in the minds of white people. And since discretion is a part of determining what is fair, that gives them free reign to be unfair to those groups they don't like. Women are one such group.

I am no feminist but I am a brilliant analyst. And there is something inherently unfair about a system that first of all lies about the "value" or "morality" of monogamous marriage. The ceremony is replete with lies about "'til death do us part" and loving someone "in sickness and in health" and other lies that humans usually fall short of. The fact that the divorce rate is near 60% proves my point.

But after that act of ersatz morality, and things don't work out, we can apply and accurately test the validity of the previous definition. To begin with, keeping in mind that this is a system run by men even though women are the numerical majority, read again this statement: "The purpose of alimony is to avoid any unfair economic consequences of a Divorce, even after property is divided and Child Support, if any, is awarded." This is a system that finds on-going disparate pay for women, a glass ceiling in the workplace and perpetual rapes and abuses a part of its culture. How can such a system therefore view women with anything even remotely approaching objectivity or "fairness"? This is a system that didn't even "allow" women the right to vote until 1920!

So "fairness" is defined by the people who make the rules. When property is divided, what is it based on? To many people, a fifty-fifty split of property is fair. But is it? To get half of what the family assets amount to is not fair to men who may have paid in much more during the marriage. But it is not fair to women either: they have to keep the children in many cases and that means that they have to deal with school, child support and child-related expenses. But even in that, women still manage to get "laid and paid" on an optimum level and I'm going to show you how. The late actor John Barrymore once quipped, "You never realize how short a month is until you pay alimony."

The divorce is final and alimony is doled out, usually to the woman (but not all the time). But this book is about women getting paid and that is my focus at this point. Women use that alimony to care for the child and in most cases, they also have to maintain the house, which they are usually rewarded. Now keep in mind that no matter how well off a woman may appear to be, she is still living in a society that is controlled by male rules. She knows that. So what is the male's main weakness? Pussy. So although it may appear as if the man is now free to cock hound now that he's divorced, the woman actually has the advantage even if she does have the children.

You see, she is getting a monthly payment and doesn't have to leave the house to get it. If she works, that's just icing on the cake. Children or no children, she's got a guaranteed income and even while paying for child care and related children's expenses, she's not going broke. The court will make sure that the former husband pays his alimony and if he doesn't, then he'll go to jail. So the man loses on that count as well.

Now the previous definition adds that in the case of alimony decisions, "instead of telling judges how and when to award alimony, most courts simply grant them broad discretion to decide what is fair in each case." Again, we find that word "fair" and what did we learn about its application when gender issues are involved? We learned that the female will always receive short shrift, either immediately or down the road.

So the alimony has been awarded, and she is now free. The alimony is going to continue until she re-marries, and this is the key: she is not required to re-marry. So now she is free to collect alimony, recruit and get free dick, get the money that the "new" relationship (or relationships) can generate and basically live the life of Riley. She gets to raise the kids which is not the "curse" that some people try to make it out to be, because once those kids grow up, they are going to kick in and take care of mommy dearest as well. And this gives her time to continue poisoning the minds of the kids against their father while making herself out to be some kind of saint, savior or self-sacrificing victim who "bore the brunt" of a bad marriage.

By the time she re-marries – if she decides to make that mistake again – she's not broke. Women outlive men on average anyway: alimony is a cash cow if the woman manages it correctly. Since she's out looking for a new dick she's going to dress better, look better and has learned from any mistakes she made during the previous marriage. And the new guy is none the wiser.

I've always said that where there is white discretion, there is racism and gender bias. This is perhaps most true in the case of the court system in general and the family courts, in particular. Burton (2007) writes that, "No mathematical guidelines exist to tell courts how to calculate alimony. In addition, each state legislature sets its own policy regarding whether and when alimony may be awarded.

And according to the US Legal. Com website (2017), "The Uniform Marriage and Divorce Act (UMDA) was an attempt by the National Conference of Commissioners on Uniform State Laws to make marriage and divorce laws more uniform. This is also known as the Model Marriage and Divorce Act. UMDA was extensively amended in 1973. UMDA is a 1970 model statute that defines marriage and divorce. The greatest significance of UMDA is that it introduced irreconcilable differences as the sole ground for divorce. UMDA has been partly enacted only in a handful of states. However, it has had an enormous impact on marriage and divorce laws in all states."

More specifically,

> The Uniform Marriage and Divorce Act (UMDA), which many states use as a model, recommends that courts consider the following factors: the financial condition of the person requesting alimony; the time the recipient would need for education or job training; the standard of living the couple had during the marriage; the length of the marriage; the age, physical condition, and emotional state of the person requesting alimony; and the ability of the other person to support the recipient and still support himself or herself (Burton, 2007).

Let's look at these factors that the courts are going to "consider" before deciding whether or not this woman is going to walk away with a shit load of cash and assets.

The financial condition of the person requesting the alimony. So if the man has a good job, he's gonna get taxed. If she has a job, that don't mean shit: she's still going to get a part of his shit as well. If there's a house, usually she gets it if there are children, even if it's in his name. Some judges will have the assets liquidated and then the proceeds are divided between the two, with her getting the lion's share. This is but a small part of what I call "the reality of alimony." It's like what Peggy Joyce one said: "Alimony is a system by which, when two people make a mistake, one of them keeps paying for it."

Another variable considered by the courts is the time the recipient would need for job training or education. If she gets alimony, she can keep getting it until she gets a job or completes training for a job. In this day and age of scam training programs and proprietary (for profit) colleges, the recipient of alimony should be able to bullshit her way through a program by taking her time, changing her major course of study, or "getting pregnant." All of this shit works and as long as she's getting training, she keeps on getting alimony from you – which is automatically deducted from your paycheck.

The couple's standard of living during the marriage is another way to determine the amount of alimony doled out. So the better off you are, the more money she is going to get. This is true only because men fall for the okey-doke and hang on to that antiquated belief that, "no wife of mine is going to work." Well the fact is, when he goes out and makes that money and she's at home, she's going to get paid anyway! If she's married to him when the money was made then, by law, she is entitled to HALF. The only salvation is a prenuptial agreement and most of these women aren't going to sign one: they wouldn't be getting married if they couldn't get PAID! What do you think this is about: LOVE?

Then there is the length of the marriage, which is an extension of the previous situation. The standard of living usually increases the longer the couple is together. And if they both work, this is definitely the case. The length of time oftentimes makes men lose their mind and enter into "joint accounts" with their wives: what a mistake. He thinks he can keep an eye on what she's spending when, unbeknownst to him, she has her own personal account PLUS his shit! She's getting laid, having kids that make him even more dependent on the relationship, and she's also getting paid.

And check this one out: "the age, physical condition, and emotional state of the person requesting alimony." Most women are going to be in better condition than men as they age. Women see to that. Remember that saying, "The way to a man's heart is through his stomach"? Who do you think was cooking that fatback, those pork chops, those steaks and all that ham? She was. She knew what she was doing and we sat there rubbing our distended bellies telling her, "that was good, honey." Meanwhile, she's going on walks and jogging with her gal pals while he's at work, stressing out and making that high blood pressure go even higher. By the time he finds out he's fucked up, she's got the reins on the money, what the split will be, who gets what and has another dude waiting in the wings – with a better job!

And the final point for consideration is "the ability of the other person to support the recipient and still support himself or herself." See? Even when the divorce takes place she STILL gets paid. The studies show that she gets all the burden because she has to have the kids and he's free to start over. First of all, if he starts over with another woman right away he's out of his damn mind. Furthermore, she might have the kids, but that alimony enables her to pay a good child care provider and she has the house as well. In other words, even when she's not getting laid by him, she's getting laid by somebody; and he has to pay, so in a way he's getting FUCKED as well.

Burton (2007) concludes thusly:

> Courts have at times awarded alimony when an unmarried couple separates, if the relation-ship closely resembled marriage or in other circumstances, such as in keeping with the couple's intentions and verbal agreements. Awards of this type are informally called palimony. Private separation agreements negotiated between divorcing individuals also can contain alimony provisions. For these reasons, it is difficult to estimate accurately the size and frequency of awards through the most common method, U.S. census data.

Alimony makes sense if there are young children being left behind by one of the spouses. But these women are using it to make a living, not for the kids, but for themselves. Some of these women are getting thousands of dollars a month that goes beyond food and clothing and shelter. The rich ones are taking men to the bank, literally. And this is just one more way that despite all the rampant gender bias, the glass ceiling and the general abuse of women, they inevitably get the last laugh – through the courts.

Speaking of courts, let's look at some instances where "child support" also represents a revenue stream for the so-called "fairer sex."

CHILD SUPPORT PAYMENTS: KA-CHING!

A woman meets a man she likes. She makes him beg and pay for pussy through dinner dates, movies, concerts, outright "help" with rent, phone bills or car payments, and then when she thinks the time is right and she believes him to be a "keeper," here comes the news: "we're pregnant!"

We? Bitch, I don 't remember asking or telling you to have a kid! But she's made the decision and now is when the real battle begins. Back in the day a reliable scam was if you got the pussy and then ditched her, she'd come back with an excuse that she was "with child" and ask you for the $400 that it cost for an abortion. The average nigga ain't thinking: he's going to do what it takes to get the bitch out of his face. You'd be surprised at how many bruthas fell for that bullshit.

But now we come to the bruthas who have to deal with child support, so-called "wealthy" and "celebrity" black men who ought to know better.

Little Bow-Wow

In the gradually declining black music culture, it has become popular to refer to black men as "dawgs"; even if you are talking about a friend, that person becomes "my dawg." Therefore it should be no surprise when a young rapper came to the fore by the name of, get this: "Little Bow-Wow."

He started off and went to the top and that included money. Where you find rich black men you find gold digging women. One article reminds us of his start:

> When Bow Wow (formerly Lil' Bow Wow) appeared on "The
> Oprah Show" in 2003, the then-16-year-old rap star was living the
> high life. He bought fancy cars, wore expensive jewelry and even
> revealed that he had a $6,000-per-month allowance. Fast-forward
> 10 years. Now age 26, Bow Wow has said goodbye to his once-
> flashy lifestyle and has also become a father. (Huffington Post,
> 2013).

As is typical of far too many young people, especially young black people, their white (Jewish) agents pacify them with money and stand back and watch them "invest" their money in trinkets and other trivia. Bow-Wow was no exception. He had a $6,000 allowance – the same single mother that allowed this kid to have that insulting nickname was the one who thought that six grand a month was a fair amount for a 16-year-old kid. His real name, Shad Gregory Moss, is really no better. Then some girl/woman "got pregnant" (set-up) and as this section of the book makes clear, that is the way that a lot of these women "get laid and paid."

Moving on:

> In this clip from "Oprah: Where Are They Now?", Bow Wow
> opens up about how dramatically his life has changed since his
> days of teenage stardom. For one, he says, he stopped focusing so
> much on material things. "We called it 'stunting,'" Bow Wow says

> of parading around his large purchases. "I don't even wear that stuff no more. I'm so laid-back and just chill." (Huffington Post, 2013).

He claims he's matured. The question is, what took so long? After you spend all that money on gold chains, watches, cars and the like, after you've cruised through ghettos and low-income areas to flash it all in front of the poor, then it gets boring. He claims that he's "so laid-back and just chill," but he's still the same immature punk that he always was. And he's still getting gamed on via the paternity route:

> … Bow Wow's perspective on material things isn't all that's different about the entertainer. He became a father in 2011, when his former girlfriend, Joie Chavis, gave birth to a little girl, Shai Moss. Bow Wow says he is still adjusting to the idea of being a parent, especially given the fact that he and his daughter, now 2 years old, live on opposite ends of the country. "Shai lives in Los Angeles and I'm in New York full-time," Bow Wow says in the clip. "It's so hard. I Skype with her and I just wish that I could just reach in there and grab her little self. [But] I can't." (Huffington Post, 2013).

So he's an absentee father, what we call a "Disneyland daddy." He comes around with gifts to shower on his daughter and hopes to curry favor with her. But the mother has her all the time and if he does something she doesn't like, she will poison that little girl's mind against him – and she will see to it that those child support payments are jacked up. Ka-ching!

Continuing:

> Bow Wow's career as a rap artist, TV host and all-around entertainer also makes fatherhood more of a challenge, he says. "I missed [Shai's] first step because I was in Australia on tour," he says. "I missed her first word." (Huffington Post, 2013).

Life is about choices. He has agents who can book his gigs. He has no real talent, a point that can be imposed on most of those guys who call themselves "rappers." They are poets with "beats" that they usually steal from old school artists. Be that as it may, he's a biological father, but he's just going through the motions like most single parents. According to an article in the Huffington Post, "Bow-Wow says that since he can't be with his daughter all the time, he understands how precious it is when they *can* get together. "For the times that I'm with her... I always try my best to take full advantage of it," he says."

Meanwhile the baby's mother is basking in the lap of luxury, no doubt I don't know what has taken place since that time, but my research uncovered that this happy father was paying $3,000 a month in child support for a while. And that was in 2013. Who knows how much it is now?

Jermaine DuPree

Another runt. These short black guys make money and they can't keep the women away. That's because the women want one thing from them: their money. This 5'4 brutha is listed in his credits as, "an American hip hop recording artist, record producer, songwriter and rapper." You can add one more title to that: sucka or, more clearly, "trick." Women get "laid and paid" because of men like these, and they can be found all over the place.

On May 10, 2011 the following was reported on a website under the title, "Jermaine Dupri Sued by Stripper for Child Support. Check this out:

> According to AccessAtlanta, troubled music producer Jermaine
> Dupri Mauldin has been sued by a woman for missed child support
> payments. Earlier this year, a judge ordered Dupri, 38, to pay
> former stripper Sarai Jones $2,500 per month in child support
> based on the results of a paternity test for Jones' 7-month-old
> daughter. Dupri was also ordered to pay Jones an additional
> $7,500. (Rose, 2011).

See? These women know what they're doing. This woman strips for a living meaning that she knows she has the kind of body that men are going to glare at. She also knows how to "shake her groove thing." Runts like Dupri come into a club and then approach the woman, thinking that their "rap" is enough to get them laid. They buy some expensive drinks and flash some jewelry and take the woman home. She sets them up knowing that she's not using birth control. And she gets him horny enough to lose his mind and abandon his condoms. Next thing you know: pregnancy and that means eighteen years of child support.

He fronts and talks a big game, but Jermaine has had some financial problems. Check out the following:

> But Dupri, whose money problems are well-documented, has yet
> to come up with the money, so Jones went back to court to force
> him to pay up. Dupri reportedly met Jones during one of his many
> side trips to Atlanta strip bar Magic City, where Jones worked as a
> stripper under the name "Obsession". (Rose, 2011).

Her working name was "Obsession" but her real name was Sirai Jones. She knew what she was doing and she knew his track record as a DJ and a cockhound. She also knew that this guy has no morals whatsoever. He dated Janet Jackson for seven years and was messing around all along. All that money Janet had couldn't get him to fly right.

Moving on:

> According to a source close to Dupri, the diminutive producer often hid Sarai (and her stripper friends) in the back room of his Atlanta recording studio while Janet visited with him in the main studio. Friends say that Janet knew Jermaine was spending her money on strippers (and she even participated in ménage à trois with them), but her attitude at the time was, *"whatever makes him happy."* (Rose, 2011).

So Janet was weak-minded and this guy was able to convince her to engage in a threesome. This is what happens when there is money to burn and guys like Dupri have less dough than the main female. But Jones had less than Dupri, so she decided she'd get hers the old fashioned way: she'd *earn* it.

So Jones set Dupri up and then all hell broke loose:

> Jermaine's world began to unravel quickly when Jackson learned of Sarai's pregnancy and ended her relationship with Dupri before moving back to California. Without Janet as collateral, Jermaine could no longer secure financial loans and creditors began pursuing him aggressively through the court system for their money. (Rose, 2011).

All flash with no cash. For instance in 2011 it was reported that,

> Last week, Dupri's $2 million Mount Paran Road mansion in Northwest Atlanta was saved from the auction block when Dupri came up with cash at the last minute. WSB-TV obtained documents showing that Dupri owes more than $493,000 in back taxes for 2007. Plus he owes more than $12,000 in property taxes on the Fayetteville home where his mother currently lives. (Rose, 2011).

But this woman Jones is going to get paid. She was getting laid and turned that into a pregnancy that links Dupri to that child for eighteen years. And then he's got all this other debt. He is going to have to let his work control him rather than the other way around. He is going to have to earn or else go to jail. And at

5'4", he'd better come up with that dough or he's going to end up being somebody's prison bitch.

He comes off as a bum. Check out the following:

> Dupri's longtime friend, local club owner Alex Gidewon, helped
> Dupri out by hiring him to deejay at the Gold Room and other
> clubs last year. According to sources, Durpri is paid up to $10,000
> for deejaying gigs around the country. (Rose, 2011).

He's going to wear himself out one way or the other. These bruthas are tying themselves to these women and in the case of DuPri, finding women who are weak minded enough to fall for the okey-doke. But as old playas know it wears you down after awhile. As the old sports maxim teaches, "There are old quarterbacks and there are bold quarterbacks. But there are no old, bold quarterbacks."

Chief Keef

Rappers talk a lot of street shit, sell woof tickets about how many women they have and how much "cheese they have stacked" (translation: money they've made) but when all is said and done, most of them are pussy-crazed suckas who pay for the premature ejaculation that they boast about in their videos. They talk about not giving a shit and about how many women they have sucking their dicks and then once outside of the studio, these 'tricks' end up getting "tricked." Such is the case of Chief Keef (whose real name is Keith Cozart).

In other words, this no-talking muthafucka is pronouncing his first name incorrectly – as so many members of their generation tend to do. They can write lyrics as long as the words are spelled all fucked up, but they can't even pronounce their own names. And this is somebody's father?

A November 29, 2013 article by Tayla Holman titled "Chief Keef Ordered to Pay Child Support for 10-month Old After DNA Test" proves my point:

> Chief Keef has been ordered to pay child support after a DNA test
> confirmed that he is the father of a 10-month-old baby. The
> Chicago rapper is currently in a drug rehab facility in California
> for the next three months to address his marijuana addiction. His
> attorney appeared before Bridgeview Judge Russell Hartigan to
> review the results of the DNA test, according to Cook County
> state's attorney spokeswoman Lisa Gordon. (Holman, 2013).

So he had doubts that he was the child's father. Why? Because more likely than not the woman was a slut. She was in a club with one of those pussy-hugging micro skirts on, ass sticking out, titties up under her neck, and he thought that she was "special." These women know what they're doing, and the men who design their clothes know too. All you have to do is design something for a young girl and these grown as women will go out and buy it as well. Why? Because young girls are their competition! These "tricks" like Bow-Wow and Chief Keef are the guys these older sistahs want because these guys don't know the game the way the old hands do. They fall for the okey-doke and get just enough fellatio to get them in the mood to forget to put on a condom. From there, whether it's his or not, he's going to get the blame. Chief Keef got caught.

And the marijuana didn't make it any better. He's just a thug who came out with some poetry that he set to music and made some money. He was lost, probably quasi-illiterate, and walking around trying to be a "gangsta." The story continues:

> "An order was entered finding him to be the father," Gordon said.As reported by the *Chicago Tribune*, Hartigan ordered Chief Keef, whose real name is Keith Cozart, to pay $2,500 a month beginning December 1 for the next 10 months, as well as a lump sum of $25,000 by December 31. He must also obtain medical and life insurance for the baby, Gordon said. Chief Keef is due in court on January 27. Apparently, Chief Keef never denied that the child was his. (Holman, 2013).

And now this "sucka" has a child that he is responsible for and that means that the woman who carried the child and then had it is also taken care of. This is just one more case of women getting "laid and paid." And this guy, Chief Keef, is just a baby himself. An irresponsible one, making you wonder just where in the hell HIS mama is at. Check this out:

> The 18-year-old has been served with two paternity cases in less than a year. In January, a middle school student who said Chief Keef impregnated her in 2011 sued him for child support, health insurance, and other medical expenses. The girl gave birth to a daughter, Kayden Kash (Kay Kay), that same year. Kayden turned two on November 28, but the mother's age is currently unknown. A judge ordered Chief Keef to pay $2,600 a month in child support, plus $500 for daycare expenses, payments he repeatedly failed to make. (Holman, 2013).

Poor kid. In 2013 he was eighteen years old meaning that now he's about 22 or 23. The mother's age is "unknown" because the media chose not to make it known. The courts know her age and I'm willing to bet that she's much older than

Keef is. If he never denied that the kid was his, then what was the paternity test for? It's because he was going by what the woman said and his attorneys were going by what they found out about this woman's past. The courts don't like this shit and now we know that he's got TWO baby's mamas. And from the pictures I've seen, both of them are butt-ugly.

As for the on-going saga involving the first kid,

> A judge sentenced Chief Keef to jail in September for failing to show up for a child support hearing. On October 21, Chief Keef was ordered to pay $11,000, which he did last week, managing to avoid jail time. He is due back in court on December 10 to address his failure to show up for multiple court dates. (Holman, 2013).

And that's how it goes. Paternity suits. Shelling out money to women you can't stand. Little girls growing up having their mother's put your name in the streets and condemning all men – along with teaching their "ho tricks" to their daughters. And the cycle of getting "laid and paid" is therefore perpetuated.

Now comes the second child:

> Chief Keef is currently expecting a son, Mon'e, with another woman. According to his Instagram, the child is due in January. When the rapper finishes his stint in rehab, which he has to pay for himself, he will head back to Illinois to work at a horse therapy facility for disabled patients. (Holman, 2013).

A loser with a hit record. Just like Jermaine Dupree and the others – totally lacking in penis control.

Allen Iverson

At just over six feet tall, this NBA scoring phenom entertained fans and made opposing defenses look ridiculous. But like so many before him, he got married at an early age and then got into major trouble with the child support people. The gossip show "TMZ" reported the following at the end of August of 2013:

> Allen Iverson's ex-wife is sick and tired of dragging him to court to squeeze out child support ... she's asking a judge to make him cough up the next 13 years worth RIGHT NOW -- a cool $1.2 MILLION. TMZ broke the story ... after the couple's nasty divorce Iverson was ordered to pay $8000/month in child support for their

> 5 kids. Problem is, Tawanna has gone to court on numerous
> occasions because A.I. won't pay. (TMZ staff, 2013).

Five kids? This translates to mean that Tawanna knew his weaknesses. The kids were probably conceived during his off-time from the basketball season. She knew what she was doing and she knew what he liked. The plan is used by women from welfare recipients to heiresses: the more kids, the more money you can get. Tawanna wasn't using birth control and evidently neither was he. Five kids! And then he turns around with his multi-million dollar contract and refuses to pay? Continuing:

> It came to a head in July when a judge **threatened Iverson with jail**, unless he forked over $40,000 in back support -- **which he did**. But Tawanna says she doesn't want to keep running into the same problem. (TMZ staff, 2013 – emphasis original).

Laid and paid. They call it "child support," but these women are the ones spending the money on the child! The check doesn't come directly to the child. It comes to HER, and she blows it on herself and the child – in that order. How do I know? Because most of these women are broke until they latch onto one of these professional athletes. Even before they get to the pros, these women know who's got the potential to get the big contract and who doesn't. Even ugly niggas like Dennis Rodman can get booty because they make the big bucks. The only thing about him is that he doesn't like black women. But it's all the same when the lights go out.

TMZ even added up the dollars that Iverson is going to owe. Check it out:

> On August 1st she filed docs asking a judge to make A.I. cover ALL the support through October 2026 (when their youngest turns 18). After the math, it comes to $1,272,000 ... which Tawanna wants put in a trust for the children. A court has yet to rule. (TMZ staff, 2013)

It really doesn't matter how the court rules. Putting money in a "trust fund" for the kids doesn't mean anything when the woman is in control. She continually programs the kids with negative information about their father and about how she's "sacrificed" so much. This stuff begins to take hold after a while and even if the money is in a trust fund, she can borrow on it. That's what a lot of people don't seem to understand: these women get "the hookup" with some well-to-do trick and can borrow on that money in the name of the children. These women got laid and they will make sure that they get paid.

Terrell Owens

I saw this asshole on his television show, surrounded by two young black women who were his "advisors." The 2012 program was called, "The T.O. Show" and I watched him walk into a jewelry store and plop down $167,000 for a pair of diamond earrings. That's right – like the true fag that these niggas appear to aspire to be, "earrings."

An article titled, "Terrell Owens Makes Payments" on an ESPN website tells another story of a professional athlete turned "trick." Check it out:

> ATLANTA -- Former NFL star Terrell Owens has made child
> support payments that he owed to the mother of his 7-year-old
> daughter, avoiding the threat of jail time. Owens appeared in
> Fulton County Superior Court in Atlanta on Thursday, after failing
> to appear for a court date in the case last week. His lawyer and a
> lawyer for Melanie Smith had come to an agreement before the
> hearing and signed it in front of the judge. Owens made the back
> payments he owed to Smith and agreed to pay her legal fees,
> according to court documents. (ESPN.go.com, 2012).

These types of black men – coons, for the most part -- have to be threatened with jail before they pay the child support that their own pussy-hunting trapped them in. These women know what they're doing, and the pain of childbearing is muted by the thoughts of a big money future. After going through all that, and then having their dreams threatened or dashed because some athlete refuses to pay? You think black women are going for that shit? No way.

Terrell Owens boasted and bragged all over the football field, almost demanded that he be admitted into the Hall of Fame (which he deserved) and ruined almost every locker room he ever entered. That was on the field. Off the field he was a pussy whipped piece of shit, a "trick" in the true sense of the world, and ended up at the mercy of attorneys and the courts:

> "We're pleased. It's too bad it took this long," Smith's lawyer,
> Randy Kessler, said after the agreement was signed. "If he's not
> going to be there physically, he needs to be there financially."
> Owens left the court without speaking to reporters. A lawyer for
> Owens didn't immediately respond to an email seeking comment.
> (ESPN.go.com, 2012).

There is no doubt that the attorney was a white man. He says that if Owens is "not going to be there physically, he needs to be there financially." Doesn't this peckerwood realize that if he's "there financially," he IS there physically! That's his money, that's his check being cashed and that his young child who is benefitting from the resources being provided!

It gets worse: check this out:

> A previous agreement requires Owens to pay Smith $5,000 a month. This was the third case Smith has brought against Owens for non-payment of child support, Kessler said. In previous instances, Owens has settled and paid up right before the cases were to go to court but then failed to make subsequent payments, Kessler said. (ESPN.go.com, 2012).

In other words, Owens went to Smith, flashed a couple of grand in her greedy ass mug, and shut her up. This woman is going to get $5,000 a month because she gapped her legs and set this professional athlete up. She had to know she wasn't marrying material; she had to know that like most athletes, he was a playa. But she wanted that money and she knew how to get it. So she got pregnant and now she's got an income without lifting a finger. This is another example of how women "get laid and paid."

Now comes the "mommy dearest" contradictions that most of these skanks offer once they get the money they seek:

> Smith, who lives in northwest Georgia, is glad to have the signed agreement, but would really like for Owens to be more involved in their daughter's life, Kessler said."What she really wants is for him to have a relationship with his child," Kessler said. Smith, who was also present in court Thursday, said her daughter has seen Owens about eight to 10 times. (ESPN.go.com, 2012).

Take note that Owens "having a relationship with his child" was not as important as Smith getting that money up front! If she had managed to trap Owens into seeing her regularly, she could have gotten paid. Or would she? She probably knew that Owens was a piece of shit and as a result, there were no guarantees. She may want Owens to see that child, but trust me: that's for babysitting purposes. If he comes and gets the child for the weekend or takes the child out, that's more time for her (Smith) to get dressed in those micro-skirts that Owens paid for and sashay out to the bar to look for a new sucker … oops! I mean suitor.

Pretending to be broke (remember that $162,000 diamond earring set this asshole paid for?), Owens then made a number of moves where he made a complete and utter ass out of himself. He's already made one: impregnating a woman that he had no intention of staying with. But wait: there's more!

> Owens has raised the possibility of lowering his monthly child support payments since he's no longer drawing an NFL salary, and Smith is willing to discuss that, Kessler said. (ESPN.go.com, 2012).

Cutting deals to whittle down his payments after making tens of millions of dollars and wasting millions on jewelry, cars and expensive furnishings for his mansion. Check out this man's Hall of Fame-like stats:

> The 38-year-old Owens played 15 years in the NFL, most recently for the Cincinnati Bengals during the 2010 season. Before his single season with the Bengals, Owens played one season with the Buffalo Bills, three with the Dallas Cowboys, two with the Philadelphia Eagles and eight with the San Francisco 49ers. (ESPN.go.com, 2012).

So many men, many of them black men, fall for the okey-doke. They say that for the want of money is the root of all evil. I disagree. I say that it's the want of pussy that is the root of all evil. Not because the women are bad, but because men are so screwed up, so animalistic in their lust for something that often smells like sardines, that we lose our damn mind. And then, when they choose, here comes a cute little baby that you can't help but love, but you're responsible for that tiny creature for 18 years according to the law. More evidence of how women "get laid and paid."

Evander Holyfield

Poor Evander Holyfield – another "trick" masquerading as a world class athlete. When all is said and done, even the mightiest fall to the almighty seductions of those who are in good enough shape to be able to convincingly sport a lift-up bra or a skirt with no draws on under it.

A September 18, 2012 story on FoxSports.com titled, "Report: Holyfield Held in Contempt" provides one more example of a woman getting "laid and paid."

> The financial blows keep coming for boxing legend Evander Holyfield. Celebrity news website TMZ reported, citing court documents, that the former heavyweight champion has been held in contempt of court in Georgia for failing to pay $563,900.91 in back child support.(FoxSports, 2012).

More than half a million dollars owed in back child support. He competed in boxing from 1984 to 2011, and according to the Xfinity.com (2017) website, "Evander Holyfield earned several hundred million dollars during a career that spanned more than two decades."

As it was reported in 2012,

> The latest charge stems from an initial payment of more than $372,000 that Holyfield owed in support of his 18-year-old daughter, Emani. TMZ reported that, according to court documents, that amount increased to $563,900.91, and Holyfield was held in contempt and ordered by a judge to pay $2,950 per month to clear the debt. Holyfield made an initial $17,700 payment, TMZ reported, but the judge also ordered that a percentage of Holyfield's income be earmarked to pay down the debt.(FoxSports, 2012).

Public humiliation after being in the ring with some of the baddest men on the planet. Brought down by pussy payments. What else can you say? And he's not just being sued in one state, either:

> According to a biography on Holyfield's website, the former boxing star made more than $230 million in the ring. But he's faced numerous financial difficulties since. The Atlanta Journal-Constitution reported that Holyfield recently foreclosed on his Fayette County mansion and has been sued for thousands of dollars in child-support cases in Georgia, Texas and California. Holyfield has fought these cases, the AJC reported, claiming that his income has fallen off since his career ended. (FoxSports, 2012).

Broke, busted with a kid who grew up to hate your guts because, thanks to her mother's on-going lectures, she has been led to believe that you hated her guts, didn't want her, and had to be forced by the courts, to do the right thing. If Holyfield hadn't been in such world-class shape for most of his life, I'm pretty sure that all this financial and personal pressure would and could have led directly to a heart attack or a stroke.

Bobby Brown

Whitney Houston was one of the most beautiful women in the world. When I saw that she was hung up on and eventually married Bobby Brown, two words came to my mind: dick whipped. That's the only way to explain why she would marry someone so unattractive with a track record so abysmal. This woman was supposed to be from a Christian background, but I guess that just goes to show what a little crack cocaine can do.

Long after Whitney died, Bobby was still in trouble with child support. An article by Paysha Stockton Rhone that appeared in People.com on February 27, 2007, titled, "Bobby Brown Arrested in Massachusetts, proves the point and offers background:

> Bobby Brown, who was arrested and jailed in Massachusetts on
> Sunday for failing to appear in court and pay child support fines,
> will remain behind bars until he pays $19,150, a judge ruled
> Monday. (Rhone, 2007).

I don't know what was on Whitney Houston's mind other than two things: (1) getting dicked and (2) hitting that crack pipe. How else to explain a woman with all the potential in the world hooking up with someone like Bobby Brown. His track record speaks for itself. Check it out:

> Brown, 40, owes suport to his former girlfriend Kim Ward, who
> lives in Massachusetts and with whom he has two teenage
> children: LaPrincia and Bobby III. The singer's attorney, Phaedra
> Parks, said she didn't expect Brown to get the money until
> Tuesday, and said he's been struggling to make the payments he
> owes to Ward. (Rhone, 2007).

All these kids. Once again, someone "famous" lands these sluts and starts dating them. Don't ask me why. When you travel all over the world you can do what you please and you have enough money to afford birth control. But these young guys (as I supposed we all did during our youthful days) see a short skirt and immediately begin wondering what the panties look like and more importantly, what the pussy looks like. Eighteen minutes (max) of pleasure for 18 years of pain once the woman claims you're the father. In the black community it seems like making babies is some kind of badge of courage and serves as an indicator of how potent you are. What it shows, in the final analysis, is how big a sucka you are.

And an un-talented sucka at that. Check this out:

> "Although this agreement was put in place when he was Bobby
> Brown the star, this agreement is being enforced when he is not
> always able to find work," Parks told the Associated Press. "He
> hasn't made an album in quite some years." (Rhone, 2007)

So what? Where are his agents and managers? Where are the people who are supposed to be watching and holding this man's money while he skips around town spending money on pussy, ordering Cristal Champagne and speeding around town in high-end sports cars? By not having any money to pay his child support this shows that he is not a responsible parent, which is what the courts look at when he eventually gets hauled up in front of them.

Continuing:

> Brown was also ordered to return to court on Thursday – the day when his next $5,500 support payment is due. "Kim always finds these hearing to be extremely difficult," Ward's lawyer, Linda Medonis, said. "This is not the route she wants it to go, but when he doesn't pay for a few months it becomes a real hardship for her." (Rhone, 2007)

Such bullshit. Kim doesn't find going to court "extremely difficult." Nobody know that bitch from Adam's house cat. She's basking in the fame she gets just like she did when she went around bragging to all of her friends that Bobby Brown was screwing her. That's how these women are – the pregnancy was set up from the get go. They knew how irresponsible that punk was. That is why women like this don't complain when they find out that he's out on the road partying with other women. Once they get the pregnancy they seek, they could care less. Kim is not stupid and hardly afraid to walk into a courtroom and point her finger at a $5,500 paycheck.

Brown is such a loser that being arrested is pretty much an acceptable form of behavior. As one account points out,

> Brown was arrested Sunday evening outside his daughter's cheerleading competition, Patrick McDermott, clerk of Norfolk Probate Court in Canton, Mass., told PEOPLE. "He went very cooperatively," he says. "According to the constable, no one was really around." (Rhone, 2007).

Of course he went cooperatively – he had no case. He was as guilty as sin and he knew it. According to Rhone (2007), "Jerry Loomis, one of the constables who arrested Brown, said he stopped the singer in the parking lot "because we didn't want to embarrass him or anyone else in there." Asked if Brown was able to see his daughter perform Loomis said, "No. He was begging us to go in there, but we felt for safety reasons we couldn't allow him. It wasn't even in the cards." So he missed his daughter's cheerleading competition – undoubtedly not the first time – and acted like it was no big deal. Kids don't forget this kind of thing, especially with the mother reminding that kid, no a daily basis, that "yo' daddy ain't shit."

As a result,

> In October, a judge ordered Brown to be arrested if he stepped foot
> in the state after the singer skipped a court hearing over $11,000 in
> delinquent child support payments to Ward. Later that month,
> McDermott said that Brown had paid what he owed to Ward;
> however, the arrest warrant has remained in place – probably in
> case Brown fell behind again, McDermott said. (Rhone, 2007).

Black men, black women and the rift between us is a direct response to trying to survive in a capitalist system – with no capital. Black men's desire for sex is well-noted because it is a societal norm for all males. Those who have resources can get the women to marry them, date them or they can just buy it outright. Those who lack resources have to use "gifts and ideological game" in order to get it. But even in that capitalism creeps into the relationship to define it. Women have to get paid in order for them to get laid, and men have to get laid in order for those payments to continue. This may sound trite and tragic – but it is also true.

Bobby Brown is proof and he continues to pay as he cavorts from female to female. He impregnates her, which is part of her game in order to get paid, and then he has to dole out more money for child support. And supporting her is part of the deal. She got "laid" and now she will get paid. Want proof? According to Rhone (2007),

> Brown, who split from Whitney Houston in September, has a
> history of missed child support payments, and was even jailed in
> March 2004 for one day after missing several payments, which he
> subsequently paid.

As the old man taught George Jackson who wrote the quote down in his great book, Soledad Brother, "Every sickness ain't death, every goodbye ain't gone, and every big man ain't strong." Women know this, have internalized it, and keep it in mind as they forge these "alienated arrangements" with black men and as such, continue to get "laid and paid.

Dennis Rodman

Even an unattractive individual can get laid, fall for the okey doke and end up paying child support in today's America. Dennis Rodman is a classic example of what I call a "troll turned trick."

Rodman had major issues. He was raised by some white people and went to some loser community colleges where he was able to dominate. But he's always been in a state of cultural confusion, the way kids who are of a different race tend to be when they are adopted by and raised by white folks. Sure, he won some NBA titles with Michael Jordan and some rebounding awards, but it was his decisions off the court that showed how confused he was. Dressing up like a woman, getting involved with tramps like Madonna and Carmen Electra – two white women who just wanted to see how big his penis was – and so on.

This kind of lifestyle sets the stage for on-going pitfalls in one's life. A March 4, 2013 article by Nate Wooley titled "Dennis Rodman Too Broke to Pay Child Support" documents that Rodman owed more than $800,000 in child support. The article, which appeared on the website InvestorPlace, claimed:

> Former basketball star and headline grabber Dennis Rodman told a court that he can no longer afford his child support payments. The player — who made news last week with his visit to North Korea, where he made friends with dictator Kim Jong-un — owes more than $800,000 in back child support, (Wooley, 2013).

Rodman is one of those black people who is evidence that a black child raised around white people is going to grow up fucked up. He was this tall kid raised by white folks who saw his potential and he became a community college star. He went on to professional ranks but unfortunately continued to think he was white. He was so daffy that his teammates couldn't stand him but white people around him always made him the center of attention so they could get some laughs and hopefully get some insulting commentary from the black players around the National Basketball Association.

Just the fact that he could get pussy shows that women place getting "paid" above "getting laid." What woman would go to bed with a nigga whose acne bumps were as big as watermelons? White bitches, that's who. Three of his most visible girlfriends prove my point: (1) Madonna (1994), who has been fucked so many times I'm surprised she can even close her legs; (2) Vivica A. Fox (1997), a true beauty but if she was dating 50 Cent and then amidst an argument charged him with being gay, continues to be someone with issues from DUIs to dating young guys and being called a "cougar"; (3) Carmen Electric (1998), another beauty who has made millions of dollars posing for Playboy, as a professional dancer and in real life, a full-time whore.

All three women have something in common: they need the photo ops that parading around with Rodman, a member of the championship Chicago Bulls teams, could bring them and they could get all the dick they craved. Judging from his face, that's probably all he was good for.

At any rate, according to Wooley (2013),

> Rodman's ex-wife Michele filed for the back payments to collect
> the total of $860,376 in child and spousal support. Rodman's
> attorney told the court that he is unable to pay due to his lack of
> funds. The attorney also cited Rodman's alcoholism as a reason for
> his lack of income and assets. (Wooley, 2013).

A 6'8", ugly alcoholic with millions of dollars to spend. In the world of the women who are "laid and paid," he is the perfect thrall. And his life has spiraled out of control because of all of his bad choices, his love of white folks and his psychosis, which white people treat as if he's merely "playfully eccentric." Just follow the money:

> Rodman — a member of the Basketball Hall of Fame and winner
> of five NBA championships — made more than $27 million during
> his NBA career. It is also believed that he earned as much or more
> than his salary in endorsements. (Wooley, 2013).

And now it's all gone. In the meantime he's posed publicly in women's clothing including a wedding gown, and he's gone to North Korea and kicked it with Kim Jong-un.

Flavor Flav and Child Support

In the same psychological nut-sack as Rodman is Flavor Flav, that zany member of the otherwise incredible rap group, Public Enemy. Another unattractive black man who attracts money-grubbing women, mostly white, Flavor Flav is as eccentric as Rodman in the world of reality.

A June 19, 2012 article by Joseph Gibson titled, "Flavor Flav Pays More Than $100K In Child Support To Stay Out Of Prison", that appeared in a website called Celebritynetworth.com" provides us with a sampling of how this guy fell into the "laid and paid" scenario.

> Flavor Flav's career has taken many different turns over the last 25
> or so years. He first found fame as the comic relief/hype
> man/sidekick to Chuck D in the rap group Public Enemy, before
> beginning a slow slide into late night talk show punchline and
> reality TV star. Those ups and downs come with their own price –
> in Flav's case, more than $100,000 in child support payments
> which he had previously owed. (Bibson, 2012).

Some background is in order because this is really some weird shit, even BEFORE we get into the issue of child support and the like.

According to one source, "After falling out of the public eye for a number of years, he reappeared as the star of several VH1 reality series, including The Surreal Life, Strange Love, and Flavor of Love." I don't know what possessed the white man to give Flavor Flav (whose real name is William Jonathan Drayton, Jr.) and this blonde bombshell Brigette Nielsen a show where they were in a relationship, cuddled up, kissing and generally making asses out of themselves. Here's some more background:

> *Strange Love* is a reality series featuring Brigitte Nielsen and Flavor Flav that aired on VH1. Sparked by their on-screen romance in the third season of VH1's *The Surreal Life*, it is a spin-off that focused solely on Brigitte and Flav. The series premièred on January 9, 2005 and ended its run on April 24, 2005. (Wikipedia, 2017).

It may have been a short-lived "reality show," but the fact is that this black man got not one, but three reality shows – and got paid for it. This is straight up freak value by white people. Brigitte Nielsen has been appearing in some pretty mediocre movies herself, including one called "Mercenaries" (with Vivica A. Fox and Cynthia Rothrock) where she played a prison guard with the bad guys. And trust me: she looked like shit boiled over.

Nielsen obviously has some issues as well, as does model Beverly Johnson, the lovely black woman who, for some reason, was kicking it with Flav for years. He's also been married twice: one to a sister named Angie Parker and then to Karen Ross.

So what happened to the "Strange Love" show? According to Wikipedia,

> Due to mutual jealousy, the couple was constantly fighting and yelling, and they went their separate ways in the end, with Nielsen choosing instead to live with her Italian boyfriend, Mattia Dessi. Flavor Flav would go on to have his own reality show, *Flavor of Love*, where he continued to search for love.

It should be stated here that Brigette Nielsen wasn't the sharpest knife in the drawer either. She seduced Sylvester Stallone and ended up with a major part in the "Rocky IV" movie, and they got married thereafter. It didn't last long and then the next thing you know, she's screwing Flavor Flav. But let us not get ahead of ourselves.

I am no big fan of Stallone, believe me. Two decades ago I wrote a 50 page essay titled, "Sylvester Stallone: Warrior or Wimp?" I wrote it after reading a book about his life and this guy was screwed up from the beginning. His mother, Toni, was a nut that was hooked on astrology and Sylvester had issues. He used to wear a Superman outfit under his school clothes and one day the principal found out. The principal called a school assembly and made Sly take off his clothes and reveal the outfit. He as a laughing stock.

So ashamed of him was Toni that she PAID a college in Switzerland to let him in. When he was three credits from graduating he dropped out to become an actor. My point here is that he is as screwed up and in search of "machismo" as Brigette was in search of, who knows that.

This explains her jealousy over sharing star billing with the diminutive Flav. But there is more about Nielsen and Sly which gives us an understanding of Flavor Flav as well. According to the *Huffington Post,*

> When Brigitte Nielsen was 22 years old, she married *Rocky* star Sylvester Stallone. At the time, Stallone was one of the biggest movie stars in Hollywood, so when he left his first wife for a woman 17 years his junior, the tabloids took them to task. Publications depicted Nielsen as a gold-digger, accused her of infidelity and asserted that she was simply using Stallone as a stepping stone for her career. But Nielsen tells "Oprah: Where Are They Now?" says that was far from the truth.(Huffington Post, 2014)

Like I said, Stallone had some issues himself. He buffed up because he was so short in stature, butchered the English language with what appears to be some kind of quasi-speech impediment, and he married a woman that stood over him. They didn't stay married long because in my view she also had issues. The used him for roles in "Rocky IV" and in "Cobra" and then, like that, they were divorced. In her words,
 "The biggest misconception while I was with Sylvester was the fact that everybody thought I married him because of money," she says. "They didn't understand that he begged me to marry. He *begged* me!" (Huffington Post, 2014).

If she didn't want to do it all the begging in the world would not have convinced her. What I figure is that she saw all the money he had so that was what convinced her – she knew she could get half his shit (getting' laid and paid) if things didn't work out. So what happened?

> When they wed in 1985, Nielsen and Stallone had only known each other a matter of months, which the Danish actress says gave her pause about becoming so serious so quickly. "I remember thinking, 'This is too early. This is not right,'" she recalls. "At the same time, everybody was going, 'Who wouldn't want to marry Rocky?'" After 19 months as husband and wife, Nielsen and

Stallone divorced. With the clarity of decades of distance since the
split, she admits that their union was a mistake. "If I would go
back in time, I shouldn't have married him (Huffington Post,
2014).

That lyin' bitch. She married him for the money and she knows it. She was
tall and blonde and couldn't get a gig in Hollywood outside of the porn industry.
She was too tall and intimidating. She was a freak. So she married someone and
used his connections. As I say, she did "Rocky IV," and then "Red Sonja" also in
1985. The next year she made "Cobra" and then in 1987 she was in the Eddie
Murphy movie, "Beverly Hills Cop."

I don't know what happened between Brigette and Stallone and personally, I
don't give a shit. All I know is that I was channel surfing one day and I saw this
little black muthafucka cuddled up with this giant white woman. "Strange Love"?
You ain't NEVER lied!

But that shit didn't last and they went their separate ways. She's white so
she'll be alright. But Flav – with that stature and that face? He gets a lot of pussy
and he continues to impregnate women (who, of course, are setting each pregnancy
up the way Tawana Iverson did to Allen):

> But, that's been taken care of now. Today, Flavor Flav showed up
> at Albany County Family Court to settle his debt with Angie
> Parker. Flav has fathered three children with Parker, and was
> facing a 180-day prison sentence if he failed to pay the $111,186 in
> child support payments he owed to her. While it's not known
> exactly how much of the sum he payed (sic) today, he must have
> cleared things up to the satisfaction of all the parties involved
> because he's out walking the streets instead of in prison. (Gibson,
> 2012).

How does somebody lay up in a studio with some white woman cracking
jokes and arguing, sucking on caviar and all that other food that lays around the
set, get chauffeured around and live the life, and "forget" that he's got three
children to take care of? How does he get behind a hundred and eleven thousand
dollars in support for those kids? If you're going to play the field and travel around
the world, at LEAST make sure the kids are being taken care of properly!

And it's not over, apparently. Back in 2012 where all this child support is
being bandied about, check out the following:

> Of course, this is a matter of ongoing and continuous child support,
> so this payment, however much it was, doesn't absolve Flav of
> future responsibilities. In fact, he has another court date in

September of this year to make sure he's kept up with his child support payments in the ensuing time. (Gibson, 2012).

So now he's got the court system all in his business. These men, all of the ones I've featured are black, just can't seem to get the point. They see some woman with huge breasts or a skirt up to the crack of her ass, and they fall for it. They apparently do not care who she is, where she's come from or where she's been. These women of the 21st century are running credit checks on men when they meet them; they are conducting background checks. They want security and safety but most importantly they want to make sure that he is the kind of guy who, if they set him up with a pregnancy, is going to be able to pay on a long-term basis. That's the politics of the game, baby: getting' "laid and paid."

As for Flav, it isn't apparent that he has much of anything going on in the immediate future, career wise. His most recent widely seen gig was in a Super Bowl commercial for Pepsi along with fellow music industry stalwart Sir Elton John. He does, however, have a new restaurant in Las Vegas, Nevada which goes by the name of Flavor Flav's House of Flavor . It opened on his 53rd birthday: March 16, 2012. So hopefully, Flav will have the financial means to keep up with his child support responsibilities and won't be facing any more prison time any time soon. (Gibson, 2012).

The restaurant didn't last. Before that he had one in Detroit, but there's still a website. But after that he had another place called, get this: "Flavor Flav's Chicken & Ribs." He and his business partners were eventually evicted from the location in a Detroit suburb called Sterling Heights because they weren't paying the rent. A loser like this, a clown on stage and a bad choice-maker in his personal life, should never even think about having children. And the women who set him up need their asses kicked as well. There should be a limit to what a woman will do in order to get "laid and paid."

Shawty Lo

Shawty Lo is another one of those rapper guys who I wouldn't know from Adam's House cat. But then again I don't know Donald Trump either, but if I was writing a book about assholes I would do the necessary research under that topic. Again, another tale of pity serves as the basis for the irresponsibility that these self-proclaimed macho types exude when on stage and in the studio:

Shawty Lo's life is clearly loaded with struggle, besides all the children and baby mamas. The Atlanta rapper was arrested on

Friday, January 18, reportedly for failure to pay child support.
(Blanco, 2013).

Pitiful. But wait: there's more:

> DJ Smallz posted a photo of Shawty Lo in cuffs while he was
> being arrested. It appears that the "Dey Know" rapper was
> detained after taping an episode of CNN's *Showbiz Tonight* to
> discuss his on again, off again *All My Babies' Mamas* reality
> show (he is wearing the same clothing on the program that he has
> on while being arrested). (Blanco, 2013).

These white people are continuing to make asses out of black people on every single level. "Basketball Wives," "The Housewives of Atlanta," "Love and Hip Hop" and so on. Some coon pitches an idea to some white man who does the market research and creates the ads to start running to promote the show. Then they head over to the Jews at the bank to get the money to fund the project which has been "greenlighted." This shit is taped and mailed all over the world for people to see just how sick black people are. Black men acting like bitches, black women getting into "cat fights," young blacks spending money on jewelry and expensive liquors and young black women dressed like whores. And you wonder why we are so disrespected around the world?

Shawty Lo is just another casualty of the white man's casting couch, fast talk and ability to write what these young bruthas consider to be "fat checks." In turn, now they get money in their pocket and they start engaging in conspicuous consumption-type behaviors and hitting the clubs to "make it rain" (throwing up money into the air in a crowd of people). Those who see this stuff know that these men are idiots and don't really care about their money. As the age old saying teaches, "A fool and his money are soon parted."

To add insult to injury he was then fodder for the media to announce (and crack up at) his total irresponsibility:

> The G-Unit affiliated rapper has been in the press lately because of
> the controversial, to say the least, *All My Babies' Mamas*.
> Although initially scheduled to appear on Oxygen, the network
> backtracked after all the controversy surrounding its glorification
> of a poor lifestyle and stereotypical content that features the artist's
> *11 children and 10 baby mothers.*(Blanco, 2013, - emphasis
> added).

Again, here is whitey pointing his camera at people who are more than willing to get on television at the expense of the race. They will humiliate themselves to no end just to be able to tell their peers "I'ze was own TV, y'all." Even the title of the show, "All My Babies' Mamas" is not only an embarrassment, but just remember that it is going to be circulated all around the world and will be placed in the archives and used whenever the white man sees fit. Not only that, but all this embarrassing footage is admissible in a court of law.

Eleven children with ten different women. After the second woman found out that he had other women, or after female number five found out about those other kids, the only possible reason why they wouldn't keep their legs shut is because he was the kind of willing dupe that they knew would have to pay in order to keep getting laid. And pay he did.

As for those bullshit television show, check out the following:

> Nevertheless, Shawty Lo started a petition to bring back the show and recently told TMZ that he has suitors from other networks that will bring the program to a television near you. "There are offers on the table," he said, before adding, "I take pride in having been actively present in all my children's lives — and I understand my family doesn't represent the typical American family, but it's my family and it works for us." (Blanco, 2013).

How sick can one brutha be? Doesn't he know that the first thing he should do is have a plan that goes beyond how much money he is offered? The first question should be "what is the desired effect or impact of the show I am about to put on the air"? Or, "what are the desired outcomes as it relates to the young people who will inevitably be my primary audience?" The same lack of forethought that he exhibited when he impregnated all these women with all these dependent children is the same thoughtlessness that is clearly most evident in his "plan." And there is no bigger snitch than the Jewish-run TMZ which is always more than happy to circulate anti-black gossip any chance they get.

Shawty Lo's logic is convoluted at best:

> … However, Shawty previously asking, "Would you rather see 11 children struggle with mothers on welfare?," in his aforementioned petition probably doesn't sit right with tax payers. Also, showcasing wads of cash, eating King Crab dinners and flossing a Rolex watch on Instagram … is a bad look if it's true that's he behind on child support payments. However, he does share a photo of him playing Monopoly with his daughters and plenty of family pics on the 'Gram, though.

White people don't need comedy clubs or any other form of humorous entertainment when they can see and read about people like Shawty Lo or any other black athlete or entertainer who continues to fall for the okey-doke. These women who are getting "laid and paid" know what they're doing and showboating one's financial status the way these black celebrities do merely makes the "targeting" of suckas that much easier.

Look at Shawty Lo: high siding (as we call it) on the internet, which reaches out to millions. Flashing a Rolex watch and he has ten kids whose child support he is behind on. Eating King Crab dinners while the mothers of his children are probably getting food stamps or feeding the kids peanut butter and jelly sandwiches. And then the ultimate insult: to call playing a game of Monopoly with his daughters and taking "plenty of family pics" a sign of positive and productive fatherhood.

DON'T HATE THE PLAYA OR THE GAME: HATE THE
SYSTEM THAT PRODUCED AND ENDORSES BOTH!

So we know that the men are prospective tricks because of the American culture they were raised in. And we know that the women, even if not outright ho's, still have a philosophy that will get them "laid and paid" when all is said and done.

The Side Chick

An article titled, "3 Reasons Why Side Chicks are Settling for Second Place ... And Lovin' It" offers up some of the reasoning and rationale for "being number two" in exchange for money and other favors. Following are the key points of that article with my analyses filtering in and out:

> What is a "side chick"? In my own simple terms, I define a side chick as a female who is involved in sëxual relations with a male who is in a committed relationship with another person. One may ask why on earth an individual would voluntarily choose to play this role in life. It sounds degrading, trifling, and just downright wrong. However, in a society where the idea of "every man for himself" becomes more widespread and the concept of a monogamous, traditional marriage becomes less and less popular with time, the side chick starts to prevail (Danielle, 2013).

"Starts" to prevail? These women have been around for as long as marriage has. In fact, they've been around longer. The fact of the matter is that a lot of these "side chicks" are married themselves and are just "stepping out" on their husbands for various reasons. Some of them just need some extra money or want to have "more fun" because the "man" in their life is, for whatever reason, ignoring their social and financial needs. A great many of today's "wives" were able to latch onto their husbands because they started off as "side chicks" with the man they "took" or with some other guy.

This article is biased against the side chick as are large numbers of hypocritical moralizers. Check it out:

> She has reared her ugly little head in pop culture media numerous times over the past year, and unlike the old days where she was plagued with a scarlet letter and owned humility, she now is bold, fierce, and daring to be judged. (Danielle, 2013).

This white man controls these media images and remember the words of Mao: "He who controls images controls minds, and he who controls minds has little, if anything, to worry about from bodies." This side chick is a star in American culture, despite her dubious deeds. She is what the "good girl" wants to be; she is in many cases, the employee in the "world's oldest profession" – prostitution! She is an adventurer and she is the one who is a metaphor for America: a slut who feigns a belief in morality but who will do anything for a dollar.

Because of the on-going mis-perception of her, a number of distorted assumptions are derived. Following are three of them:

> Why are side chicks settling for second place and loving it? I found three reasons: **Convenience** – It takes time to develop and maintain a healthy relationship with a significant other. Trust is a very important part of relationships and is established over time. Side chicks have the pleasure of not having to be concerned with the emotional stress behind opening themselves up to trust. They know their role in a clearly defined, simple sëxual relationship and not much is required of them. They get theirs and get out, avoiding any headaches. (Danielle, 2013 – emphasis original).

What was just described is the American way! These college bitches – that's how they roll. They date, get screwed and take money and if the guy is an athlete, that's all the better. Maybe they can set him up with a pregnancy. But the point is that as soon as they are about to graduate, the guy gets dumped, she goes back home or to another city where she feigns borderline virginity, and then turns out another who she can dupe into marrying her. On campus she's the side chick, but she's a side chick on a mission.

Now, reason number two why side chicks love their roles:

> **Thrill --** Some find excitement in living a secret life. Obviously to be in an undercover relationship, there are always strategic steps made in finding out the best time to partake in sëxual relations with their taken partner. A lot of the hookups may take place late at night, on long lunch breaks, out of town, etc. To side chicks, the "creeping" never gets old. They live for thrill of not knowing where or when the next orgasm may occur. (Danielle, 2013 – emphasis original).

The next "orgasm"? These bitches don't care about busting a nut: they want to get paid! They know men ain't shit and the way to entice them and keep them coming back it to convince them that the man they're with is "all that and a bag of chips." Even if he CAN'T screw (and most can't), she'll lie and say he can and that's all he needs to hear because he sho' ain't satisfying the woman at home. If he was, he wouldn't be banging THIS bitch – and paying her for the right to do so!

The previous statement by Danielle tries to make something scientific and strategic out of something that is surreptitious and sluttish. Let's accept a basic and irrefutable fact: *The woman is a ho*. She wants a man but she doesn't want to be controlled, told what to do or hounded. Men represent baggage. She just wants to make some money and maybe go on some interesting dates to concerts, high-end restaurants and trips out of town. What is so complex about that?

Third point is one that needs analysis. It is where Danielle offers the following:

> **Short-term Cure** – In an odd and crazy way, side chicks feel needed. They believe their secret lovers are in relationships where they are unhappy, so she fills an important void. (Danielle, 2013 – emphasis original).

So one lonely person finds lonely picking up somebody else's leftovers? What kind of bullshit is this? It doesn't represent short term care; it represents sick desperation! This slut is no "good Samaritan" out there looking to give up booty so that a man can feel "whole." She's out there trying to get laid and paid, looking for something to do because her girlfriends have men in their lives. It is not rocket science: it's the way things have been for centuries. This article by Danielle calls them 'side chicks' when, in reality, they are just straight up hos. And so are the men who finance their charade.

Danielle clearly doesn't know her ass from a hole in the ground, as shown in her next attempt at morality:

> In closing, I personally feel that to lower yourself to this level of "importance" is sad. Those being fulfilled in this role suffer from insecurity issues. Feeling needed, living the thrill, and calling the situation convenient is all a cover-up for what is really a void inside of one's soul. I'm a firm believer in the famous Bible verse "do unto others as you would have them do unto you." The most important part in all of this is respect, honesty, and integrity for another individual … (Danielle, 2013).

First of all, side chicks are now "lowering" themselves any more than a housewife, who is nothing more than a legal prostitute with benefits. These women get these guys to marry them and in many cases use the incomes to buttress their own accounts in the name of "taking care of the household." A prostitute is someone who sells her body for money; what do you think these "married women" do before they tie the knot? They go out on dates, suck dick, give up pussy and pussy whip the man into dropping to one knee and asking for their hand in marriage. This shit has been going on for centuries and no one says anything. In my book, that's "lowering yourself" in a more long-term basis and not only that, but then you get children involved in the whole shebang.

Secondly she says that side chicks suffer from insecurity issues. Women, in general are insecure. And so are the men who believe that somehow they are not "whole" unless they find some woman to latch on to and play "mama" for them. Lay out his clothes, tell him when to come home, cook his food, tell him what to do, control the money. That's a mother –figure, man! How much more insecure can you get than that. Women are under equal pressure and are judged by their own female pals: if one of them turns thirty and hasn't been married, they assume something's wrong with her or she's a dyke. America is filled with insecure people looking to latch on to someone else to "fulfill" their lives. What you end up with is two unfulfilled muthafuckas.

Danielle must have gotten a case of the Holy Ghost, writing that, "The most important part in all of this is respect, honesty and integrity for another individual." That is bullshit. The most important part is to have all those things first, and foremost, *for your self!* If you don't love yourself, how can you love anybody else? The greatest number is one and number one is supposed to be YOU!

Danielle (mercifully) concludes with the following:

> There are several victims involved in these circumstances. The one being cheated on is not alone in suffering from betrayal, it is just that the two cheaters are forcing betrayal on themselves. One should always rise above the temptations and hold integrity and respect at a higher regard. (Danielle, 2013).

The concept of "cheating" has to be looked at. The term implies that marriage is somehow "fair" and the perfect goal of the game. It is not. It is a scam where you have to sign up with the state, pay for various tests and other fees and then stand before a crowd of people who claim to be your friends and lie your ass off. "Til death do you part" is an ideal, but in reality very few of the people probably go that far. In fact, when it gets to "in sickness and in health," most people are ready to cut bait.

The fact of the matter is, you already had sex and it was so good and you feel so comfortable that you want to keep on getting it. But now you bring in extra baggage that is going to impede on those sexcapades: electric and gas bills, car payments, mortgage payments and/or rent, kids and their clothes and food, related costs. By the time you get through working a job (which it is almost required that you have) who have time for fuckin'?

The "side chick" is no victim: she's playing it safe. She gets primo dick and his money *sans* the responsibility and the brats running all over the house fuckin' shit up.

CONCLUSION

Girls inherit the guile and knowledge of older women"
                                                    - Anonymous

Chairman Mao once wrote that, "He who controls images controls minds, and he who controls minds has little, if anything, to worry about from bodies." The white man knows this and has traditionally used his version of reality via movies and television, to control the minds of the masses. He has set standards and initiated trends and fads, and has basically established the "American values" that so many people emulate and learn from.

Women getting laid and paid is nothing less than knowing the white man's system from top to bottom and expertly exploiting his values and priorities while lying about what the white male REALLY is. Women get paid to lie to men about male virility, stability and their status. In return, they get to control the purse strings. The white man in 2016 is so obsessed with global domination, profit and control that he's willing to do anything to show everyone that he's still the one on top. He uses a number of arenas to do this and one of those avenues is the media.

CLOSING REMARKS

There you have it, my contribution to the age-old debate regarding male-female relationships and how power tends to skew them. As a sociology professor I taught long ago the difference between a dyad (a group of two) and a triad (a group of three). Not only is there the obvious numerical difference, but when a person is added to a group of two, "power shifts" begin to take place. Relationships tend to get skewed one way or the other. In the case of American relationships, what is being done is a variation of what white folks did when they were back in jolly ol' England and other European countries. The women had no rights, the men were either queer or biased, and all the power was in the hands of men.

In my view and what I have presented herein is that there is not much difference today in America. These people who run the media want to singularize or personalize sexism into the actions of this person or the abuse of that single victim. Rarely do they offer any major detail into the gender bias that is locked into the ideology of white supremacy which, after all, is the guiding principle of American society.

Therefore the title of this book – "The American Casting Couch: A Metaphor for Sexual Manipulation in American Politics and Popular Culture" is multi-faceted in its offering of viewpoints that address various aspects of male-female relationships.

For one thing the men who are engaged in what is now called "sexual harassment" at the workplace are married in many instances. You don't think their wives know what kind of devilment these men are up to at work? These white women like to play ignorant when their men are caught or arrested for major embarrassing crimes. You don't think that Bernie Madoff's wife knew that this asshole had stolen fifty billion dollars? You don't think that Harvey Weinstein's wife knew what he was like? Divorcing him after the fact is just an attempt to protect HER reputation and avoid future complicity-related charges. I always write that, "The hand that rocks the cradle rules the world," and any dirt that this white boy has imposed on the world is known about by his woman. She was right there and opted to keep quiet. And in this case, silence is consent.

In another book I've written - *Transformers: American Sex and Role Changes in America* - I propose a change in the sex roles of American society but that doesn't necessarily mean a change in the race of the people calling the shots. The white female is as committed to white supremacy as her man is although she may be more tactical, seductive and cunning. He was the brute who paved the way for the system that she now benefits from. He is the one who put into motion the "white privilege" that has opened the door for her not to "change" the system, but to continue it with the lessons that she learned from watching HIM at work. She talks a good game but when all is said and done she is as racist and diabolical as he is. "The hand that rocks the cradle rules the throne."

There is no doubt that Harvey Weinstein was a serial abuser and rapist and is deserving of any punishment he gets. But let's make it retroactive and apply it to the "founding fathers" and other "great white men" who used heir power to rape, seduce and bamboozle women and anyone else they had power over. The "casting couch" is alive and well and as integral a part of American history and tradition as racism itself.

REFERENCES

Æsop. *Fables,* retold by Joseph Jacobs. Vol. XVII, Part 1. The Harvard Classics. New York: P.F. Collier & Son, 1909–14; Bartleby.com, 2001.

Blanco, Alvin Aqua (2013, January 20). Shawty Lo Arrested For Failure To Pay Child Support? Retrieved from http://hiphopwired.com/2013/01/20/shawty-lo-arrested-for-failure-to-pay-child-support-photos/#sthash.pzl1N13T.dpufNews,

Burton, W.C. (2007). *Burton's Legal Thesaurus*. Retrieved from http://legal-dictionary.thefreedictionary.com/Alimony.

Bussman, C. (2014, November 12). Twenty Presidents Who Were Rumored to Have Mistresses. Retrieved from http://www.rantpolitical.com/2014/11/12/15-presidents-who-were-rumored-to-have-mistresses/

Carr, Coeli (2014, August 14). The male bad-in-bed list. Retrieved from http://www.msn.com/en-us/news/other/the-male-bad-in-bed-list/ss-AAd6Aj?srcref=rss&FORM=MH146Q&OCID=MH146Q#image=11

Chancellorfiles (2006). Penis size and racial groups. Retrieved from https://chancellorfiles.wordpress.com/2006/12/10/penis-size-and-racial-groups/

Crilly, R. (2014, November 23). Marion Barry, scandal-plagued ex-mayor of Washington, dies. *The London Telegraph*. Retrieved from http://www.telegraph.co.uk/news/worldnews/northamerica/usa/11248647/Marion-Barry-scandal-plagued-ex-mayor-Washington-dies.html

Danielle, Patrice (2016, April 9).Naturallymoi.com. 3 reasons why side chicks are settling for second place … And loving it. Retrieved from http://naturallymoi.com/2016/04/3-reasons-why-side-chicks-are-settling-for-second-place-and-lovin-it/

ESPN.go.com (2012, July 19). Terrell Owens makes payments. Retrieved from http://espn.go.com/nfl/story/_/id/8180722/terrell-owens-agrees-pay-child-support-promises-more

Farrell, W. (1993). *The myth of male power: Why men are the disposable sex.* New York, New York: Berkley Publishing.

Feiffer, J. (1965). *The Great Comic Book Heroes Paperback*. Seattle, Washington: Fantagraphic Books.

Fletcher, Connie. (1990). *What cops know: Today's police tell the inside story of their work on America's streets.* New York: Pocket Books

Fletcher, M.A. & Bock, J. (1994, August 1). NAACP leader denies sexual harassment allegations. *Baltimore Sun*. Retrieved from http://articles.baltimoresun.com/1994-08-01/news/1994213100_1_chavis-harassment-naacp-board

Forbes magazine (2014, September 23). Forbes 400 – Facts and figures on America's wealthiest.

FoxSports (2012, September 18). Report: Holyfield held in contempt. Retrieved from http://www.foxsports.com/boxing/story/evander-holyfield-judge-court-orders-back-pay-child-support-debt-091812.

Gibson, J. (2012, June 19). Flavor Flav Pays More than $100K in Child Support to Stay Out of Prison. CelebrityNetworth.com. Retrieved from http://www.celebritynetworth.com/articles/celebrity/flavor-flav-pays-100k-child-support-stay-prison/

Hakim, D. & Rashbaum, W.K. (2008, March 10). Spitzer is linked to prostitution ring. *New York Times*. Retrieved from http://www.nytimes.com/2008/03/10/nyregion/10cnd-spitzer.html

Healy, B. (2014, December 5). Abigail Johnson, after years of training, gets to put her stamp on Fidelity. *The Boston Globe.*

Holman, T. (2013, November 29). Chief Keef Ordered to Pay Child Support for 10-month Old After DNA Test. *Inquisitr*. Retrieved from http://www.inquisitr.com/1046968/chief-keef-child-support-10-month-old/

Huffington Post (2013, April 30). Bow Wow Isn't 'Lil' Anymore: Rapper Opens Up About His Baby And Being A Dad. Retrieved from http://www.huffingtonpost.com/2013/04/30/bow-wow-lil-rapper-baby-dad_n_3181067.html

Huffington Post. (June 27, 2014). Brigitte Nielsen: I Didn't Marry Sylvester Stallone For The Reason Everyone Thought. Retrieved from http://www.huffingtonpost.com/2014/06/27/brigitte-nielsen-sylvester-stallone-marriage_n_5536778.html

McCarthy, M. ()2016, March 16). *Sporting News*. Porn star Lisa Ann warns 25 percent of NBA players have faced blackmail. Retrieved from http://www.sportingnews.com/nba-news/4697284-porn-star-lisa-ann-warns-25-of-nba-players-are-blackmailed

Miller, B. (1999, September 8). Cisneros Pleads Guilty to Lying to FBI Agents. The Washington Post. Retrieved from http://www.washingtonpost.com/wp-srv/politics/special/cisneros/stories/cisneros090899.htm

Miller, M.E. (2016, March 15). A Miami woman killed a teen burglar as he fled her home, police say. Should she be charged? The Washington Post. Retrieved from http://www.msn.com/en-us/news/crime/a-miami-woman-killed-a-teen-burglar-as-he-fled-her-home-police-say-should-she-be-charged/ar-BBqtGa8?li=BBnb7Kz&ocid=iehp

MSN.com (2016, March 11). The top 20 traits women want in a man. Retrieved from http://www.msn.com/en-us/lifestyle/lifestylewomen/the-top-20-traits-women-want-in-a-man/ss-AAeHzO0?ocid=iehp

Naturallymoi.com (2012, November 4). Gabrielle Union on marriage: "I just like saying 'my boyfriend'. Retrieved from http://naturallymoi.com/2012/11/gabrielle-union-on-marriage-i-just-like-saying-my-boyfriend/

Naturallymoi.com (2016, April 9). Ladies: 5 things you must know about dating a black man. Retrieved from http://naturallymoi.com/2016/04/ladies-5-things-you-must-know-about-dating-a-black-man/

New York Daily News (2016, July 6). New Iron Man is black – And a woman. Retrieved from http://www.nydailynews.com/entertainment/new-iron-man-black-woman-article-1.2701328

Page, A. (2013, July 13). Baby Drama! Celebrities With Major Child Support Issues. Retrieved from http://madamenoire.com/287670/baby-drama-celebrities-with-major-child-support-issues/15/

Pearce, M. (2013, September 26). Cory Booker's Twitterstripper: 'It's not a sex scandal!" Los Angeles Times. Retrieved from http://articles.latimes.com/2013/sep/26/nation/la-na-nn-cory-booker-stripper-20130926

Rhone, Paysha Stockton (2007, February 27). Bobby Brown arrested in Massachusetts. People.com. Retrieved from http://www.people.com/people/article/0,,20013443,00.html

Rose, Sandra (2011, May 10). Jermaine Dupri Sued by Stripper for Child Support. Retrieved fromhttp://sandrarose.com/2011/05/jermaine-dupri-sued-by-stripper-for-child-support/

Scott, Bartie (2016, March 7). Forbes' wealthiest women in the world. Forbes magazine. Retrieved from http://www.msn.com/en-us/money/savingandinvesting/forbes-wealthiest-women-in-the-world-2016/ar-BBqc8dC?li=BBnb7Kz&ocid=iehp

Shilliday, Beth (2015, October 7). Matt Barnes Attacks Former Teammate Derek Fisher For Dating Wife Gloria Govan. Hollywoodlife.com. Retrieved from http://hollywoodlife.com/2015/10/07/matt-barnes-attacked-derek-fisher-dating-gloria-govan-ex-wife-teammates/

Simmel, G. (1990) The philosophy of money. London, England: Routledge Books.

Stelly, Matthew C. (2016). *Transformers: Sex and Role Changes in America.* Lexington, Kentucky: CreateSpace Publishing.

Stitt, R. (2016, January 19). NY Jets' Antonio Cromartie's Child Support Bill is $336,000 For His 8 Children. Financial Juneteenth. Retrieved from http://financialjuneteenth.com/ny-jets-antonio-cromarties-child-support-bill-336000-8-children/

TMZ staff (2013, August 31). Allen Iverson's ex-wife: I want $1.2 million right now. Retrieved from Retrieved from http://www.tmz.com/2013/08/31/allen-iverson-tawanna-iverson-child-support-1-2-million/

Wikipedia (2016). Misandry. Retrieved from https://en.wikipedia.org/wiki/Misandry

Wikipedia (2016). Anthony Weiner sexting scandals. . Retrieved from https://en.wikipedia.org/wiki/Anthony_Weiner_sexting_scandals

Wikipedia (2016). Eliot Spitzer. Retrieved from https://en.wikipedia.org/wiki/Eliot_Spitzer#Prostitution_scandal

Womanist Musings. (2016). When Black Women Sell Out: "It's Free Swipe Yo EBT." Retrieved from http://www.womanistmusings.com/when-black-women-sell-out-its-free/

Xfinity.com (2017). From rags to riches: How 10 jocks went broke. Retrieved from http://my.xfinity.com/slideshow/sports-richestorags/5/

Wooley, Nate (2013, March 4). Dennis Rodman too broke to pay child support. InvestorPlace.com. Retrieved from http://investorplace.com/2013/03/dennis-rodman-too-broke-to-pay-child-support/#.VyUKHMtwXcs